REVOLUTIONARY WAR

Quiz and Fact Book

Jonathan N. Hall

Taylor Publishing Company

Dallas, Texas

To my parents, James and Ruth Hall, who first stimulated my interest in history by reading the Bible to me at a young age. And to my wife Marlene for her tolerance, my daughter Simone, and friends Sally Peters and Marti Seaton for their help in editing.

Copyright © 1999 by Jonathan Hall
All rights reserved.

No part of this book may be reproduced in any form or by any means—including photocopying and electronic reproduction—without written permission from the publisher.

Designed by David Timmons

Published by Taylor Publishing Company
1550 West Mockingbird Lane
Dallas, Texas 75235
www.taylorpub.com

Library of Congress Cataloging-in-Publication Data:

Hall, Jonathan, 1951–
    The Revolutionary War quiz and fact book / Jonathan Hall.
      p. cm.
    Includes bibliographical references (p.261).
    ISBN 0-87833-226-X (pbk.)
    1. United States—History—Revolution, 1775–1783—Miscellanea.
2. United States—History—War of 1812—Miscellanea. 3. Questions and answers. I. Title.
    E209.H33   1999
    973.3—dc21   99–11678
                                         CIP

Printed in the United States of America
10 9 8 7 6 5 4 3 2 1

Contents

Foreword

The American Revolution came about, fundamentally, because the English North American colonies matured to the degree that their worldview became substantially different from that of their mother country. British politicians and statesmen proved to be indifferent to these changes. After a weak attempt at diplomacy failed, an eight-year military conflict resulted to solve the issue. It is impossible to overemphasize the importance of the American Revolution. It is the defining event that established the foundation of this country and its rise to greatness. The successful struggle to win its independence made possible everything that would follow in America. If General George Washington and his ragged Continental army of citizen soldiers were not able to eventually prevail in the military contest with the numerically and professionally superior British army, the fate of people living in North America today would have been quite different.

In the 1950s, Walter Millis published his seminal volume entitled *Arms and Men: A Study in American Military History*. In it he wrote, "The United States was born in an act of violence," when describing the American War for Independence. Millis then described how this war affected not only the military segment of American culture, but also the entire breadth of its national character. Wars used to be considered as strictly military exercises conducted by the armed forces of a country, involving just a narrow aspect of the overall society. The American Revolution transcended that notion. This war would permeate the far reaches of this new nation.

Realizing the consequences of this turbulent period, many writers have fixed their attention on this remarkable historical era. Today, library and bookstore shelves are groaning under the weight of this mass of literature. More is being added on a daily basis. We are truly in an information age, deluged by data. What is needed at this time is an effective way to interpret, categorize, and comprehend this overwhelming body of material. Meticulously researched, skillfully analyzed, and engagingly written, this book performs this function admirably. It will be a welcome addition to the holdings of the aficionado and scholar alike. Jonathan Hall's work pertaining to the American Revolution and the nation building that occurred beyond will serve as an invaluable reference for both the chair side and the desktop.

Hal T. Shelton, Ph.D.
Author, *General Richard Montgomery and the American Revolution*

Introduction

The memorable men of the Revolutionary era still evoke admiration and emulation in today's world. They performed heroic and dangerous deeds in the face of danger and hardship, often against seemingly insurmountable obstacles; yet they endured and prevailed against Great Britain, then the world's greatest power. They left a legacy of lasting accomplishments for the benefit of their country's posterity. They were true heroes, men of admirable character holding to eternal principles that should never be forgotten, men who will always be exemplary.

Even in their own time, our nation's founders were recognized as great men. England's renowned William Pitt, a contemporary, said of the Continental Congress, "For myself, I must declare and avow, that in all my reading and observation . . . and I have studied and admired the master states of the world—that for solidity of reasoning, force of sagacity, and wisdom of conclusion, under such a complication of difficult circumstances, no nation, or body of men, can stand in preference to the general congress at Philadelphia." George III said after George Washington retired that Washington was "the greatest character of the age."

Jefferson, Madison, and others are revered because of their influence on the founding and the philosophy of the American government. But also worthy of our respect are the soldiers, the many amateurs and the small core of professionals, who lost many more bitterly contested battles than they won, but who believed in the Revolution with a strong devotion that enabled them to fight on through extensive sufferings at great sacrifice and personal cost.

Though the Revolution occurred more than two hundred years ago, these men and events are relevant today. In considering who we are as a nation, what we stand for, and what we desire for our future, we can benefit by pondering the era of our country's foundation. Would our nation today be capable of accomplishing what was done over two hundred years ago? In today's culture of political correctness, would a revolution ever be considered the right response by enough of the population to succeed? What would the objectives be and what type of government would be established? Would George Washington or Nathanael Greene be allowed to remain in command after so many setbacks and defeats? Would current Americans believe in a cause with sufficient fervor and conviction to cause them to endure the hardships and devastations suffered by their forefathers, including the destruction of their own personal property?

This book covers the peoples, places, and occurrences of the Revolutionary era. For easy learning, understanding, and remembrance, this story is told chronologically, in quiz format, to factually and concisely portray the most important and interesting highlights of the era that established America's independence. The book allows each reader to gain a comprehensive knowledge of the era, to learn who did what, what happened, when, where, and why.

Prelude to War: 1763–1774

"I am not a Virginian, but an American."

Q. Name the treaty that ended the French and Indian War, known in Europe as the Seven Years' War.

A. The Treaty of Paris, signed on February 10, 1763, eliminated France as a contestant for the North American continent. France ceded both Canada and all of its territory east of the Mississippi River. Only Spain, with territory west of the Mississippi, was left to challenge England. Soon after the signing of the treaty, the relationship between the colonists and the mother country deteriorated.

Q. In 1763 a war with Native Americans broke out on America's northwest frontier. An estimated two thousand settlers were killed and many forts captured. Who was the Ottawa chief that assembled a confederation of tribes and led them during the war?

A. Chief Pontiac. The Native Americans had depended on trade goods from the French. British traders who replaced the French were ordered to cease supplying the Native Americans with powder; also the British discouraged intermarriage between the races and began appropriating Native American lands without compensation. In response, Pontiac instigated a war. He was assisted by an antiwhite Delaware prophet who preached a return to traditional Native American ways.

Q. How many of the ten English forts west of Niagara did Pontiac's confederation capture in 1763?

A. Pontiac's confederation of Hurons, Potawatomis, Senecas, Chippewas, and other tribes captured eight forts.

Q. The failure to capture what fort contributed to the dissolution of Pontiac's confederacy?

A. Pontiac failed to capture Fort Detroit after the longest siege ever conducted by North American tribes. The siege, lasting from May through October, was abandoned when Pontiac's allies began to lose hope of victory and Pontiac learned he would no longer be receiving any aid from the French. A Peoria tribe member later murdered Pontiac in 1769.

Q. Fort Pitt also held out during a siege. What tactic did Captain Simeon Ecuyer employ to help defend the fort?

A. At the suggestion of General Jeffrey Amherst, who was governor-general of British North America from 1760 to 1763, Ecuyer employed an early form of biological warfare. Blankets and handkerchiefs infected with smallpox were sent out to the Native Americans surrounding the fort and caused an epidemic to break out.

Q. While on their way to relieve the siege of Fort Pitt, an army of about five hundred, under former Swiss officer Colonel Henry Bouquet, defeated approximately the same number of Native Americans at what battle?

A. At the battle of Bushy Run, Bouquet withdrew one side of his surrounded army, ambushed the attacking Native Americans, and routed them, thus enabling his men to continue to Fort Pitt and lift the siege on August 10, 1763.

Q. How many troops did the British have in America after the French and Indian War ended, more or less than 3,000?

A. The British left 6,000 troops and decided the colonists should be taxed to pay for them.

Q. What was the Proclamation Line of 1763?

A. A part of the Royal Proclamation of 1763 decreed a line of demarcation on the crest of the mountains dividing Native American land to the west from that of the colonists. The British enacted the proclamation to keep peace with the Native Americans by prohibiting colonists from settling their land. However, the proclamation provoked colonist hostility, and an insatiable hunger for new land drove many to ignore it.

Q. In the years following the French and Indian War, the British Parliament decided to tax the American colonies to help pay off the large war debt and to assist in the cost of maintaining troops for the defense of the western frontier. Which of Parliament's subsequent revenue raising acts served as a catalyst to arouse and unite the colonies to active opposition?

A. The Stamp Act of 1765 required colonists to purchase stamped paper for all official documents, including licenses, legal papers, and various printed material, a measure that affected almost everyone. Colonists prevented officials from even taking a position to collect the tax, and the Stamp Act Congress met to petition Parliament.

Q. At the instigation of what colony did the Stamp Act Congress convene in New York in October 1765?

A. At the instigation of the Great and General Courts of Massachusetts, delegates gathered from nine colonies, demonstrating the capacity of the colonies to unify in opposition to the mother country.

Q. Name the only state where an official occupied a position and collected revenue for the Stamp Act?

A. Georgia, under governor Sir James Wright, was the only state where an official occupied a position and collected revenue. Parliament rescinded the act in 1766 after receiving numerous petitions from British merchants. British trade with the colonies had declined by 25 percent as a result of American nonimportation. At the time Parliament refrained from using military force as advocated by George Grenville, the first lord of the treasury.

Q. The testimony of what American helped to persuade Parliament to repeal the Stamp Act in 1766?

A. On February 13, 1766, Benjamin Franklin fielded 174 questions from the House of Commons, helping the members to decide for repeal.

Benjamin Franklin
(1706–1790)
Printer, publisher,
statesman, philosopher,
inventor

Q. Parliament imposed a new revenue act on the colonies in 1767. Since the colonists had complained about internal taxation, this act taxed glass, lead, painter's colors, tea, and paper imported into the colonies. It also increased the power of revenue officers to enforce the law and established new courts of vice admiralty. Who was responsible for promoting these new acts?

A. The acts were named for Charles Townshend, who ascended to the leadership of the House of Commons in 1766. The colonists resisted by reviving nonimportation of British goods. Under pressure from the merchant class especially, the British government repealed all of the Townshend duties except for the one on tea.

Q. In 1768 the British landed two regiments in Boston to intimidate the colonists. Tensions finally erupted in the Boston Massacre of 1770. Five colonists were killed including the mob leader, a free African American. Name him.

A. Crispus Attucks, who was of mixed blood, part Natick Indian and part Negro.

Q. Though the British soldiers who killed the five colonists had fired only after one soldier had been beaten and knocked down with a club, they were arrested and charged with murder. What prominent Boston lawyer defended Captain Thomas Preston and his men?

A. John Adams defended them and won an acquittal for Captain Preston and all but two of his men, who were convicted of manslaughter but were later released and discharged from the army. As a result of this decision, public pressure forced the evacuation of all British troops to Castles William, a fortress on a Boston Harbor island.

Q. Where was the first colonist killed by British soldiers?

A. In New York City, in the so-called battle of Golden Hill, on January 19, 1770, one man was killed. Citizens and soldiers had clashed because soldiers were distributing a handbill that denigrated the patriots.

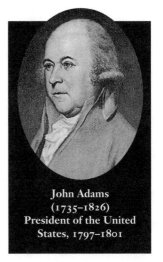

John Adams
(1735–1826)
President of the United
States, 1797–1801

Q. Beginning in 1768 in North and South Carolina, backcountry men (called Regulators) organized to seek representation in the provincial assembly, to administer justice, and to oppose corrupt civil authorities. After these Regulators invaded the courtroom of Judge Richard Henderson and appointed their own judge, North Carolina Royal Governor William Tryon raised an army of 1,000 men to restore royal authority. At what battle, on May 16, 1771, did Tryon disperse 2,000 Regulators?

A. At the battle of Alamance, Governor Tryon drove the Regulators from the field in an hour of fighting that left nine dead on each side. One Regulator leader was executed, six were hung, and pardons were offered to the rest. An estimated six thousand men took an oath of allegiance to the king in the weeks following the battle. During the Revolutionary War, Regulators fought on both sides.

Q. In what year did the Boston Tea Party take place?

A. About fifty Boston patriots, disguised as Mohawks, instigated the Boston Tea Party, aboard the British merchant ship *Dartmouth* and two other ships, on December 16, 1773.

Q. Who organized the Sons of Liberty, the patriots who, disguised as Native Americans, dumped 342 chests of tea into Boston Harbor in response to Parliament granting a monopoly on tea to the British East India Company?

A. Samuel Adams. This act provoked the English and started the chain of events that culminated in the Revolutionary War. Tea parties were also held in other port cities. As a result, the East India Company could not sell its tea anywhere in the colonies.

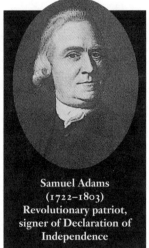

Samuel Adams
(1722–1803)
Revolutionary patriot,
signer of Declaration of
Independence

Q. What Native American tribe did Virginia militia fight in 1774?

A. The Shawnees, under Chief Cornstalk. In the battle of Point Pleasant, against a force under Andrew Lewis, the tribe suffered painful losses. Afterwards the Shawnees sought to live at peace with the whites.

Q. What was the name given to the war fought against the Shawnees in 1774?

A. Lord Dunmore's War, named after Virginia's governor, John Murray. White settlement on Native American land and Native American retaliation were the underlying causes of hostilities. However, Daniel Greathouse's atrocious murder of six Native Americans from a group he had invited over for entertainment inflamed the Shawnees to go to war. Many future leaders on both sides of the Revolutionary War fought in Dunmore's War.

Q. What Parliamentary act extended the boundaries of Britain's Canadian provinces to the Ohio and Mississippi Rivers and granted religious rights to Quebec's Roman Catholics?

A. The Quebec Act of 1774. In addition to the Quebec Act, Parliament enacted other acts, dubbed the Intolerable Acts, which finally served to incite the colonies and unite them in rebellion.

Q. What American city's port was closed by the Port Bill in 1774?

A. The port of Boston was closed to all trade until remuneration was made for the tea destroyed in the Boston Tea Party. Though

Benjamin Franklin advised payment for the tea, and more than one hundred merchants were willing to pay, radical leaders prevented the restitution. While the port was closed, other colonies aided Boston by sending food overland.

Q. Under the Massachusetts Governing Act, the British Parliament altered the Massachusetts charter and replaced previously elected colonial officials with royal officials to govern the colony. Who was sent as the commander in chief and governor?

A. General Thomas Gage assumed the position in May 1774. Due to extensive opposition to the Crown, Gage was reluctant to use force against the colonists until reinforcements arrived. Gage wrote the British government that he would need 20,000 regulars plus additional troops to ensure British authority in America. Instead, the government sent only 1,000 men for reinforcements.

Q. After the port of Boston was closed, where did Gage relocate the capital of Massachusetts?

A. Salem.

Q. In what city did the first Continental Congress meet?

A. They met in Philadelphia's Carpenter's Hall, beginning in September 1774.

Q. "The distinctions between Virginians, Pennsylvanians, New Yorkers and New Englanders, are no more. I am not a Virginian, but an American." Who spoke these words at the first Continental Congress?

A. Patrick Henry. Henry was well-known throughout the colonies. He had been a lawyer and a member of the Virginia House of Burgesses. His Seven Resolutions, given in response to the Stamp Act in 1765, were published in other colonies and had nearly helped foment a revolution then. One of his

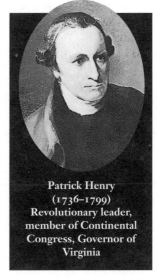

**Patrick Henry
(1736–1799)
Revolutionary leader,
member of Continental
Congress, Governor of
Virginia**

resolves, which was not adopted by the House of Burgesses, declared that Virginia's legislature was autonomous.

Q. What colony did not send a delegate to the first Continental Congress?
A. Georgia.

Q. On which side did the Tories fight in the war, Britain or America?
A. Tories, also called Loyalists, sympathized with and fought for the British. In New York State more men probably fought for the British than for the Americans. During and after the war, many Tories fled the colonies. Over one half of all the Loyalists who fled the thirteen colonies were New York citizens.

Q. Patriotic colonists frequently resorted to what favorite punishment for Tories found in their midst?
   a. Tar and feathers
   b. Whipping
   c. Jailing
A. The answer is a. Patriots preferred to punish Tories with tar and feathers, an infliction dating from the Middle Ages. The patriots would strip a victim, coat him with hot tar, and dump feathers on him. It usually took weeks for anyone to recover from the third-degree burns incurred during the ordeal.

Q. In what colony were the first minutemen regiments organized?
A. They were organized first in Massachusetts in September 1774 to purge Tories from the militia. One-third of the men from each regiment were to be ready at a minute's notice. Eventually Maryland, North Carolina, New Hampshire, and Connecticut all had minutemen. Massachusetts's minutemen ceased to be once Washington's army was formed.

Q. At what age was a man required to enroll in the militia?
A. Every man from age sixteen to sixty was required to enroll in a company from his own township and to possess a gun, ammunition, and proper accessories.

FACT

Tories were persecuted severely during the war. Usually their greatest loss was all of their property, though a few were brought to trial and hanged on charges of treason. Colonies viewed Tory property as a source of revenue. Congress recommended the seizure of Tory personal property late in 1777, and all colonies enforced this measure before the war ended. Also, in most colonies large Tory estates were parceled into small lots and sold to the common people. An estimated 80,000 to 100,000 Loyalists fled the colonies before, during, and after the war. All Loyalists who had lived behind British lines for at least a year were provided transportation out of the colonies and sufficient provisions for one year's sustenance. Five thousand Tories submitted claims to the British government for compensation. The British government eventually compensated 2,560 of them for about half of their claimed personal losses.

Q. What was the approximate population of the American colonies on the eve of the war?

A. The population was about 2.5 million. An estimated one-sixth were slaves. Compare this to Great Britain's population of 9 million. The military manpower of the colonies is estimated to have been about 175,000, while Britain's was about 2,350,000.

Q. What was the largest city in the colonies during the war?

A. Philadelphia. With a population of 34,000, it was the second largest city in the English-speaking world. New York was the second largest American city with 22,000 inhabitants, followed by Boston with 16,000, and Charleston with 12,000. In contrast, London, England, boasted a population of 750,000 inhabitants.

Q. What was the most populous state in the colonies at the war's beginning?

A. The most populous state was Pennsylvania with about 300,000 people. Delaware was the least populous state with approximately 40,000 people.

Q. What fraction of the colonists, known as "patriots" or Whigs, were thought to be devoted to the cause of independence?

A. As first estimated by John Adams, one-third of the population was for independence, one-third was Loyalists, and one-third wanted to be left out of the conflict.

Q. At the time of the war's beginning, were the majority of the colonists originally from the mother country?

A. Yes. About 61 percent of the colonists traced their origins to England. As for the rest, 14 percent were Scotch and Scotch-Irish from Northern Ireland, 9 percent were Germans, 6 percent were Dutch, 4 percent were southern Irish, and 7 percent were from miscellaneous other countries.

Q. Name the reigning king of England during the war.

A. King George III (1738–1820) assumed the throne in 1760. George was also the ruler of the duchy of Hanover in Germany.

Q. Who were the Hessians?

A. They were German mercenary troops hired to serve in the British army for the same rate of pay as British troops. Since most of them (20,000) were from the German state of Hesse-Cassel, they were called Hessians. Altogether about 30,000 German mercenaries served the British during the war, though no more than 20,000 were in America at one time.

Q. What percentage of the British army in America were Hessian troops?
   a. 15 percent
   b. 33 percent
   c. 50 percent

A. The answer is b. Until 1777 Philip von Heister was the Hessian

FACT

B esides Hesse-Cassel, five other German states supplied troops: Hesse-Hanau (2,500), Brunswick (6,000), Anspach-Bayreuth (2,400), Waldeck (1,300), and Anhalt-Serbst (1,200). The 4,500-mile trip to America was hazardous. On every transport of 900 to 1,000 troops that arrived in America, 130 to 200 men were ill while 30 to 40 had died en route. Only about 17,313 German troops returned to Germany when the war ended. Nearly 8,000 died during the war and about 5,000 deserted. Many also stayed in America after the war. The renowned warrior Frederick the Great was against sending German troops to America.

commander in chief. When he was recalled, Wilhelm von Knyphausen assumed command until 1782, when he was then succeeded by Wilhelm von Lossberg.

Q. Were the majority of the British people in favor of a war against the Americans?

A. No. Numerous British people, including many in high positions in the government and the military, opposed the war. During the Seven Years' War (1756–1763), England had been able to raise 300,000 troops. During the Revolutionary War, England barely succeeded in raising 50,000 troops. George III hired Hessians after Russia, Holland, and Frederick the Great of Prussia turned down his request for troops.

Q. How many troops did Britain have in America at the start of the war?
   a. 3,300
   b. 8,500
   c. 16,000

A. The answer is b. The largest concentration was in Boston where General Thomas Gage had 4,000 troops. Gage had lived in America for twenty years and had married an American woman. Prior to the breakout of fighting, Gage recommended to Secretary of War Viscount Barrington that maximum force should be sent to crush resistance to Britain's authority.

Q. Did Britain have more or less than 1,000 troops in Canada at the start of the war?

A. Only 700 men, out of a total British army of 48,000, were stationed in Canada.

Q. Name the British governor of Canada at the war's beginning.

A. Sir Guy Carleton had been appointed in 1775. He commanded British troops in Canada until 1778.

Q. Four major British generals commanded armies in America for extended periods of time during the war. Name them.

A. John Burgoyne, Sir William Howe, Sir Henry Clinton, and Lord Charles Cornwallis.

Sir Henry Clinton
(1738–1795)
British general during
American Revolution

Q. Is it true that British generals had to buy their rank?

A. No. While other officers bought their commissions, generals were appointed directly by the king. Most had political connections, evident by the fact that twenty-three of the generals in the war were also members of Parliament.

Q. On average, how long did it take a ship to travel from Britain to America?

A. It took two months to travel to America and about six weeks for the return trip.

1775

"I do not think myself equal to the command
I am honored with."

Q. Who addressed the House of Lords in January, submitting a
motion asking for withdrawal of British troops from Boston, in an
attempt to reconcile with the colonies?

A. William Pitt, the earl of Chatham, submitted a motion that was
defeated by a vote of sixty-eight to eighteen.

Q. Where did a battle nearly take place in February, almost two
months before Lexington and Concord?

A. Salem, Massachusetts. British colonel Alexander Leslie, commanding an expedition of 240 men, was sent to Salem to seize a
few brass fieldpieces. He came to a hoisted drawbridge and saw a
large crowd and armed militia on the other side of the stream. A
Salem clergyman, Thomas Barnard, and Captain John Felt persuaded Leslie to leave without the fieldpieces and explain that he
did not find any guns.

Q. What British action precipitated the battles of Lexington and
Concord?

A. Under orders from General Gage, Lieutenant Colonel Francis
Smith marched out to Concord with 700 men to destroy the colo-
nial arms depot there. He also attempted to capture Samuel
Adams and John Hancock, who were in Concord. Smith led
Gage's best troops, the grenadier and light infantry companies
from each regiment and the 400-man Royal Marine battalion.

Q. Where did Paul Revere's friend, John Pulling, show a lantern signaling the route by which the British were leaving Boston?

A. Pulling signaled with two lanterns from the Old North Church to indicate the British were going by water, across the Charles River, instead of by land over Boston Neck.

**Paul Revere
(1735–1818)
Revolutionary patriot,
silversmith, engraver**

Q. Name one of the two couriers, besides Paul Revere, who rode to warn the minutemen at Lexington and Concord.

A. William Dawes and Dr. Samuel Prescott also rode as couriers to warn the minutemen. (Paul Revere was captured and later released.)

Q. The patriots observed signs that Gage was planning some kind of military operation. All the longboats had been gathered around a warship close to shore, and the grenadiers and light infantrymen had been withdrawn from regular duty. Some historians also believe the patriots were tipped off to Gage's plans from what person in his headquarters?

A. Gage's wife, Margaret Kemble, who was a patriotic American from New Jersey.

Q. On what date were the battles of Lexington and Concord fought?
A. April 19, 1775.

Q. On Lexington Green, Captain John Parker commanded about seventy-seven militiamen. What did Parker tell them to do after he saw that the British outnumbered them three to one?

A. Seeing their hopeless situation, Parker told the militiamen to disperse. As they began to leave, a shot was fired. Then British regulars under Major Pitcairn fired two volleys, killing eight and wounding eight of Parker's men. After the second volley, Parker's men fled. Later in the day, many of them returned and sought revenge by firing on the British column as it retreated from Concord.

Q. Who ordered the Americans to advance against the British at Concord?

A. In the absence of Colonel Barrett, Major Buttrick gave the order.

Q. After searching the town and finding few arms, the British retreated from Concord and were harassed along their line of march by a continuing gathering of patriots. Where did the worst fighting take place during the British retreat?

A. At Menotomy (now Arlington). Actually the fighting at Menotomy can be included in the list of the larger battles of the war. As many as 5,500 men may have fought there.

Q. Was there any American general among the patriots around Lexington and Concord?

A. Yes. The only American general involved in the battle, William Heath, was responsible, along with Dr. Joseph Warren, for placing many Americans in the path of the retreating British at Menotomy.

FACT

It is remarkable that one of the patriots fighting at Menotomy that day was an 80-year-old farmer, a former veteran of the French and Indian War, Captain Samuel Whittemore. He stood alone after his companions fled. He shot and killed three British soldiers before they shot, clubbed, and bayoneted him, leaving him for dead. Though Whittemore suffered no fewer than thirteen bayonet wounds, he lived for eighteen more years.

Q. Which side lost more men at Lexington and Concord and in the fighting during the British retreat?

A. For the British, 273 men were killed, wounded, or missing. For the Americans, forty-nine were killed, forty-one wounded, and five missing. Most of the British were killed during their retreat when patriots shot at them continuously from behind trees and stone fences and from houses.

Q. Approximately how many shots were fired by the patriots to inflict 273 British casualties at Lexington and Concord and during the retreat that day?

a. 10,000

b. 35,000

c. 75,000

A. The answer is c. Historian Christopher Ward stated that only one of every 300 bullets fired by the Americans hit the enemy. This meant that only one of every fifteen marksmen hit their mark.

Q. On what date did Charleston, South Carolina, learn of Lexington and Concord, April 30 or May 10?

A. On April 19 Israel Bissel rode to inform the rest of the colonies of the battle. He reached New London, Connecticut, 100 miles away, the next day. He arrived in New York on April 23 and Philadelphia on April 24. The news finally reached Charleston on May 10.

Q. Who led the surprise raid of Fort Ticonderoga on May 10, capturing a small British garrison of forty-eight and, more important, about one hundred cannon?

A. Ethan Allen and the Green Mountain Boys, assisted by Benedict Arnold, captured the fort without the loss of a man. A sentry tried to fire a musket point-blank at Allen as he and Arnold rushed into the fort, but the sentry's gun did not fire when he pulled the trigger. Allen then forced the fort's commander, Captain William Delaplace, to surrender his garrison with no further resistance.

Q. After capturing Fort Ticonderoga, Allen sent Seth Warner to capture what other British post on May 12?

A. Warner captured Crown Point without any resistance. The captured material from both forts greatly aided the American cause as seventy-eight serviceable guns, six mortars, three howitzers, thousands of cannonballs, and 30,000 flints, among other items, were added to the American arsenal.

Q. Whose idea was it to attack Fort Ticonderoga, sometimes referred to as the Gibraltar of America?

A. The idea actually originated from two separate sources. Arnold, while he led the Connecticut militia serving around Boston, had the idea to attack the fort to obtain badly needed artillery. Samuel Adams, upon the recommendation of an agent whom he had sent to Canada, also suggested the idea to Governor Trumbull of Connecticut, who contacted Allen. Some members of Congress were appalled at the taking of Ticonderoga because they still hoped for a reconciliation with England. While Lexington and Concord had been defensive actions, the king would consider the seizure of Ticonderoga and Crown Point hostile provocations.

Q. Near which major city was the battle of Bunker Hill fought?

A. Boston. Immediately after Lexington and Concord, patriots gathered to besiege the British in Boston. When the patriots learned that the British planned to seize Dorchester Heights, they moved swiftly to fortify Bunker Hill.

Q. What American traitor informed General Gage a month in advance that the Americans planned to fortify Bunker Hill?

A. Dr. Benjamin Church, a well-respected patriot who had been a delegate to the Massachusetts Provincial Congress in 1774, informed Gage.

Q. On what hill was the battle of Bunker Hill actually fought?

A. The battle was fought on Breed's Hill on June 17.

Q. Who was overall commander of the American troops around Boston at the time?

A. General Artemus Ward, who had served in the French and Indian War as a major of militia, had been commissioned general and commander in chief of Massachusetts troops on May 19. By early June, Ward commanded over 15,000 men from Massachusetts, New Hampshire, Connecticut, and Rhode Island. Under Ward, Colonel John Stark commanded the New Hampshire troops, Major General David Wooster headed the Connecticut troops, and Brigadier General Nathanael Greene led the Rhode Island troops.

General Artemas Ward
(1727–1800)
Revolutionary general,
Congressman

Q. Identify the American commander who placed the troops on Breed's Hill.

A. Colonel Israel Putnam, another veteran of the French and Indian War, wanted to force the British to attack on ground of his choosing rather than wait for the British to decide where to attack. Putnam believed that Americans could fight better from behind fortifications that protected their legs. Men greatly feared leg wounds, which frequently led to amputation and a slow death. Putnam also spouted the famous order, "Don't fire until you see the whites of their eyes," a saying used at least as early as 1745.

Q. The chief engineer for the American army, Colonel Richard Gridley, marked out the position on the hill. Who actually commanded the American troops in the battle?

A. Colonel William Prescott actually commanded the troops on the hill, and Colonel John Stark commanded the troops behind the walls and fences extending down to the Mystic River. William Howe, under General Gage, commanded for the British.

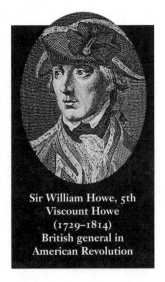

Sir William Howe, 5th
Viscount Howe
(1729–1814)
British general in
American Revolution

Q. Early in the morning on June 17, a British warship bombarding the rebel entrenchments on Breed's Hill awakened General Gage. He called a council of war with major generals William Howe, John Burgoyne, and Henry Clinton, who all had arrived in Boston on May 25. Which of these generals advised Gage to allow him to go up the Mystic River with 500 troops, land behind the rebel position on Charlestown Neck, and position the troops on Bunker Hill to fire down on the enemy and cut off their retreat, while another general led a frontal assault on the rebel lines?

A. General Clinton advocated this plan, which may have squashed the Revolution right then and there. However, Gage did not know what preparations the Americans may have made to oppose the landings and feared placing his forces between two parts of the rebel army. Besides, Gage believed the untrained rebels behind improvised fortifications could not withstand a frontal assault by regular troops.

Q. What British blunder seriously weakened the effectiveness of their attack?

A. The British brought forward twelve brass fieldpieces but discovered they had twelve-pound balls in their side boxes instead of the required six-pound balls. Admiral Samuel Graves also hampered the British effort by refusing to send a warship up the Mystic River to bombard Stark's men on the American left flank. This action could have severely damaged the American position. However, Graves did not want to risk destruction to a ship on the river's shoals, which he had never bothered to chart.

Q. How many times did the British charge the American lines at Bunker Hill?

A. The British charged three times. On the third charge, the Americans retreated because they had run out of ammunition. Of the approximately 3,000 Americans in the battle, 441 were casualties. The British suffered about 1,150 casualties, or 40 percent of their 2,500 men.

Q. Five hundred British reinforcements had been sent over for the third assault through the initiative of what British general?

A. General Henry Clinton's action saved the day for the British army.

Without reinforcements, they would have been unable to mount a third attack.

Q. Of which colonial leader at Bunker Hill did a veteran say, "I tell ye that if it had not been for _____ there would have been no fight"?

A. Colonel William Prescott. Because of his personal example, his men kept up their work, building their defenses, and stayed there to fight without rest, food, or water. During the French and Indian War, the British had offered Prescott an officer's commission in their army.

Q. After Bunker Hill, what British general said, "A dear bought victory, another such would have ruined us"?

A. General Henry Clinton.

Q. Did the Americans generally think of Bunker Hill as a defeat or a victory?

A. At first the Americans regarded Bunker Hill as a defeat, and no one wanted to claim the honor of having directed it. However, over time it came to be seen as a great victory of raw recruits over veteran soldiers. The Americans had fought bravely and only retreated because of lack of ammunition.

Q. What member of Congress nominated George Washington as the commander in chief of the Continental army in June? Washington assumed command around Boston in July.

A. John Adams nominated Washington, a Virginian, partially because he recognized the need to gain the support of the southern colonies in a fight that had so far involved only New England. When chosen for the position of commander in chief, Washington said, "I beg it to be remembered by every gentleman in this room that I this day declare with the utmost sincerity that I do not think myself equal to the command I am honored with." Though he humbly accepted the position, it is noteworthy that as a delegate in Congress, Washington wore his military uniform from the French and Indian War.

Q. Samuel Adams had seconded John Adams's nomination of Washington. Were Samuel and John related to each other?

A. Yes, they were second cousins.

Q. The Continental army originated from the militias of four colonies. Name three of the colonies.

A. Connecticut, Massachusetts, New Hampshire, and Rhode Island.

Q. Who designed the first money for the Continental Congress in 1775, to provide payment to the army?

A. Paul Revere, who was a silversmith. He also learned to manufacture gunpowder and cast cannon. Later he discovered a process for rolling sheet copper and made the boilers for a steam ferry built by Robert Fulton. During the war, Revere was the official courier between the Massachusetts Provincial Assembly and the Continental Congress.

Q. How many lashes did the Congressional Articles of War allow for punishing a soldier in the Continental army in 1775?

A. In 1775 39 lashes were allowed; this was raised to 100 in 1776, though Washington favored 500. At the time, the British army allowed up to 1,000 lashes.

Q. On June 17, when Washington was appointed to head the Continental army, four major generals were also appointed. Identify them.

A. Artemus Ward, already commanding troops around Boston, was chosen first. The other three were Israel Putnam, the only officer voted for unanimously; ex-British officer Charles Lee, whom Washington requested; and Philip Schuyler, an experienced soldier from one of New York's leading families. In addition, Horatio Gates was appointed adjutant general. Congress chose eight brigadier generals, seven of whom were New Englanders, as were most of the troops.

Q. The pay established by Congress for a major general was $166 a month. Was this five, fifteen, or twenty-five times larger than a private's pay?

A. The pay for major generals was twenty-five times that of a private, who was paid $6 2/3 a month. Congress paid brigadier generals a monthly rate of $125, captains $20, lieutenants $13 1/3, and corporals $7 1/3.

Q. What was the larger unit in the Continental army, a brigade, regiment, or battalion?

A. A brigade had two or three regiments. The term "battalion" was used synonymously with regiment. One of Washington's problems in organizing the army around Boston stemmed from the differences in the sizes of units in various states. Companies ranged in size from 32 to 95 men, and while Rhode Island and New Hampshire fielded 590 men in a regiment, Connecticut had 1,000.

Q. What Virginian raised a company of ninety-six riflemen in ten days?

A. Daniel Morgan. He marched his men the 600 miles to Boston in twenty-one days—without losing a man—an average of more than twenty-eight miles per day. His riflemen as a group were very undisciplined, and Washington wished that many of them had never come.

Q. Many of the New Englanders had never before seen rifles like the ones Morgan's men carried. What was the difference between a rifle and a musket?

A. The barrel of a musket was smooth. In a rifle spiral grooves were cut inside the barrel to make the bullet rotate in flight, which increased its accuracy. Rifles were invented in central Europe as early as 1500.

Q. Although the American rifle with a 300-yard range was much more accurate than the standard flintlock musket with an 80 to 100 yard range, it had several disadvantages. What were they?

A. It could not be equipped with a bayonet, was heavier, and took longer to load than a musket. Rifles could not be manufactured as quickly as muskets; each one had to be made completely by hand. Rifles varied greatly in caliber; thus each rifleman had to pour and shape his own bullets as precisely as possible for his own rifle. Many colonists used British muskets until later in the war when the French supplied the Americans with the "Charleville" musket. The French musket was lighter than the British musket and shot a smaller bullet, thus conserving on lead, which was scarce.

Q. What additional weapon was carried by bayonet-less American riflemen?

A. Many carried tomahawks.

Q. What was the standard musket used by the British?

A. The "Brown Bess" dated from around 1700. It weighed over eleven pounds, had a 46-inch barrel, and shot a bullet seven-tenths of an inch in diameter. It also came equipped with a 17-inch bayonet. The average soldier could shoot two to three rounds a minute. Hessians were expected to shoot four to five rounds per minute.

Q. What kind of rifle was patented by British colonel Patrick Ferguson in December 1776?

A. Ferguson patented the breech-loading rifle. Unfortunately for the British cause, due to the decision of General William Howe, fewer than 200 breech-loading rifles were used during the war. Ferguson had formed a corps of volunteer riflemen equipped with his rifle and had been assigned to Howe's army without Howe's consent. Ferguson was wounded at Brandywine. The conservative Howe, who probably realized the rifles would influence a change in tactics, put the rifles in storage. In the American Civil War, generals also opposed the introduction of breechloaders into the U.S. Army.

Q. Around Boston, Washington never had sufficient powder. What were the most rounds of ammunition per man that he had enough powder to supply?

A. Washington never had enough powder to supply more than thirty rounds per man. At one point there was only enough powder for nine rounds per man.

Q. Because of the ammunition shortage, what weapon did Benjamin Franklin suggest using?
A. Franklin suggested using bows and arrows. Though his suggestion was rejected, several thousand iron-pointed pikes on 12-foot shafts were procured for Washington's army.

Q. How many rounds of ammunition did a British soldier carry?
A. He carried sixty rounds. A soldier could carry a pack of over one hundred pounds into battle.

FACT

Ferguson's rifle was truly revolutionary. In a test performed before King George in the summer of 1776, Ferguson proved his rifle to be more accurate and faster firing than any other. With his rifle, Ferguson achieved four feats never before accomplished. He fired six shots in one minute, fired four shots a minute for five minutes at a target 200 yards distant, fired four shots while moving at four miles an hour, and fired his rifle after water had been poured down its barrel. In wet weather the typical flintlock went off only about one in four times. Also, a British flint was only reliable for about six shots before it needed resharpening (American flints were good for about sixty rounds). Thus, Ferguson proved the superiority of his rifle over any other of the period. Yet, like many other new innovations, the establishment regarded it skeptically and resisted its introduction.

Q. Who were the first Native Americans to aid the colonists against the British during the war?

A. The Stockbridge Native Americans of Massachusetts began to aid the colonists in 1775, with some of them enlisting as militiamen. At the time, George Washington was against the enlistment of Native Americans in the army. The Stockbridge Native Americans were Christianized and practiced agriculture, but they were not suited to camp life and were soon dismissed.

Q. In September Washington apprehended Benjamin Church, surgeon general of the army, for spying for the British. Nathanael Greene had brought Washington a coded letter taken from a prostitute who was attempting to deliver it to the British. Two amateur cryptologists deciphered the letter, which Church had written, providing intelligence on Washington's plans and forces. What punishment did the Articles of War provide for Church?

A. Church was cashiered from the army, to the disappointment of Washington, who wanted to hang him but was prevented from doing so by the Articles of War. In 1777 Church finally received his due punishment when he sailed for the West Indies on a schooner that disappeared forever.

Q. Who succeeded General Gage as commander of British forces in Boston?

A. In October General William Howe succeeded Gage, who remained as governor of Massachusetts. Both of them had fought in the French and Indian War and had much experience in American affairs.

Benedict Arnold
(1741–1801)
Revolutionary officer,
traitor

Q. Both Benedict Arnold and Ethan Allen wrote to the Continental Congress advocating an invasion of Canada. Allen wrote that two or three thousand men could take Montreal. He believed that many Canadians would flock to the American cause. Was he justified in this belief?

A. No. Though some Canadians did join to fight the British and two Canadian regiments were formed, most Canadians stayed loyal to England.

Q. In an attempt to make Canada a fourteenth colony, Congress sent an expedition to capture Montreal and Quebec. Who first commanded the expedition?

A. General Philip Schuyler, whom Washington had placed in command of the troops in the northern theater. However, due to illness, Schuyler relinquished command to Major General Richard Montgomery.

Q. Montgomery's plan to attack Montreal and Quebec was delayed by a two-month siege of what fort?

A. St. Johns. British Major Charles Preston commanded this fort on the Richelieu River. He finally surrendered on November 2, but his stubborn resistance had forced the Americans to fight a winter campaign in Canada.

Q. Ethan Allen tried to capture Montreal with 110 men. Montreal was a city of 5,000 inhabitants, with a small British garrison of about 40 men. Did he succeed in his plan?

A. No. The garrison recruited between four and five hundred Canadians and captured Allen. He was shipped to England and did not return to America until exchanged in 1778. Allen never fought against the British again.

Q. Did the Americans capture Montreal in 1775?

A. Yes. Under Montgomery, the Americans captured Montreal in November after Carleton had abandoned it. They held it until June 1776 and abandoned it in the face of an approaching British army.

Q. Washington sent a second expedition of over one thousand men to assist Montgomery in attacking Quebec. Who did he place in command?

A. Colonel Benedict Arnold, along with Captain Daniel Morgan, led the men up the Kennebec River in Maine and then through the wilderness. They did not reach the Saint Lawrence River until November 9. Due to the late start and accompanying harsh weather conditions, lack of food, and very difficult terrain, many men turned back, fell ill, or died. Consequently, only about 675 men made the trip, which took twice as long as expected. Montgomery's expedition of 300 men came down later from Montreal and joined Arnold's men in front of Quebec.

Q. Also occurring in December was the first battle of the war fought in Virginia. Name this battle, which was also the first fight between British soldiers and colonists since Bunker Hill.

A. In the battle of Great Bridge, fought on December 9, Colonel William Woodford led patriots in stopping Governor Dunmore's attack at the end of a causeway near Norfolk, Virginia. The patriots inflicted 60 casualties on the British at a cost of one wounded.

Q. What was unusual about the composition of Dunmore's army at Great Bridge?

A. About 300 to 600 black slaves joined Dunmore's army in the attack. Dunmore had induced them to join by offering to free any who would fight for Britain. All told, perhaps 800 black slaves joined Dunmore by July 1776. Dunmore officially designated them "Lord Dunmore's Ethiopian Regiment."

1776

"These are the times that try men's souls."

Q. On what date did the combined American force finally attack Quebec?

A. On January 1. After camping outside the city for several weeks in the cold, Montgomery and Arnold led the American attack in a snowstorm. They chose to attack then because many of the men's enlistments expired on January 1. In the first minutes of the attack, Montgomery was killed and Arnold wounded in the leg. With the loss of their leaders, the American attack, made simultaneously from opposite ends of the town, broke apart, and the Americans retreated. The British captured 426 Americans, killed and wounded another 60, while only 5 were killed and 13 wounded on their side. It was the first major American defeat of the war.

Q. On the first day of the year, Lord Dunmore bombarded a Virginia town and the patriots burned Tory homes in retaliation. According to historian Lynn Montross, "As Virginia's largest town went up in flames the loyalist cause perished with it." Name this town where 6,000 inhabitants then lived.

A. Norfolk, Virginia.

Q. Who wrote the famous 47-page pamphlet, *Common Sense*, which convinced many Americans to seek independence from England?

Thomas Paine
(1737–1811)
Revolutionary, agitator, pamphleteer, philosopher, author of *The Age of Reason*

A. Thomas Paine, who had only arrived in America in November 1774, published *Common Sense* anonymously in Philadelphia in January 1776. Within three months 120,000 copies were sold. Eventually a total of 500,000 copies were sold.

Q. Identify the battle known as the "Lexington and Concord of the South," fought in North Carolina by Americans against Americans.

A. Moores Creek Bridge, fought in February, was a victory for the patriots. This battle effectively ended Loyalist power in North Carolina. Thirty Tories were killed in the three-minute battle, and almost the entire 850-man force was captured while fleeing.

Q. Why did General Howe say, "The rebels have done more in one night than my whole army could do in months"?

A. On the night of March 4, 1,200 men erected field fortifications on Dorchester Heights. Since they could not dig in the frozen ground, at the suggestion of General Rufus Putnam, they used prefabricated timber frames and filled them with gabions, fascines, and bales of hay. They also constructed abatis and surrounded the works with barrels of dirt to roll down the hill in case of attack. Howe estimated that 12,000 men must have been employed to build the fortifications.

Q. What were gabions, fascines, and abatis?

A. Gabions were wicker baskets filled with earth. Fascines were made by tying brushwood together into long bundles. Abatis were felled trees, with branches intact (and sometimes sharpened), placed strategically around a fortified position.

Q. Why didn't Howe attack the fortifications on Dorchester Heights?

A. Though Howe planned a night attack, he could not elevate his artillery enough to bombard the obviously strong fortifications. An attack would have resulted in severe losses, similar to those at Bunker Hill. The attack was called off, but the decision was blamed on a severe storm that arose during the night.

Q. The Americans had besieged the British in Boston since the summer of 1775. Why did the American position on Dorchester Heights suddenly reveal the British occupation of Boston to be untenable and force the British to evacuate the city?

A. The artillery the Americans had installed on Dorchester Heights could bombard British shipping in the harbor. Following the seizure of the Heights, Howe soon sailed away to Halifax, Nova Scotia. Though the British did not burn Boston, they did loot the city. Nevertheless, they were allowed to leave unmolested on March 17. They never returned to Boston for the duration of the war. Howe left in such a hurry that he forgot to warn three British transports, carrying over six hundred troops of the Seventy-first Regiment of Highlanders, destined for Boston. The vessels were all captured by Captain Seth Harding in the *Defence* and Captain Nicholas Biddle in the *Andrea Doria*.

Q. Identify the man who led an artillery train of more than fifty pieces on forty-two sleds over snow, from Fort Ticonderoga to Boston, a distance of over three hundred miles.

A. Henry Knox, the former Boston bookseller who at the age of twenty-five commanded Washington's artillery. Knox arrived at Fort Ticonderoga on December 5, 1775. He then dragged the artillery to Cambridge by January 24, 1776. His feat enabled the Americans to force the British to evacuate Boston.

Henry Knox
(1750–1806)
Revolutionary general,
Secretary of War under
Washington

Q. Who was the last royal governor of New Jersey?

A. William Franklin, son of Benjamin Franklin. He was arrested in June, exchanged in 1778, and returned to England in 1782. Father and son did not reconcile to any extent until 1784 when they began to exchange letters.

Q. The yearlong American attempt to annex Canada was finally thwarted when a 2,000-man force, under General John Sullivan, was defeated in what battle?

A. In the June battle of Trois-Rivières, Canada, the Americans suffered 400 casualties with 200 surrendering against a dozen British losses, in an uncoordinated attack through a wilderness against British entrenchments. The Americans then left Canada after a minor battle at Ile Aux Nois, having lost a total of 5,000 casualties in all their Canadian invasions.

Q. Who was the first congressman to introduce a resolution in Congress for a declaration of independence, stating: "That these United Colonies are, and of right ought to be, free and independent States, that they are absolved from all allegiance to the British Crown, and that all political connection between them and the State of Great Britain is, and ought to be, totally dissolved"?

A. On June 7 Richard Henry Lee of Virginia introduced the resolution, which also called for foreign alliances and a confederation plan for the colonies. On June 10 Congress appointed a committee to prepare a declaration of independence by July 1.

Q. What British admiral attacked Charleston, South Carolina, in June?

A. Admiral Sir Peter Parker led an attack that failed because he could not get past Fort Sullivan on Sullivan's Island.

Q. From a half-finished Fort Sullivan, built of palmetto logs sixteen feet apart and filled with sandy soil, who repelled the British attempt to take Charleston?

A. On June 28 Colonel William Moultrie, under the overall command of General Charles Lee, repelled the British attack. The fort was renamed Fort Moultrie in honor of his defense there. With less than 450 men and thirty cannon, Moultrie fought off nine British ships possessing five guns for his every one. In a ten-hour duel, with the heaviest shelling General Lee had ever witnessed, the fort absorbed all the British cannon balls hurled at it with little harm done. At a cost of less than forty killed and wounded, the

Americans inflicted about 225 casualties, destroyed one frigate, and deterred the British from invading the southern colonies for another three years.

Q. General Henry Clinton commanded the British army in the Charleston expedition. After landing over three thousand men on Long Island, why did he cancel a planned attack across a ford to Sullivan's Island?

A. Clinton had been informed that the ford between the two islands was only eighteen inches deep at low tide. Instead Clinton learned, too late, that the ford contained seven-foot holes which would swallow up his men.

Q. The first execution ever of an American soldier by a military court occurred during the Revolutionary War. Who was executed and why?

A. Thomas Hickey was publicly hanged on June 27 in New York City in front of 20,000 people. He worked for Governor Tryon as a conspirator in a plot to deliver George Washington to the British. He was caught after he passed counterfeit currency and then bragged about his involvement with the British.

Q. Of what day did John Adams write, "It ought to be solemnized with pop and parade, with shows, games, sports, guns, bells, bonfires, and illuminations, from one end of the continent to the other, from this time forward, forevermore"?

A. John Adams wrote this of July 2, 1776, when Congress first voted for Henry Lee's resolution for independence by a vote of twelve for and none against, with New York abstaining. Congress accepted the final draft on July 4. Not until July 9 did New York finally give its assent to the Declaration of Independence.

Q. Allegedly, at the signing ceremony for the Declaration of Independence, President John Hancock stated, "We must be unanimous; there must be no pulling different ways; we must all hang together." Who then quipped, "Yes, we must indeed all hang together, or most assuredly we shall all hang separately"?

A. Benjamin Franklin.

Q. Who wrote the Declaration of Independence?

A. Thomas Jefferson, then thirty-three years old, wrote the document. He was one of a committee of five, including John Adams, Roger Sherman, Robert Livingston, and Benjamin Franklin, who had been appointed by Congress in early June to prepare a declaration of independence.

Thomas Jefferson (1743–1826) President of the United States, 1801–1809

Q. Fifty-six members of the Continental Congress signed the Declaration of Independence. Later, for their act of treason, what did fifteen of them share as a common experience?

A. Their action was considered so dangerous that the names of the signers were kept secret until January 18, 1777. By 1781 the British had destroyed the homes of fifteen of the signers. A few were captured by the British and treated cruelly in prison.

FACT

Jefferson wrote the first draft in two days and made fifteen changes before submitting it to Congress on June 28. In preparing the Declaration of Independence, Jefferson incorporated suggestions from John Adams and Benjamin Franklin. Franklin had written a declaration the previous July, but had been persuaded not to bring it before Congress at that time. Before reaching its final form, congressional delegates improved the document. They deleted two long paragraphs and made other minor changes. The document was signed first by the president of the Congress, John Hancock, on August 2, after it had been engrossed on parchment. The last of the delegates to sign the Declaration was Thomas McKean of Delaware, who is believed to have signed it in 1781.

Q. What was the first state to declare independence?

A. Rhode Island declared its independence in the first week of May. New York was the last state to declare, waiting until July 15.

Q. Did Thomas Jefferson own slaves?

A. Yes, Jefferson owned about two hundred slaves. One-third of the signers of the Declaration of Independence were slave owners.

Q. George Washington also owned slaves. Did he own more or less than Jefferson?

A. Washington owned 135 slaves. He freed some during the war, and in his will, he freed the rest.

George Washington
(1732–1799)
President of the United States, 1789–1797

Q. Where did the largest expeditionary force ever assembled by the British, up to that time, land in August?

A. General William Howe landed 15,000 of his 32,000-man army on Long Island.

Q. Shortly after the British arrived in New York, which of Washington's generals fell ill and had to relinquish command of Long Island?

A. General Nathanael Greene, who was familiar with the lay of the land, was replaced by General Sullivan, who was not.

Q. Which side was victorious in the battle of Long Island, fought in August?

A. The British under General Howe were victorious. They defeated American forces under General John Sullivan and Lord Stirling, inflicted 970 casualties and captured 1,000 men, including Sullivan and Stirling, while incurring 400 casualties themselves.

Q. What American general faced over nine thousand British with less than one thousand men after the rest of the American army had fled?

A. General William Alexander, or Lord Stirling. He was taken prisoner and exchanged the following month. He received a promotion to major general in February 1777.

Q. The British general facing Stirling, as a member of the House of Commons, had once boasted that with 5,000 men he could march from one end of the American continent to the other. Who was he?

A. General James Grant, who with 7,000 men at hand waited for 2,000 more reinforcements before attacking Stirling.

Q. Washington reinforced Brooklyn Heights, but after council decided to retreat. During darkness and fog, the miraculous boat evacuation of 9,500 men in nine hours across the East River to Manhattan Island saved Washington's army from destruction. Who commanded the Twenty-first Massachusetts Regiment that handled the boats?

A. John Glover. His regiment of fishermen and seafarers were mostly from Marblehead, Massachusetts.

Q. Name the pass that Howe's forces found virtually undefended, which enabled them to outflank Washington's army on Long Island.

A. Jamaica Pass.

Q. What term for army enlistment did Congress agree to after the battle of Long Island?

A. After prodding from Washington, Congress agreed to a three-year enlistment.

Q. Name the inventor of the submarine.

A. David Bushnell invented a one-man submarine, the *Turtle*, built of oak, banded with iron, and coated with tar, in 1775.

Q. On September 6, while Howe's fleet lay anchored around New York City, Sergeant Ezra Lee in David Bushnell's submarine the *Turtle* attacked the British man-of-war *Asia* in New York Harbor. Was the attack successful?

A. No. Lee could not screw through the copper hull to attach the explosives and was forced to withdraw. The British later eliminated the *Turtle* when they sank the sloop that carried it on the Hudson River.

Q. What was the first battle in which the Continental army beat the British in a stand-up fight out in the open?
A. In mid-September the British crossed over from Long Island to Manhattan Island. In the battle of Harlem Heights, Continental army units counterattacked an elite British reconnaissance force out in the open and drove them from the field.

Q. At the battle of Pelham Bay, who commanded the 750 men who held off 4,000 British troops for a day, enabling Washington's army to escape a trap on Manhattan Island?
A. John Glover's Massachusetts regiment of Marblehead fisherman saved the day. They were the same men who had rowed the army across the East River to escape from Long Island.

Q. When fire broke out in New York City on September 21, why weren't the alarm bells rung?
A. They had been melted down for ammunition.

Q. Did the patriots set fire to New York City?
A. Yes. Patriots—several were caught and hanged by the British—set about a dozen fires. About one-fourth of the city (600 houses) burned to the ground in the fire. Washington denied knowing about a plot to burn the city.

Q. Why did Nathanael Greene favor the burning of New York City?
A. He argued that the patriots would never be able to regain the city—two-thirds of the residents were Tories anyway—and burning it would deny a place of barracks for the British army. Washington had questioned Congress about the issue, and they had answered that no damage should be done to the city. Congress was confident that Washington would be able to retake the city.

Q. Name the patriot who when caught spying on British troops on Long Island reportedly said before his execution, "I only regret that I have but one life to lose for my country"?

A. Nathan Hale. He actually may have said these words, which paraphrased a line from Joseph Addison's *CATO*, America's favorite play during the eighteenth century. As an officer from Connecticut, Hale had responded to Washington's call for paid volunteers to spy on the British. The former schoolmaster was caught when recognized by a Tory relative, Samuel Hale. He was brought to Howe and searched. Incriminating documents were found on him. Since he was out of uniform, he was hung as a spy.

Q. Could Hale have used invisible ink to write the information he was carrying, thus hiding its contents?

A. Yes. An American had invented invisible ink three years earlier. However, Hale's commanding officer, Colonel Thomas Knowlton, did not supply him with any invisible ink or a code to write messages in cipher.

Q. Who commanded a corps of about five hundred Tories around New York City called "the Queen's American Rangers"?

A. Major Robert Rogers, commander of the famous Rogers's Rangers, had been an American hero during the French and Indian War. Rogers lived in England from 1769 to 1775, then returned to America. Washington had jailed him on suspicion of spying for the British. He escaped to the British and was commissioned to recruit the Queen's American Rangers. He was later defeated in a skirmish near White Plains at Mamaroneck. When Colonel John Haslet's Delaware Continentals made a surprise night attack, the first instance of Americans fighting against each other in large regular army units took place. Rogers was stripped of his command and returned to England.

Q. In what battle did the British make the first formal cavalry charge of the war?

A. At White Plains the British cavalry charged up Chatterton Hill and drove off Alexander McDougall's troops. During the war, both sides made only limited use of cavalry in battle. Instead, they used cavalry primarily for reconnaissance or harassment.

Q. What British commander invaded New York from Canada in October?

A. Sir Guy Carleton invaded New York with an army of 13,000 men.

Q. In what body of water is Valcour Island located?

A. Valcour Island is in Lake Champlain in the state of New York. Lake Champlain is 125 miles long and is a link between the St. Lawrence and Hudson Rivers. It was the natural invasion route for both sides during the war.

Q. Carleton knew the Americans had been building a squadron of vessels to thwart any British move down the lake. In ninety days, he constructed a fleet that sailed down Lake Champlain with Captain Thomas Pringle in command. Carleton met the American squadron at Valcour Island. Who commanded the American squadron?

A. Benedict Arnold constructed and commanded the outgunned American squadron. Carleton had 28 vessels, which could throw more than 1,300 pounds of metal, more than twice that of the Americans. Also, he had experienced seaman while Arnold had almost none. Arnold kept his vessels hidden behind Valcour Island. When the British fleet passed the island, they spotted Arnold's vessels and had to beat against the wind at a disadvantage to attack Arnold.

Q. What were the immediate and long-term results from the battle of Valcour Island?

A. Arnold's squadron fought a six-hour battle, and both sides suffered losses. However, Arnold had used up three-quarters of his ammunition and knew the superior British fleet could finish him off the next day, so he slipped by the British in the night. During the British chase the next day, Arnold lost most of his squadron as he retreated down the lake. His men burned Crown Point and retreated to Ticonderoga. Though Arnold had been tactically defeated, he had won a strategic victory. He had delayed Carleton's invasion by forcing Carleton to build a fleet. After victory, Carleton thought it was too late in the season to begin a campaign, so he retreated back to Canada. Arnold's heroic effort might just have saved the Revolution by buying another year's time for the Americans to gather an army to defeat the British invasion from Canada the next year.

Q. Arnold was short of grapeshot and chain shot in the battle. What were they used for?

A. Grapeshot consisted of clusters of iron balls, which scattered when discharged from a cannon. It was very effective against gun batteries, ships, and massed formations. Chain shot, made from a chain connected to iron balls, was used against a ship's rigging.

Q. What Hudson River fort did Howe's army capture in November?

A. A 13,000-man attacking force took Fort Washington, capturing over 2,500 Americans while suffering 500 casualties. It was here that Margaret Corbin carried water to the men serving the guns until her husband was severely wounded, after which she took his place. Four days after Colonel Robert Magaw had surrendered Fort Washington, Fort Lee also fell to the British. The garrison, including Nathanael Greene, barely escaped. The loss of Fort Washington marked the greatest American loss of men until 1780.

Q. Where was General Charles Lee taken prisoner on December 13?

A. During the retreat across New Jersey after the fall of Fort Washington, Lee delayed obeying Washington's command to join forces. He was then caught in a tavern by a British patrol under Banastre Tarleton while away from camp. Ironically, Lee was captured by men in the same regiment in which he had served in the British army. Lee had been writing a letter to Horatio Gates in which he characterized Washington as "most damnably deficient."

Q. In the middle of December, who wrote a pamphlet that began with the words, "These are the times that try men's souls: The summer soldier and the sunshine patriot will, in this crisis, shrink from the service of his country; but he that stands it Now, deserves the love and thanks of man and woman"?

A. Thomas Paine wrote *The Crises* while retreating across New Jersey with Washington's army. Paine was an aide-de-camp to General Greene. After the loss of New York and during the ensuing retreat, the morale of the army plummeted to a very low point. Some men were deserting to the British. Washington himself wrote to his nephew that without reinforcements soon, "I think the game is pretty near up." The 6,000 men he had at the time would be reduced to only 1,400 when enlistments expired on December 31.

Q. Which river did Washington's army cross to attack the Hessian troops at Trenton, New Jersey?

A. The Delaware River. Washington was determined to raise his army's morale by obtaining a victory over an isolated outpost of 1,400 Hessians under Colonel Johann Rall.

Q. When did Washington cross the Delaware River to attack the Hessian troops in Trenton?

A. On the night of December 25, the army was ferried across by John Glover's regiment.

Q. What type of boats peculiar to the Delaware did Washington use to cross the river?

A. Durham boats, named after their builder, Robert Durham, who had been building them since 1750. The boats were forty to sixty feet long, eight feet wide and two feet deep, and each had a mast with two sails. Durham boats were able to transport horses and artillery as well as men.

Q. Did Rall have prior knowledge that Washington was marching toward him?

A. Yes. Though Rall had the information, he probably had not read it. While drinking wine and playing cards in the middle of the night at a party, he had been handed a note informing him that the

American army was marching against the town. He put the note into his pocket unread. It was found in his pocket after his death two days later.

Q. In the battle of Trenton, why did Colonel Charles Scott of the Fifth Virginia Regiment tell his men to fire at the legs of the enemy?

A. Because each man wounded in the leg would require two men to carry him off the battlefield.

Q. What future American president was wounded in the battle?

A. James Monroe was one of the few Americans wounded in this battle, in which over one hundred Hessians were killed and wounded and over nine hundred were taken prisoner.

Q. Name the two other commanders Washington assigned to cross the Delaware with separate forces to assist in his attack on Trenton.

A. Lieutenant Colonel John Cadwalader was to cross with almost two thousand men near Bordentown, and General James Ewing was to cross with about seven hundred men at Trenton Ferry. Ewing thought that the river's icy condition made it impossible to cross. Cadwalader brought 600 men across, but did not see how he could get his artillery across and essentially did nothing. Thus Washington's plan to attack Princeton and New Brunswick next was ruined.

Q. Writing of the battle of Trenton, what historian wrote, "Yet it may be doubted whether so small a number of men ever employed so short a space of time with greater or more lasting results upon the history of the world"?

A. George Otto Trevelyan. Washington's men, some without shoes, had marched and fought continuously for as many as fifty hours in the most miserable of weather. Washington's victory caused the British to abandon their posts along the Delaware River and immensely raised the morale and prestige of the army in a time of desperation. The victory also raised Washington's stature as a general in the eyes of his countrymen and his opponents.

1777

"If Washington is the general I take him to be, he will not be found there in the morning."

Q. Why has 1777 been referred to as "Year of the Hangman"?

A. Some superstitious people thought the last three digits of 1777 represented gibbets for patriot leaders if they failed to succeed in the Revolution.

Q. In what battle did Washington risk his life by riding between the opposing lines to rally his troops?

A. In the battle of Princeton, fought on January 3, 1777. Washington, on his white horse, rode out in front of his troops to rally them and escaped unhurt from a volley fired by the British. The victory at Princeton enabled the American army to regain control of New Jersey. The victory was made possible because on December 30, 1776, more than half of Washington's army agreed to serve another six weeks for a bounty of ten dollars. Troop enlistments had been due to expire on January 1.

Q. Before the battle of Princeton, British troops arrived in front of Washington's army, pinning the Americans against the Delaware River near Trenton. What British general allowed Washington's army to escape by failing to attack in the evening, bragging that he would "bag the fox" in the morning?

A. General Charles Cornwallis. Cornwallis should have listened to General Sir William Erskine who said, "If Washington is the general I take him to be, he will not be found there in the morning." Washington's army escaped the trap by slipping away quietly in the night while leaving their campfires burning. They hid their getaway by muffling the artillery wheels with cloth and moving down a side road. They marched around Cornwallis's army, then attacked the rear guard at Princeton before Cornwallis could come to their relief.

General Charles Cornwallis, 1st Marquis Cornwallis (1738–1805) British general in American Revolution, defeated at Yorktown

Q. Where did Washington's army gather for winter quarters after the victories at Trenton and Princeton?

A. The army spent the winter of 1776–77 at Morristown, New Jersey. Washington had planned on staying there only a few days, but ended up staying for five months. Though the army was in deplorable condition, Washington frequently sent out men to harass British foraging parties. They often succeeded in preventing the British from gathering supplies.

Q. What new state was granted independence on January 16 and essentially became a free republic?

A. Vermont. Previously known as the New Hampshire Grants, it was formed from land west of New Hampshire.

FACT

The first cannonball fired by the Americans at the battle of Princeton entered Nassau Hall at Princeton College and passed through the portrait of George II without touching the frame. The college trustees later paid Charles Wilson Peale to paint Washington's portrait and then used the former King's frame.

Q. Where did the first mass inoculation in America occur?

A. It occurred at the army's Morristown encampment in February. All of Washington's troops at the camp were inoculated against smallpox, which had been rapidly spreading through both the British and American armies.

Q. During the winter of 1776–77, did Congress offer men a greater bounty to enlist than the colonies did?

A. No. Congress offered a bounty of $20 and a hundred acres of land to any man who would enlist for three years or for the duration of the war. New England colonies began enlistment offers with an additional $33.33. Later Massachusetts offered a total of $86.66 to enlist. This made Washington's task of raising men for his army very difficult.

Q. During an attack on Boonesborough in April 1777, Daniel Boone and his men had to run through a party of Shawnees blocking their path to the fort. Name the famous frontiersman who saved Daniel Boone's life twice that day.

A. Simon Kenton shot one Shawnee and clubbed another one with his rifle as they attempted to tomahawk and knife Boone while he lay semiconscious on the ground, felled by a bullet to his ankle. Kenton then lifted Boone up and carried him into the fort. Like Boone, Kenton had also entered Kentucky in 1775 from the Ohio River. During the entire early period of Kentucky, Kenton helped feed and establish settlers, led scouts who warned the settlements of attacks, worked to defend the settlers, and chased Native American war parties across the Ohio River.

Q. In late April, over two thousand men, under former New York governor William Tryon, raided Danbury, Connecticut, where they burned nineteen houses, other buildings, and many supplies. Who was appointed a major general due to his actions harassing the British retreat from Danbury?

A. Upon learning of the British raid, Arnold, who had been sulking because he had been passed over for promotion in February, rode immediately to the vicinity and took command of some of the troops under generals David Wooster and Gold Silliman. For his attempt to block the British retreat, during which he shot an attacking Tory demanding his surrender, Congress appointed Arnold a major general in May, citing his "gallant conduct." Congress had previously passed over Arnold and promoted five brigadier generals to major generals. After his promotion, Arnold then sought to be ranked ahead of these five brigadiers; however, Congress ignored him.

Q. Name the famous Frenchman who arrived in America in June and assisted Washington for the remainder of the war.

A. Marie Joseph Paul Yves Roch Gilbert du Motier, or the Marquis de Lafayette, one of France's richest men, arrived with Johann Kalb, known in America as Baron de Kalb.

Q. How old was Lafayette when he reported to George Washington? He had already been commissioned a major general by Congress in July.

Marquis de Lafayette
(1757–1834)
French patriot, general in
Continental army

A. Nineteen. Lafayette volunteered to serve without pay and supported the patriot cause with a substantial amount of his money.

Q. Name the American agent in Paris who sent Lafayette, de Kalb, and many others from Europe to join the American army.

A. Silas Deane. Congress had sent Deane to France in 1776 to negotiate with the French government. Deane also found four engineers for the Continental army, but he exceeded his authority by contracting commissions with too many men, both qualified and unqualified, and later turned against the Revolution.

Q. During the spring, Howe tried unsuccessfully to draw Washington's army into battle on open ground. Failing in this stratagem, he decided to move on Philadelphia, the colonial capital. What route did Howe take by boat after leaving Sandy Hook on July 23, Chesapeake Bay or the Delaware River?

A. He traveled by way of the Chesapeake Bay after pausing at the Delaware capes. It took his fleet an incredible thirty-two days to reach the landing at the head of the Elk. At one point before sailing, Howe's cavalry and troops boarded the fleet of 260 warships and transports and spent almost two weeks, beginning on July 8, pent up in the holds of the vessels, during the hottest season of the year.

Q. As Howe's army moved toward Philadelphia, an advance guard of Cornwallis's "grand division" fought and routed about sixteen hundred men under General William Maxwell on September 3. It was the only battle of the war fought on Delaware soil. Name the battle.

A. The battle of Cooch's Bridge, named for Thomas Cooch, an American colonel whose home was nearby, was also probably the first battle where the Stars and Stripes was unfurled.

Q. What battle did Washington's army fight to defend Philadelphia?

A. The battle of Brandywine. Howe had been closing in on the colonial capital of Philadelphia in anticipation of ending the rebellion with its capture. On September 11 Washington fought the battle of Brandywine, with a 10,000-man army against Howe's 15,000-man army, to prevent Howe from capturing Philadelphia. After losing 1,200 men (twice that of the British), Washington was forced to withdraw.

Q. What was Brandywine, a creek, mountain, or town?

A. A creek. Washington positioned his army behind the natural defensive barrier of Brandywine Creek. Howe would have to attack to advance on Philadelphia.

Q. Although there were numerous fords where the enemy could cross, at what ford did Washington concentrate his men?

A. Chadd's Ford.

Q. What role did Howe assign to General Wilhelm von Knyphausen during the battle?

A. General Knyphausen had to hold the American army's attention with 5,000 men and keep them in position behind Chadd's Ford with an artillery barrage and threat of attack. Meanwhile Howe and Cornwallis marched the rest of the army around Washington's right flank and crossed at another ford. The plan, which was very similar to the plan of battle on Long Island, nearly succeeded in trapping Washington's army. Washington moved to meet the threat only when he heard artillery fire coming from the direction of the rear of his army.

Q. Is it true that the British were responsible for cracking the Liberty Bell after they entered Philadelphia on September 23?

A. No. Before the British entered Philadelphia, the Liberty Bell was removed from the state house belfry and stored in Zion's Church in Allentown, Pennsylvania, until the British vacated Philadelphia. The bell was restored to its resting place on June 27, 1778. It is not known with certainty when the bell was cracked, but it probably happened in 1835 during the funeral of Chief Justice John Marshall. The crack caused a distortion in the bell's bong, and it was rung for the last time in 1846. The bell now resides in Philadelphia's Independence Hall.

Q. In what country was the original Liberty Bell cast, France, England, or America?

A. England. In 1751 the Assembly of the Province of Pennsylvania ordered the bell through their agent in London, Robert Charles. Thomas Lester of London was to cast a bell weighing about two thousand pounds and measuring twelve feet in diameter.

Q. On the Liberty Bell are the words, "Proclaim liberty throughout all the land unto all the inhabitants thereof." What was the source for this inscription?
   a. Thomas Lester of London
   b. The Bible
   c. Benjamin Franklin

A. The answer is b. The words are found in chapter 25 in the book of Leviticus. The full inscription on the bell, as ordered by the Assembly of the Province of Pennsylvania, reads:

Proclaim liberty throughout all the land unto all the inhabitants thereof,
Leviticus XXV, V, XL
By order of the Assembly of the Province of Pennsylvania for the State
House in Philadelphia.

Q. When told that General Howe had taken Philadelphia, who replied, "I beg your pardon, sir, Philadelphia has taken Howe"?

A. Benjamin Franklin responded with this quip at a dinner party in France.

Q. Name the American general called "Mad Anthony."

A. Anthony Wayne started as a colonel in January 1776. He was promoted to a brigadier general in February 1777 and would serve with Washington throughout the war.

Q. Soon after the Battle of Brandywine, where did British General Charles Grey massacre Anthony Wayne's men in a surprise nighttime bayonet attack?

F A C T

The Liberty Bell was shipped to America in 1752 and was hung in September. The first time it was rung, it cracked. Rather then send it back to London to be recast, the Philadelphians had two local bell founders, named John Pass and John Stow, recast it. They melted the bell and added an ounce and a half of copper per pound to reduce the metal's brittleness. The new bell lacked the former bell's clarity of tone. Pass and Stow cast yet another bell. Many people did not like the sound of this bell either, so another bell was ordered from Thomas Lester. When the new bell arrived, it did not sound any better than the American bell, which the Philadelphians decided to keep. It is not known what happened to Lester's bell.

A. At Paoli the surprised Americans lost approximately three hundred men while less than ten British were killed or wounded. Wayne's division of 1,500 men had been detached with orders to attack the British baggage train. Meanwhile, a Tory informed the British of the location of Wayne's camp. Wayne never forgot the humiliation and later revenged the attack in a similar fashion.

Q. At what battle did the American army retreat because of defective cartridge boxes and rain-ruined musket cartridges?

A. At White Horse Tavern on September 16. Many regiments could not even fire a shot.

Q. In what battle did Washington's army make a surprise attack on Howe's divided army near Philadelphia?

A. At Germantown on October 4. Washington's nearly successful attack was repelled with heavy losses to the Americans. It was the first battle of the war in which an American army directly attacked a major part of a British army.

Q. Why did Washington decide to attack at Germantown so soon after the defeat at Brandywine?

A. Washington had received two intercepted letters that informed him that Howe was dispatching about 3,000 men to Billingsport to aid the British navy in opening up the Delaware River to bring in supplies. Howe's army was thus reduced to about 9,000 while Washington's army was being reinforced by 900 Continentals under General Alexander McDougall, 1,000 Maryland militia under General William Smallwood, and other troops numbering about 11,000. A war council of general officers unanimously favored an attack; thus, for only the second time in over two years—the first instance being at Trenton—Washington ordered an offensive action by his whole infantry.

Q. What tactical error by Washington significantly influenced the American defeat at Germantown?

A. Washington attempted to coordinate columns of troops approaching on four roads and separated by a distance of between six to seven miles. Washington rode with General John Sullivan in the center column. On Sullivan's left, General Nathanael Greene commanded a column that contained two-thirds of the American army. On the far left, General William Smallwood commanded militia that never reached the battle. On the far right, General John Armstrong made only light contact and did not participate in the main battle.

Q. What fortified place contributed to the British victory at Germantown, because from there British troops delayed and harassed the American attack?

A. The Chew House. Washington's decision to reduce Chew House before advancing with the rest of his army may have cost him a victory.

Q. Who advised Washington not to leave the Chew House behind him without subduing it?

A. Henry Knox advised Washington that an occupied castle could not be left in his rear. Washington always respected Knox, who had read the military classics in his book shop.

Q. Germantown was a defeat for Washington, his army losing 1,000 men compared to 500 for the British. He was also forced to withdraw from the field of battle. Why then was the battle a great morale booster for his army?

A. Despite the battle loss, this was the first time Washington's army routed some of Britain's best troops in a direct frontal assault that narrowly missed victory. In addition, the French were greatly impressed that Washington's army could bounce back so soon from its defeat at Brandywine only a few weeks before. This feat was something expected only of a veteran army.

Q. What French general did American diplomat Silas Deane agree to make a major general, predating his commission to August l, 1776, and in effect, enabling him to surpass Generals Greene and Sullivan in seniority and replace Knox as artillery chief?

A. General Philippe Charles Jean Baptiste Tronson de Coudray. Congress attempted to resolve the dilemma by making him a major general of the staff with no authority over commanders of the line. Friction was avoided when de Coudray drowned after falling off a ferry.

Q. For the 1777 British campaign, General John Burgoyne had planned a three-prong attack in New York State. What was the objective of the attack?

A. Albany, New York. Burgoyne would lead one army from Canada, through the Lake Champlain route. Another army would travel from the west via Lake Ontario and the Mohawk River, and Howe would move northward from New York City, on the Hudson River. Burgoyne believed that by controlling the Hudson River, New England could be isolated and the rebellion ended. Burgoyne led an army of almost 8,000 composed of 4,000 British, 3,000 Germans, 400 Native Americans, 250 French Canadians and American Loyalists, plus as many as 2,000 women and children.

Q. Why was Burgoyne called "Gentleman Johnny"?

A. His soldiers gave Burgoyne the nickname because he treated them humanely. In the Revolutionary War era, when soldiers were not treated well, Burgoyne took heed of their personal comforts and did not exercise cruel punishments. He tried to inspire them and teach by example, not by force.

General John Burgoyne
(Gentleman Johnny)
(1722–1792)
British army officer
in American Revolution,
dramatist

Q. By his actions, what British general doomed Burgoyne's strategy to control the Hudson River and isolate New England from the rest of the colonies?

A. Instead of moving up the Hudson River to assist Burgoyne, General William Howe transported his army from New York to Pennsylvania to attack the colonial capital at Philadelphia. Only when it was far too late to save Burgoyne's army did Howe send an expedition to meet them.

Q. Name the secretary of state for the colonies, who was supposed to be coordinating British strategy.

A. Lord George Germain held the position from 1775 until 1782. He acted too late and with insufficient force to ensure cooperation between Howe and Burgoyne.

Q. Name the commander who abandoned Fort Ticonderoga to Burgoyne's army without a fight.

A. In July Major General Arthur St. Clair abandoned the fort, which Polish engineer Tadeusz (Thaddeus) Kosciuszko had strengthened. St. Clair's garrison of 2,300 men was expected to hold the fort for at least several weeks to delay Burgoyne's advance and buy time to gather an army against him.

Q. Why did St. Clair abandon Ticonderoga without a fight?

A. The British occupied the supposedly inaccessible Mount Defiance after Burgoyne's subordinate, Major General William Phillips, proclaimed, "Where a goat can go, a man can go, and where a man can go he can drag a gun." Once in position on Mount Defiance, the British could fire their artillery down into the fort. Seeing his predicament, St. Clair abandoned Fort Ticonderoga, crossed Lake Champlain, also abandoned Ticonderoga's sister fort, Mount Independence, and fled toward Hubbardton, Vermont.

Q. After the American army fled Fort Ticonderoga, what was the next battle for Burgoyne's army?

A. In a rearguard action at Hubbardton, troops, led by Colonel Ebenezer Fraser, halted the pursuing British corps, with heavy casualties incurred on both sides.

Q. What fatal mistake did Burgoyne make after the battle of Hubbardton?

A. Instead of returning to the Hudson River and a wagon road, Burgoyne tried a shortcut through twenty-three miles of forest to Fort Edward. His army's journey consumed twenty-four days, thus buying time for the Americans to gather a large army against him. Due to Burgoyne's penchant for luxury, he insisted on bringing all his own baggage and liquor, which alone required thirty carts. He also brought wagons to carry the women and extra supplies and forty-two cannon. All of these additional encumbrances prevented him from making a speedy advance.

Q. Why did Burgoyne choose the difficult route through the forest from Skenesboro to Fort Edward, a route that he had previously rejected?

A. Burgoyne said that he feared the retrograde motion would have a harmful effect on his troops and encourage the Americans. He may also have been influenced by the advice of the Tory Philip Skene, who had an interest in Burgoyne cutting a road from his property to the Hudson River.

Q. What did General Schuyler do to slow Burgoyne's advance?

A. He put a thousand axmen to work felling trees, destroying bridges and digging ditches. He also removed the inhabitants of the area and their cattle and destroyed crops that could feed Burgoyne's army.

Q. What incident turned many of the Loyalist inhabitants against Burgoyne when he invaded New York?

A. The murder of Jane McCrea. Native Americans attached to Burgoyne's army killed and scalped Jane McCrea, who was engaged to Tory officer David Jones in Burgoyne's army. No one felt safe from the Native Americans, and most of the 500 attached to Burgoyne's army departed soon after the McCrea murder because of the severe restrictions Burgoyne now began to impose on them.

Joseph Brant
(Thayendanegea)
(1742–1807)
Mohawk Indian chief,
leader in Cherry Valley
massacre

Q. Name the Mohawk chief who led four tribes of the Iroquois League—the Mohawks, Senecas, Cayugas, and Onondogas—against the Americans during the war?

A. Thayendanegea (Joseph Brant) was also commissioned a colonel in the British army. He was greatly influenced by his friendship with Englishman William Johnson, who had influenced the Iroquois to join the British against the French during the French and Indian War. Brant had acquired an education, had converted to Anglicanism, and helped translate religious texts into his native language. He also restrained Native Americans from committing atrocities.

Q. Identify the two remaining tribes of the Iroquois League, who sided with the Americans during the war?

A. About three hundred Oneidas and Tuscaroras were persuaded to join the Americans by Presbyterian minister Samuel Kirkland. They were enlisted into the army by Philip Schuyler.

Q. Did more Native Americans fight for the British or for the Americans during the course of the war?

A. Approximately thirteen thousand Native Americans fought for the British, far more than fought for the Americans.

Q. What caused the battle of Bennington to be fought?

A. Burgoyne had been informed he could obtain abundant supplies at Bennington. He detached an expedition of 800 men under Lieutenant Colonel Friedrich Baum to obtain cattle, horses, and carriages. He needed 1,300 horses for Major General Baron von Riedesel's horseless dragoons. Baum had to march his men southeast forty miles to obtain these supplies.

Q. What side won the battle of Bennington on August 16, a battle where American militia fought British and German regulars?

A. Two thousand American militia under John Stark annihilated the greatly outnumbered force under Baum. When a German relief force under Colonel von Breymann arrived and began forcing the militia to retreat, Colonel Seth Warner's Continental regiment arrived in time to turn the battle around. The

General John Stark
(1728–1822)
Revolutionary general

battle weakened Burgoyne's army by about nine hundred men. After the battle, Stark, who had previously resigned his colonel's commission because he had been passed over for promotion, was officially appointed a brigadier general in the Continental army.

Q. While Burgoyne's army marched from the north, Colonel Barry St. Leger marched from the west through the Mohawk River valley. In early August, St. Leger's force of 2,000 men laid siege to what fort?

A. They besieged Fort Stanwix, commanded by Colonel Peter Gansevoort with 750 men.

Q. At what battle did a combined force of Loyalists and Native Americans under Mohawk chief Joseph Brant ambush and turn back Nicholas Herkimer's relief force bound for Fort Stanwix?

A. The August 6 battle of Oriskany, which, according to one authority, was "the bloodiest encounter in proportion to the numbers engaged, that occurred during the war." Only about 400 of the 600 Americans participating in the battle of Oriskany returned on foot to Fort Stanwix after the Native Americans, who also suffered heavy losses, broke off the fighting.

Q. At the battle of Oriskany, the participants engaged each other at close quarters. The Native Americans would attack a man after he fired and before he could reload. What tactic did the Americans adopt to defeat this stratagem?

A. During a lull in the battle caused by a downpour of rain, Herkimer instructed his men to pair off so that while one man had fired and was reloading, the other would be ready to fire. The tactic worked.

Q. Why did St. Leger abandon the siege after only a few weeks?

A. St. Leger's Native American allies forced him to abandon the siege after they panicked upon hearing that a second relief force of 3,000 Americans was marching toward Fort Stanwix. The Native Americans, demoralized by their losses at Oriskany, had also sustained great losses at Fort Stanwix. Under Colonel Marinus

Willett, fort defenders had sallied forth, plundered the Native American camp, and carried off twenty-one wagon loads of spoils while the Native Americans were away fighting at Oriskany.

Q. Who led this second expedition marching to relieve Fort Stanwix?

A. Benedict Arnold. Though his force was actually smaller than St. Leger's, Arnold frightened St. Leger's army through a ruse. By offering a pardon from a death sentence, Arnold persuaded the German Hon Yost, deemed an idiot, to travel to St. Leger's camp. Once there Yost was to try to convince St. Leger that Arnold's force would overwhelm him. Yost's effort was successful partly because the British and Native Americans feared Arnold more than any other American officer, due to his previous daring exploits in the course of the war.

Q. General Philip Schuyler was commander of the northern department of the American army until after the battle of Bennington. Who replaced him?

A. General Horatio Gates replaced Schuyler, an aristocratic New Yorker hated by his own army of New Englanders. Gates had never commanded a large body of troops on the field of battle.

Q. Who did Washington detach with 500 riflemen to reinforce Gates?

A. He sent Colonel Daniel Morgan to reinforce Gates.

Q. After Bennington, Burgoyne halted to wait for additional supplies to arrive before crossing the Hudson River to move against Albany. Meanwhile an ever increasing number of Americans troops gathered and prepared defensive positions in the path of Burgoyne's army. Name the two battles Burgoyne was forced to fight after he crossed the Hudson River and started moving toward Albany.

A. Burgoyne was forced to fight the battle of Freeman's Farm on September 19 and the battle of Bemis Heights on October 7. Both battles were fought in the same location and together are considered the battle of Saratoga.

Q. What action of Gates allowed the British to occupy the Freeman's Farm battlefield at the end of the day?

A. It was really his inaction. He refused to send the reinforcements requested by General Benedict Arnold during the battle, or to attack Riedesel's column near the Hudson River. Gates only allowed 3,000 of his 7,000-man army to fight the battle.

Q. Why did General Gates remove Arnold from a position of command in the days following the battle?

A. Many in the army credited Arnold with the Americans' success in halting the British advance at Freeman's Farm. Gates grew angry and retaliated by not even mentioning Arnold's role in his report on the engagement to Congress. Gates publicly claimed credit for the victory when actually Arnold was the man chiefly responsible for it: Arnold had commanded the troops on the battlefield while Gates stayed in his tent. Arnold, angered by Gates's behavior, confronted Gates to protest and ended up quarreling with Gates, calling him "irritating, arrogant and vulgar." Gates relieved Arnold of command. Arnold, popular with most of the officers and many of the men, stayed in camp at their urging.

Q. Burgoyne probably would have won a victory if he had attacked the American position the next day. Why did he cancel the planned attack on the twenty-first?

A. He received a note from General Henry Clinton, written on September 12, informing him that Clinton expected to "make a push" against two forts on the Hudson in about ten days. Burgoyne thought this would draw troops away from Gates. Burgoyne's assumption was a mistake as reinforcements kept arriving in the American camp until there were 11,000 men.

Q. Clinton did not plan to come to Burgoyne's aid, but intended to create a diversion. What two forts did he attack forty miles up the Hudson River from New York City?

A. Having received reinforcements on September 24, Clinton now had 7,000 regulars. He took 4,000 men and attacked Forts Clinton and Montgomery, capturing both of them at about the same time. Clinton advanced up the Hudson as far as Livingston Manor, forty-five miles downriver from Albany and eighty-five miles from Saratoga. Further advancement was made difficult because of resistance from 5,000 American militia under General Putnam and 1,500 under Colonel Samuel Parsons. Clinton then received orders from Howe to abandon his campaign and send reinforcements to Philadelphia.

Q. Why was Clinton's messenger, Daniel Taylor, executed as a spy?

A. Taylor was carrying a message detailing Clinton's capture of the two forts to Burgoyne when he was captured. He swallowed the hollow silver bullet that contained the message. Administering an emetic, the Americans retrieved the bullet and executed Taylor.

Q. What famous Polish engineer laid out the American defensive positions at Bemis Heights?

A. Tadeusz (Thaddeus) Kosciuszko's work contributed greatly to the American victory at Bemis Heights. He had come to America in 1776. Since he was a well-trained soldier, he was commissioned a colonel. He served in the Continental army throughout the entire war.

Thaddeus Kosciuszko
(1746–1817)
Polish patriot, general in
Continental army

Q. On October 7, against the counsel of Generals Baron von Riedesel and Simon Fraser, both of whom advised retreat, Burgoyne sent a reconnaissance force of 1,500 men to ascertain the American position around Bemis Heights. The Americans, under Daniel Morgan and Enoch Poor, began to push the British back toward their camp. At that point, who suddenly entered the battle, took command of three regiments, and turned the orderly British retreat into a decisive American victory?

A. Benedict Arnold acted against the orders of Gates, who had stripped him of command. Arnold led the American forces on the field and aggressively pressed the attack against the British defenses. Shouting "Victory or death," he led a charge into Breymann's redoubt. At the close of the battle, Arnold was severely wounded in the same leg that he had wounded at Quebec.

Q. Name the British general whose inspiring leadership almost single-handedly rallied the British to halt the American advance.

A. Simon Fraser. Daniel Morgan ordered marksman Tim Murphy to shoot Fraser. Murphy mortally wounded him on his third shot. Soon afterwards British resistance crumbled and they retreated. Burgoyne lost another important commander when Lieutenant Colonel Heinrich von Breymann's own men shot and killed him. Breymann had been sabering those who were fleeing the battlefield.

Q. Why did Burgoyne surrender his army ten days after the battle of Bemis Heights?

A. After accepting the counsel of other officers for the first time in the campaign, Burgoyne attempted to retreat north on October 8. His escape route was blocked by New Hampshire militiamen under newly promoted Brigadier General John Stark. Burgoyne then holed up and fortified his camp near Saratoga in the hope that Henry Clinton would come and reinforce him. On October 17 with no relief in sight, low on food and supplies, under constant harassment by American riflemen, and surrounded by over 13,000 Americans, he signed terms that were basically his own. Burgoyne had considered breaking off negotiations after he noticed American militia leaving for home, but his officers told him his own men would probably no longer fight.

Q. As a consequence of Burgoyne's surrender, the British withdrew garrisons from three locations. Name two of the locations.

A. Ticonderoga, Crown Point, and Fort Clinton.

Q. By the terms of the Convention agreement signed at Saratoga, Burgoyne's army of over 5,000 men would lay down their arms and march to Boston. After swearing not to participate in the war again, the army would sail back to England. What arrangement did Congress actually implement after the army of prisoners arrived in Boston?

A. Congress disputed the agreement after Burgoyne wrote a letter complaining about his troops' quarters in Boston. Congress kept Burgoyne's troops, known as the "Convention Army" as prisoners in the colonies for four more years. On April 5, 1778, Congress permitted Burgoyne and two staff members to return to England. There Burgoyne sat out the remainder of the war. At the end of the war, only half the Convention Army remained. The rest had died, deserted, or were paroled or exchanged.

Q. Why is the battle of Saratoga often considered the turning point of the war?

A. After Burgoyne's surrender, the French decided to enter the war against the British.

Q. Which two American-held forts, located on the Delaware River just below the mouth of the Schuylkill River, kept the Royal Navy away from Philadelphia and made it difficult for Howe to supply his troops after the British arrived there in September?

A. Forts Mercer and Mifflin. The British took what was left of each fort after a 40-day siege in November. They had leveled Fort Mifflin, located on Mud Island, bombarding the fort for five days with as many as six ships on the line. The bombardment caused the remainder of the garrison (150 out of the original 450 under the command of Colonel Samuel Smith) to abandon the fort. Then the British gained possession of Fort Mercer, on the New Jersey shore, commanded by Colonel Christopher Greene. The garrison had abandoned the fort after burning it to the ground. In one attack on Fort Mercer, the Americans devastated a force of 2,000 Hessians, killing 180 and wounding 200, while losing only 14 killed and 23 wounded.

Q. General Horatio Gates enjoyed a surge of popularity and public acclaim after the victory at Saratoga. Some Americans believed Gates would be a better commander in chief of the army than Washington, especially when they compared Gates's recent success to Washington's defeats at Brandywine and Germantown. Name the general who was forced to resign from the army following accusations of conspiring to have Gates replace Washington as commander in chief.

A. Irish-Frenchmen general Thomas Conway. Conway wrote letters disparaging Washington's military abilities to President of Congress Henry Laurens, Patrick Henry, and General Gates. Gates wrote back to Conway in a similar vein. Word of this reached Washington, who proceeded to correspond with Gates and Conway, upon which Gates denied writing anything disparaging. Conway became aware of Washington's and many of his officers' dislike toward him and wrote a letter to Congress conveying a wish to resign. To his surprise, Congress accepted his resignation.

Q. Name the first of only two major generals who were dismissed from the army during the war?
A. Adam Stephen only lasted from February 1777 to November 1777 as a major general. A court-martial found him guilty of misconduct. He had lied to Washington about a skirmish at Piscataway, reporting success when in fact he had actually been repulsed. He also had been drunk at the battles of Brandywine and Germantown.

Q. What was the last battle of 1777?
A. As General Howe probed Washington's positions at Whitemarsh, fifty-eight miles northwest of Philadelphia, a battle—really no more than a skirmish—was fought on December 4. Soon thereafter, Howe, who did not believe in winter campaigns, left Washington alone and retired with his army to Philadelphia. He thus fulfilled Benjamin Franklin's prophecy made upon learning that the British had captured of Philadelphia. Franklin had remarked that Philadelphia had in fact captured Howe.

Q. Where did the Continental army retire for winter quarters after the battle of Whitemarsh?
A. They retired to Valley Forge, Pennsylvania. At Valley Forge about eleven thousand of Washington's men endured great hardship and deprivation. They often lacked enough winter clothing, fuel, and food. General Greene wrote, "One-half of our troops are without breeches, shoes and stockings; and some thousands without blankets." It has been estimated that up to 2,500 men may have

perished at Valley Forge in the winter of 1777–78. Meanwhile, twenty miles away, Howe's troops billeted comfortably in Philadelphia.

Q. Is it true that in 1777 more Americans were killed in military engagements than in any other year of the war?

A. Yes. In 1777, 1,389 Americans were killed in 265 land engagements and 24 were killed in 42 naval engagements involving Continental or state navies. The American total of killed, wounded, or captured in 1777 was 6,551 in both land and sea engagements. The highest one-year total for American killed, wounded, or captured was 7,643 in 1780, largely due to the number of prisoners taken by the British at Charleston.

1778–1779

"Sir, you do not know retreating British soldiers. We cannot stand against them."

1778

Q. What was the Battle of the Kegs?

A. In January, submarine inventor David Bushnell and a friend released twenty floating kegs and mines into the Delaware River to destroy British ships downriver. They dumped the cargo in the dark, but too far above the ships to avoid British discovery in daylight. A barge crew spotted one of these torpedoes and hauled it aboard, where it exploded. Once alarmed, the British crews started firing at any log, driftwood, or keg that floated near their ships.

Q. Name the Prussian who came to Valley Forge in February. He is remembered for the invaluable training and discipline he instilled into Washington's army there.

A. Friedrich Wilhelm Augustin Baron von Steuben, a former staff officer under Frederick the Great, volunteered for service in the Continental army. Washington appointed him acting inspector general. While at Valley Forge, von Steuben wrote *Regulations for the Order and Discipline of the Troops of the United States*, a manual of drill regulations that became a standard for the American army. Von Steuben claimed to have held the rank of general, but had only been a captain. He could not speak English. Instead he issued commands in French and aides translated them into English.

Q. What was dubbed the "Squaw Campaign"?

A. For this campaign, begun in February, General Edward Hand and 500 militia invaded the Ohio country and attempted to capture British military stores from Native Americans. The campaign failed miserably in its objective and only succeeded in killing four Native American women and one boy.

Q. Who did Congress want to lead an expedition into Canada early in the year?

A. Lafayette was to proceed from Albany with 2,500 men, raise a general revolt among the Canadians, and destroy works and vessels at St. Johns, Chambly, and Ile aux Noix. He found only 1,200 men at Albany and nothing prepared for the expedition. Congress finally called off the adventure.

Q. By what means did the Americans prevent the passage of British ships up the Hudson River?

A. In April, Americans placed a chain across the river at West Point. The chain was 500 yards long and consisted of 750 links weighing 125 pounds each.

Q. What fort was built to protect the chain?

A. At the urging of George Washington, Tadeusz Kosciuszko, as chief engineer, supervised the construction at West Point. By 1780 the fort consisted of twenty-one separate redoubts, forts, and batteries.

Q. Identify the British general who succeeded William Howe as the commander in chief of the British army in the American colonies.

A. General Henry Clinton succeeded Howe in May. He at once requested permission to resign because he believed he did not have the necessary means to conduct the war and that the war was impractical to win.

Q. Was Lafayette's first independent command an unqualified success?

A. No. Washington had sent Lafayette out with 2,100 men to observe Howe's movements around Philadelphia. Clinton, now in

FACT

Upon learning of the American negotiations with the French, Prime Minister Lord North dispatched the chief of the secret service in France, American Paul Wentworth, to offer conciliations to the Americans to prevent France from entering the war. Ben Franklin applied pressure to the foot-dragging French to entice them into signing the treaty by meeting with Wentworth. During their conversation, in which Franklin kept holding out for independence, Wentworth produced a letter declaring that England would fight for another ten years rather than yield to American independence. "America," Franklin shot back, "is ready to fight fifty years to win it." Fearful of an American reconciliation, the French quickly moved to sign the treaty.

place of Howe, learned of Lafayette's position and sent out 5,000 soldiers under Generals Grant and Erskine. On May 20 at Barren Hill, Pennsylvania, Lafayette's troops barely escaped a British trap by using a road unknown to the enemy.

Q. What was the first country to ally itself with America by declaring war on Britain during the Revolutionary War?

A. France, which had secretly agreed to a formal alliance with America in December 1777 and had signed a treaty on February 6, 1778, declared war on Britain on July 10, 1778. With the fight against the Americans weakening the British, the French hoped to break up the British Empire and perhaps regain some of what they had lost in the Seven Years' War. According to the terms of the treaty, America could not make peace with England without France's consent. By signing the treaty, France had broken the so-called "family compact" with Spain that prohibited entering into wars or alliances without mutual approval.

Q. The British government realized that they would soon be fighting the French. Therefore, they sent a group of peacemakers to the colonies. These men possessed the authority to suspend all the acts passed since 1763. What was the name given to this peace commission?

A. The Carlisle Commission, named for Frederick Howard, the fifth earl of Carlisle, arrived in Philadelphia in June to negotiate with Congress. Commission member George Johnson tried to bribe two leading men in Congress, Joseph Reed and Robert Morris, to accept British conditions for negotiations. The bribe attempt, and threats of further violence if negotiations were not concluded, aroused American indignation. Also, the British would not accept the conditions of American independence and a withdrawal of all British troops. Congress refused to meet with the commission. The commission finally sailed away from the colonies in November.

Q. In June a week-long riot raged in London. Mobs looted businesses, assaulted prominent politicians, and attacked their homes, including that of the prime minister. They even attacked the Bank of England and released inmates from prisons. Was this violence protesting the continuing British war effort against the Americans?

A. No. A Scottish lord, George Gordon, led a mob of about sixty thousand to Parliament with a petition requesting repeal of the Catholic Relief Act of 1778. The Catholic Relief Act had restored the civil rights of English Catholics. After Parliament voted to postpone consideration of the petition, the mob began to riot. George III called in the army. According to the government, the army killed or wounded 458 people to quell the rioting. Unofficially others reported a much higher toll.

Q. The French had already been secretly aiding the Americans. What percentage of the gunpowder used by the Americans during the first two years of the war did France supply?
a. Thirty percent.
b. Sixty percent.
c. Ninety percent.

A. The answer is c. Ninety percent.

Q. On May 8 General Henry Clinton arrived in Philadelphia to replace William Howe as commander in chief. Why did Clinton choose to evacuate Philadelphia by land instead of by ship as instructed?

A. He did not have room on the ships for his army and the 3,000 Tories who wanted to flee to New York.

Q. After wintering at Valley Forge, what was the Continental army's first battle?

A. Monmouth Courthouse. Clinton had orders to desist from offensive operations in the North and to return to New York, where he was to prepare for an invasion of the Carolinas and Georgia. Clinton evacuated Philadelphia on June 18 and retreated across New Jersey, toward New York. His army covered only thirty miles in the first six days of marching. Clinton's baggage train consisted of over 1,800 wagons and stretched out over twelve miles. A council of war on June 24 discouraged Washington from attacking the British; however, Washington sent out 1,500 troops under Brigadier General Charles Scott to harass the British. Finally, on June 27 Washington ordered an attack on the British rear guard at Monmouth Courthouse.

Q. During the midst of the battle, which general did Washington relieve from command?

A. As soon as he arrived on the scene of battle, Washington relieved Charles Lee for his reluctance to attack the rear of the British column. Lee, who had at first declined command of the advance force, said, "Sir, you do not know retreating British soldiers. We cannot stand against them."

Q. Why did Washington decide to attack the British at Monmouth Courthouse?

A. He saw a chance to inflict a defeat on Clinton's divided army as it retreated. The battle, which lasted all day, ended in darkness. It was the longest battle of the war and finished in a stalemate. When Washington sought to renew the contest the next morning, he discovered that the British had disappeared. They had imitated his useful tactic of slipping away during the night.

Q. Whose troops made up the British rear guard at Monmouth Courthouse?

A. Lord Cornwallis's.

Q. During the battle, Mary Hays took the place of her husband, a wounded artilleryman, to help keep firing a cannon. By what name is she remembered today?

A. Molly Pitcher. Hays had been carrying water to cool the cannon before her husband was wounded. Washington awarded her a sergeant's commission and half pay for her courage.

Q. Is it true that Monmouth Courthouse was the last major Revolutionary War battle fought in the North between the main armies of each side?

A. Yes. However, there were lesser battles fought between segments of each army.

Q. What two American generals fought a duel on July 4, 1778?

A. John Cadwalader shot Thomas Conway, of the infamous Conway Cabal, in the mouth for remarks he had made about Washington.

FACT

After the battle, the story was told of a woman camp follower who carried water to cool the cannon until her husband was wounded. The slang term for a female camp follower was "Molly," and one who drew water was a "pitcher," hence the name Molly Pitcher. It was also said that a cannonball passed between her legs and tore her petticoats. Government records prove that her real name was Mary Hays McCauley, as indicated by a pension granted to a Mary Hays McCauley, whose husband, William Hays, had served in the artillery at Monmouth. William Hays died in 1787, and Mary remarried to John McCauley.

Thinking he would die, Conway wrote a letter of apology to Washington. However, instead of dying, Conway recovered. He returned to France in 1779 to serve in the French army.

Q. In July the first French army arrived in America. What city did Washington propose to attack in combination with the French under Comte d'Estaing?

A. Washington proposed that the French combine with General John Sullivan to attack the British at Newport, Rhode Island. The British had held Newport since December 1776.

Q. Was the first allied operation of the war, at Newport, Rhode Island, a success?

A. No. Supposedly, Sullivan insulted d'Estaing, who became angry and departed with his sixteen ships after a brief fight against Admiral Howe's fleet of twenty ships. A severe storm wrought extensive damage to both fleets during their maneuvers. In the aftermath of the storm, Howe withdrew his fleet to New York and d'Estaing headed to Boston for repairs.

Q. After d'Estaing left Newport, 5,000 militia deserted Sullivan's army within a few days. This circumstance forced Sullivan to abandon his siege of British general Robert Pigot's forces on Newport Island. The British then pursued and attacked Sullivan's army. What was so unusual about Christopher Greene's Rhode Island regiment, which repelled three successive assaults by Hessians?

A. It was an all black regiment. After Greene's triumph, Sullivan's men withdrew successfully, the day before the arrival of 5,000 British reinforcements under Generals Clinton and Grey.

Q. During the war, the Tories and their Iroquois allies generally allowed settlers to leave the area if they surrendered without a fight. At what location did over three hundred Americans under Colonel Zebulon Butler counterattack and lose their lives to a party of almost six hundred Iroquois and rangers under Major John Butler.

A. At Wyoming Valley, Pennsylvania, the Tories and Iroquois duped the Americans into a trap. They surrounded and killed at least 227 of the Americans, in what became known as the Wyoming Valley Massacre.

Q. Who did the state of Virginia autho-rize to command a force of several hundred frontiersmen to capture the British fort at Kaskaskia and if possible Detroit?

A. George Rogers Clark, a colonel in the Virginia militia, captured forts at Kaskaskia, Cahokia, and Vincennes. He took the forts without a fight and without losing a man. However, he was never able to mount an attack on Detroit. The colonies controlled Illinois territory for the remainder of the war.

George Rogers Clark (1752–1818) Revolutionary officer, conqueror of Old Northwest

Q. What future state in particular was known as the "dark and bloody ground" during the war?
A. Kentucky.

Q. What two tribes fought Kentucky settlers during the war?

A. Shawnees and Cherokees. During the war, they killed as many as two hun-dred people at the Kentucky settle-ment of Ruddle's Station. The Shawnees also captured Daniel Boone and adopted him into their tribe. Boone later escaped in time to warn Boonesborough of an impending attack. During the September attacks, fifty men in the fort held out for two weeks. They killed thirty-seven Native Americans and lost only two men themselves before the fighting ceased.

Daniel Boone (1734–1820) Pioneer

FACT

General George Rogers Clark's four brothers were also officers during the Revolutionary War: Lieutenant Colonel Jonathan Clark, Lieutenant Edmund Clark, Lieutenant John Clark, and Lieutenant Richard Clark. George was the only Revolutionary War general who never suffered a defeat.

Providentially, Boonesborough was saved from destruction when rains fell, extinguishing the burning fort and collapsing an almost completed tunnel the Native Americans were digging under the fort's walls.

Q. What was the first important southern city to fall to the British?

A. Savannah, Georgia, fell to British lieutenant colonel Archibald Campbell on December 29, 1778. Upon discovering a hidden trail through a swamp, Campbell outflanked the American position and routed American general Howe's men. In the lopsided victory he captured forty-eight cannon, twenty-three mortars, and even the ships in Savannah's harbor.

1779

Q. Is it true that by 1779 fewer Americans were fighting with Washington than with the British?

A. Yes. At the time Washington's army mustered less than four thousand men while over sixty-five hundred Americans were listed on the roles of British regiments.

Q. The British had decided to move south to take advantage of perceived Loyalist strength in the region. South Carolina governor William Campbell and Georgia governor James Wright had pled for assistance and greatly exaggerated the number of Loyalists. What was the greatest mistake the British made in trying to maintain Tory loyalty?

A. The British did not supply permanent protection. After entering an area, they would soon leave. The Tories would then be at the mercy of the patriots. For example, after Campbell captured Augusta, Georgia, he formed the Loyalists into twenty militia companies. Campbell's precipitate withdrawal from the vicinity allowed the now stronger patriots to devastate the property of the unfortunate Tories who remained.

Q. After learning that Nova Scotia desired to become a part of the United States, why was George Washington opposed to a plan to invade the Canadian Province with the French?

A. Washington rejected the idea, first proposed by Lafayette, because he feared the French would retain control of Canada when the war ended.

Q. Where did George Rogers Clark capture Colonel Henry Hamilton? Hamilton was known as "Hair Buyer" because he had promised to reward Native Americans for American scalps.

A. Clark captured Fort Sackville at Vincennes for a second time in February. He tricked Hamilton into believing he had a thousand men. Clark did this by marching his 170 men, half of which were French volunteers, repeatedly behind the hills to give the impression of a much larger force. Consequently, Hamilton surrendered Vincennes without a fight.

Q. Loyalist governor William Tryon led 600 troops in a raid against Horseneck Landing, Connecticut, on February 26. General Israel Putnam opposed him unsuccessfully with 150 militia and two cannons. Tryon wrecked the salt works, plundered the town, and carried off horses and cattle. Though similar to many such raids during the war, what memorable action by Putnam evoked admiration from foe and friend alike?

A. Just when the enemy was preparing to attack, the sixty-year-old general escaped by charging on horseback down a hill with such a precipitate slope that pursuing enemy horsemen from the hill's other side halted upon reaching the summit, too fearful to continue the chase.

Q. What was General Clinton's objective as he headed up the Hudson River in May?

A. He planned to capture West Point in hope of stemming the flow of men and supplies out of New England to the other colonies. However, he captured only two American forts, located at Stony Point and Verplanck's Point, opposite each other on the river.

Q. In what battle did General Anthony Wayne lead over thirteen hundred men on a surprise nighttime bayonet attack?

A. In July Wayne led the attack on the fort at Stony Point, New York, held by Lieutenant Colonel Henry Johnson and 600 men. Only a few designated men were allowed loaded weapons. At a cost of 15 dead and 80 wounded, Wayne's men captured the fort, killing 63, wounding 73, and capturing over 500 prisoners. Thus Wayne avenged the surprise British attack on his command at Paoli. Though an attack on Verplanck's Point failed, the American victory at Stony Point discouraged Clinton from attacking West Point.

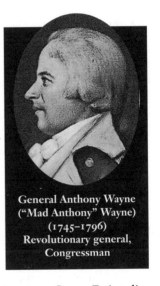

General Anthony Wayne ("Mad Anthony" Wayne) (1745-1796) Revolutionary general, Congressman

Q. Wayne had announced that cash prizes ranging from $500 to $100 would be awarded to the first five men who succeeded in entering the fort. Who was the first man into the fort?

A. French volunteer Francois de Fleury won $500 for being the first man to enter the fort.

Q. Emulating Wayne's bayonet attack at Stony Point, who led a bayonet attack at Paulus Hook, New Jersey, in August?

A. Major Henry Lee attacked the British at Paulus Hook. His men killed 50 and captured over 150 of the enemy without firing a shot. Though Lee then fled British reinforcements arriving from New York City, the attack greatly boosted the army's morale.

Q. In what state was the battle of Stono Ferry fought?

A. South Carolina. After British colonel Augustine Prevost threatened Charleston, he left a rear guard of 900 men on the islands south of the town. On June 20 General Benjamin Lincoln led a 1,200-man attack there, which was beaten back. Nevertheless, the British retreated after the battle.

Q. Due to Native American depredations on the frontier in New York and Pennsylvania, Washington sent an expedition against the Iroquois in New York. Who did he place in command?

A. General John Sullivan commanded a summer expedition of 4,000 men. Citing his age, Horatio Gates had declined the opportunity to command the expedition.

Q. Where was the only significant engagement in Sullivan's campaign?

A. The only real battle occurred at Newtown, where Sullivan's army drove off 600 Tories and Native Americans, suffering only light casualties. In the almost bloodless sweep through the Iroquois homelands, the crops and homes of over forty Native American villages were destroyed. Though the power of the Iroquois nation was broken, some warriors attacked frontier settlements the following year.

Q. Name the Iroquois capital where Sullivan burnt 128 houses described by him as "mostly very large and elegant."

A. Genesee, New York.

Q. What battle was Comte d'Estaing's last action in American before he sailed back to France?

A. Comte d'Estaing joined with General Benjamin Lincoln in an attack on Savannah, Georgia, in October. The Americans and French lost 800 men in the failed attack, while the British lost 140 men.

Q. Name the famous Polish citizen, a brigadier general in the Continental army, who died in the failed attack to retake Savannah from the British.

A. Casimir Pulaski died from a battle wound. His Revolutionary War career was generally poor. He could not speak English, quarreled with fellow officers, and refused to take orders from General Washington. Pulaski formed his own independent command (the Pulaski legion) after resigning from his position as Commander of the Horse, which Congress had created in September 1777. He was also not very successful as an independent commander. Pulaski suffered defeat when he was surprised at Little Egg Harbor in October 1778, and he was badly beaten near Charleston, South Carolina, in May 1779.

Casimir Pulaski
(1748–1779)
Polish officer in
American Revolution,
mortally wounded in
siege of Savannah

1780–1783

"We fight, get beat, rise, fight again."

1780

Q. Who was the second American general dismissed from the army after he was found guilty of disobedience in a court-martial?

A. General Charles Lee underwent a court-martial because of his disobedience to Washington's orders at the battle of Monmouth Courthouse. Initially he was suspended from command for a year. When Lee's suspension ended, Congress dismissed him from the army because he had written them an offensive letter. During and following his trial, the contentious Lee nearly fought one duel with Steuben and was wounded in another duel with Colonel John Laurens, which prevented him from accepting yet another duel with Anthony Wayne. Lee was finally dismissed from the service in January 1780.

General Charles Lee
(1731–1782)
Revolutionary general,
court–martialed,
dismissed from service

Q. The worst disaster of the war for the Americans, in terms of losses to the army, occurred at what location?

A. At Charleston, South Carolina, where a 5,400-man army surrendered after British general Henry Clinton besieged the city from February 11 to May 12.

Q. Name the American general who surrendered at Charleston.

A. General Benjamin Lincoln allowed the 10,000-man British army to bottle him up in the city and was then persuaded to surrender.

Q. How did the Charlestonians also contribute to Lincoln's decision to surrender?

A. During the siege, the townspeople threatened that if Lincoln tried to leave with his army, they would burn his boats and assist the enemy in attacking him.

Q. What battle resulted in the closing off of Lincoln's escape route from Charleston?

A. On April 14 Banastre Tarleton surprised General Isaac Huger's men at 3:00 A.M. at Monck's Corner and inflicted heavy casualties.

Q. At the Battle of Waxhaws in May, British troops slaughtered surrendering men and bayoneted wounded men. Who commanded the British troops that massacred Virginia regulars and militiamen there?

A. Lieutenant Colonel Banastre Tarleton, who became the most feared British commander in the South. Tarleton's victory at Waxhaws in May wiped out the last organized force in South Carolina. Tarleton, as commander of the British Legion, a mobile force of mostly Loyalist dragoons and light infantry, was generally very successful and won many engagements in the southern campaign.

Q. After Henry Clinton captured Charleston, how did his policies encourage South Carolinians to further resistance?

A. Clinton released South Carolinians on parole. But he required them to take an oath of allegiance and actively support the British or they would be punished. Thus, men who had believed that Washington had given up on the southern states were motivated to take up arms again.

Q. Name the present-day city that the Spanish commander Captain Don Fernando de Leyba successfully defended against a force of 300 regular British troops and 900 Native Americans

(Menominees, Sauks, Foxes, Winnebagos, Ottawas, and Sioux) on May 26?

A. St. Louis, Missouri. He held off the attack with 29 Spanish regulars and 281 town residents.

Q. Where was the last significant conflict in the northern colonies before the British began concentrating on the southern colonies?

A. In June, with a command of about 5,000 troops, General Wilhelm von Knyphausen advanced into New Jersey on orders from Clinton. His troops failed to dislodge General Nathanael Greene's men near Springfield. After suffering light casualties, Knyphausen withdrew his troops back to New York.

Q. What June 20 battle, only the second fought in North Carolina at that time, greatly dissuaded Tories from organizing and joining Cornwallis as he prepared to invade North Carolina?

A. At the battle of Ramsauer's Mill, 400 North Carolina militia, under Colonel Francis Locke, beat 1,300 Tory militia. Of the 250 Carolina militiamen actually engaged in the battle, 150 were killed or wounded. The larger Tory force suffered about the same number of casualties.

Q. Identify the man known as the "Swamp Fox."

A. Francis Marion served throughout the war as the most able of all the partisan leaders. He provided especially valuable service to General Nathanael Greene.

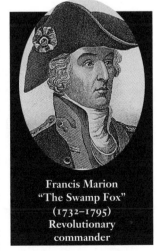

Francis Marion
"The Swamp Fox"
(1732–1795)
Revolutionary
commander

Q. At the start of the war, Marion served as a captain in the South Carolina militia. Why wasn't he captured at Charleston with the rest of the militia?

A. In order to leave a party where the host locked his guests inside, Marion had jumped out of a second floor window and broken his ankle. He was recuperating at home during the time of the surrender.

Q. What British officer named Marion the "Swamp Fox"?

A. Banastre Tarleton originated the name when he quit chasing Marion near Ox Swamp in South Carolina.

Q. Name one other major partisan leader in the southern colonies besides Francis Marion?

A. Both Andrew Pickens and Thomas Sumter participated in many of the engagements fought in the South.

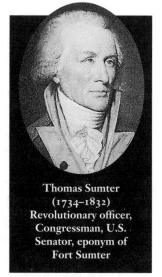

Thomas Sumter
(1734–1832)
Revolutionary officer,
Congressman, U.S.
Senator, eponym of
Fort Sumter

Q. Sumter led South Carolina partisans to their first victory after the fall of Charleston on July 12. Name the location.

A. At Williamson's Plantation, Sumter, with 350 men, attacked a Tory force of about 400 and destroyed it, killing between thirty and forty while losing only one man. He also won a victory at Hanging Rock in early August. As a result, many demoralized men flocked back to the patriot cause.

Q. What American general fled the battlefield while leading the American army during the August battle of Camden, one of the worst defeats ever inflicted on an American army?

A. At Camden, Horatio Gates commanded over 3,000 men, against 2,000 under British General Cornwallis. However, when Cornwallis attacked, about 2,000 American militia immediately ran away from the battle. Gates, already positioned in the rear, also fled. He abandoned about 1,000 Continentals to fend for themselves. In the ensuing fight, they were almost annihilated while fighting the fiercest bayonet battle of the war. Gates managed to get to Hillsboro, North Carolina, about 200 miles away in three and a half days. He never led troops into battle again.

Q. The second of the two American major generals killed in action during the war died at Camden. Name him. (Richard Montgomery, the first major general killed, died at Quebec.)

A. German volunteer Baron Johann de Kalb died along with eight to nine hundred other men. De Kalb commanded the army after Gates fled. He died three days after the battle, suffering from eleven battle wounds. British losses included 68 killed and about 350 wounded. They took about 1,000 prisoners in the battle.

Q. What nourishment, which adversely affected his army's health, did Gates inadvertently serve his troops the day before the battle?

A. He served them molasses instead of the promised rum. Consequently, severe diarrhea debilitated many of his men.

Q. Detached from Gates, Sumter's 700 men captured a British wagon train and about 150 prisoners just prior to Camden. Upon learning this, who did Cornwallis send after Sumter to attempt recovery of the men and goods?

A. Tarleton, with 160 men, caught up with and surprised Sumter's men in camp at Fishing Creek. The British killed 150, captured 300, and recovered the wagon train. At this battle the British reached the pinnacle of their success in the South.

Q. One American general also became a British general. Who was he?

A. Benedict Arnold. In May of 1778 Washington appointed Major General Arnold military governor and commander of troops in Philadelphia. There the 38-year-old Arnold met and married the prominent, 19-year-old, pro-British Peggy Shippen. Charges were later made that Arnold used his position for profit. In 1780 a court-martial found him guilty, and Washington reprimanded him. The combination of his wife's influence, an extravagant lifestyle, embitterment at past injustices (being passed over for promotion), and resentment over criticism from fellow officers, including Washington, all influenced Arnold to initiate contact with the British to obtain money.

Q. For what prize were the British willing to pay Arnold 10,000 pounds?

A. The British agreed to pay Arnold 10,000 pounds for the delivery of West Point, where he had been appointed commander on August 5. If Arnold delivered the fort with a substantial body of troops, his reward would be 20,000 pounds. The plot was discovered, and Arnold fled to the British. They still awarded Arnold 6,315 pounds and commissioned him a general.

Q. Who hung as a spy for acting as a go-between for General Clinton and Benedict Arnold?

A. In September, British major John Andre was caught traveling through American lines in civilian clothes and with documents hidden in his boot. Washington offered to exchange Andre, a friend of Peggy Shippen (Arnold's wife), for Arnold, but Clinton refused.

Q. Did the British ever capture West Point during the war?

A. No. They never even attacked West Point during the war.

Q. Who did Washington appoint as commander of West Point after Benedict Arnold fled?

A. Brigadier General Nathanael Greene.

Q. Identify the man who replaced Gates as commander in the South after the battle of Camden.

A. Congress finally allowed Washington to designate the southern commander. Washington chose Nathanael Greene, who had served with distinction in the Continental army since 1775. Next to Washington, Greene has been regarded as the most capable general in the Continental army. Before Washington chose Greene, Congress, acting without Washington's advice, had selected three men who failed miserably as commanders—Robert Howe (lost Savannah), Benjamin Lincoln (lost Charleston), and Horatio Gates (lost Camden).

Q. What important battle, fought October 7 in South Carolina, was a miniature civil war pitting an American militia against a Loyalist militia led by a single British officer?

A. In the battle of King's Mountain, American militia (frontiersmen), numbering about 900 men under Colonels William Campell, Isaac Shelby, Jack Sevier, and Benjamin Cleveland, totally annihilated a Loyalist force of 1,100 men.

Q. What British officer commanded the Loyalist force, which he had raised, at King's Mountain?

A. Major Patrick Ferguson died in the battle. Ferguson had provoked the "over-mountain" men, who came mostly from the present-day Tennessee, to gather against him by threatening to come over the mountains, waste their country, and hang their leaders if they did not cease their opposition to the king. Many of them had not even previously participated in any of the fighting. At King's Mountain, they gave Ferguson his answer.

Q. What was the strategic consequence of King's Mountain on Cornwallis?

A. Cornwallis abandoned his invasion of North Carolina.

Q. Is it true the American victors at King's Mountain committed atrocities at the end of the battle?

A. Yes. In response to Tarleton at Waxhaws, American patriots killed perhaps 100 Loyalists who had laid their weapons down.

Q. Who was the "South Carolina Gamecock"?

A. Thomas Sumter earned the title because of his courageous character. He had served early in the war but resigned in 1778. In 1780, after the British burned his home, he began raising partisan forces. Sumter died in 1832, the oldest surviving general of the Revolutionary War.

Q. What trick did Colonel William Washington use to secure the surrender of 100 Loyalists in a fortified barn?

A. At Rugeley's Mill, South Carolina, he manufactured a fake cannon to induce their surrender.

1781

Q. The year did not start out well for the Continental army. Regiments from what state mutinied on January 1?

A. Tired of poor living conditions and a lack of pay, and believing their three-year enlistments were up, Pennsylvania regiments mutinied and killed one of their officers. The mutineers then marched toward Philadelphia to confront Congress. Congress diffused the situation by promising the mutineers back pay. Many of them were discharged, and the remainder were furloughed until March. A smaller group of New Jersey men mutinied later in the month. Washington quelled the mutiny with other Continental units and executed two of the ringleaders.

Q. In January where did General Stirling attempt a surprise attack with 2,500 men on 500 sleighs?

A. He crossed the ice and snow to Staten Island, but was detected. Very few of the enemy and hardly any loot were captured.

Q. General Greene arrived in Hillsboro, North Carolina, in December 1780. He found a demoralized and poorly equipped army of only 2,000 men with whom he was to reconquer South Carolina, currently occupied by 8,000 British troops. In late December, he moved his army into South Carolina. What rule of warfare did Greene violate when he invaded South Carolina?

A. Greene divided his army in the face of the enemy. Greene dispatched Daniel Morgan with 600 troops to western South Carolina while he stayed in the East. Greene did this partially to help in feeding his troops.

Q. Learning of Greene's divided army, Cornwallis then divided his army and sent Tarleton after Morgan. Morgan was one of many American officers who had retired after feeling slighted by a lack of promotion from Congress. He resigned in 1776, but had recently rejoined the army after the defeat of Gage at Camden, and had belatedly been promoted from colonel to brigadier general. In what battle, described as "one of the most brilliant tactical operations ever fought on American soil," did Morgan use a double envelopment to win a complete victory over the British under Colonel Tarleton?

A. At the battle of Cowpens (Cowpens was a popular grazing area for Carolina farmers), fought in South Carolina on January 17. American militia performed perhaps their greatest feat of the war here. The battle has frequently been compared to Hannibal's victory over the Romans at Cannae. Morgan planned a clever strategy and used untrained militia to attain his triumph over Tarleton's army. Though both armies were of about equal strength (1,100 men), in trained regulars Tarleton's men outnumbered Morgan's two to one. In the lopsided victory, the Americans lost only 12 killed and 60 wounded while the British lost 100 killed, 229 wounded, and 600 captured. After the battle, Morgan supervised as the Americans withdrew to escape Cornwallis's pursuing army. Suffering from acute rheumatism, Morgan then retired from the army again, this time for the remainder of the war.

Q. How many lines did Morgan employ to fight Tarleton's advance?

A. Three lines. The night before the battle Morgan visited all of his men at their campfires and explained his plan. He wanted a select group of riflemen to man the front line, fire two shots, aiming particularly at officers, and then to retreat to a second line of militia about 150 yards behind them. The militia line was to fire two rounds also and then move sideways. Another 150 yards back, a line of about 450 men, mostly Maryland and Delaware Continentals, would wait for and meet the remaining British.

Q. Who commanded the second line of militia at Cowpens?

A. Colonel Andrew Pickens.

Q. Unusual in the Revolutionary War, the cavalry played an important part in the American victory at Cowpens. Name the cavalry commander.

A. Colonel William Washington, a distant cousin of George Washington.

Q. Daniel Morgan had served with General Braddock's expedition in the French and Indian War, and as a teamster, he had knocked down a British officer during an argument. What punishment did he receive?

A. Morgan received 499 lashes on his back. He never forgave the British for their injustice and cruelty.

Q. After the battle of Cowpens, Cornwallis chased Greene's army for 230 miles before the Americans escaped across a river, from North Carolina to Virginia. There Greene's army received reinforcements and supplies. Name the river which Cornwallis could not cross in pursuit.

A. Greene's army escaped across the Dan River by using all the boats in the vicinity. Without boats, Cornwallis's 3,000 men could not pursue. Having left most of his supplies behind to hasten his pursuit, Cornwallis then retreated to Hillsboro, North Carolina.

Q. How had Greene prepared for his retreat ahead of time?

A. He had ordered scouts, including General Kosciuszko, to reconnoiter the rivers for fords and to build boats on wheels, which could be easily transported from one river to another.

Q. A Spanish expedition, under Don Eugenio Pourre, captured a British fort in Illinois territory, on February 12. Name the fort.

A. The Spanish captured Fort St. Joseph, without a fight, in what is presently the state of Michigan. The Spanish held the fort for one day. Later, they tried to claim the territory on the basis of the captured fort.

Q. Known as "Financier of the Revolution," who was appointed superintendent of finances in February?

A. Robert Morris undoubtedly helped to save the Revolution from financial collapse. He established the Bank of North America, and by using every possible resource including his own personal credit, he financed the Yorktown campaign. When Washington's army was crossing the Delaware, many soldiers threatened to desert because they knew they were traveling far from home. Washington called upon Morris to pay them in hard money, which they had not seen for years. Morris collected enough specie to give the army a month's pay. Rejuvenated, the soldiers cheerfully advanced to Yorktown. Though his own personal fortune survived the war, Morris died bankrupt.

Q. Tarleton's legion wore green dragoon coats. What American legion also wore green dragoon coats?

A. Lee's legion. At Haw River on February 25, Lee pretended to be Tarleton. He drew up his men alongside 400-mounted Loyalists under Colonel John Pyles and proceeded to kill 90 and wound most of the rest without a loss.

Q. After which British victory did a member of Parliament say, "Another such victory would ruin the British army"?

A. Guilford Courthouse on March 15. Soon after escaping from Cornwallis, Greene received reinforcements and recrossed the Dan River to dissuade North Carolina Loyalists from joining Cornwallis's army. There Greene received more reinforcements, giving him over 4,000 men. He positioned his army at Guilford Courthouse in three lines, as Daniel Morgan had earlier suggested, and waited for Cornwallis to attack. Eager for battle, Cornwallis marched his 2,000 veteran troops twelve miles without breakfast and assaulted Greene's three lines. He won a pyrrhic victory, driving Greene from the battlefield, but lost 532 men, over one quarter of his army, while Greene lost 251 men.

Q. At Guilford Courthouse, at a crucial point, Cornwallis needed to make a decision to prevent the Americans from overwhelming his troops. What was the order that harmed his own men?

A. Cornwallis ordered his artillery to fire point-blank into an intermingled mass of British and American troops. At that instant they were fiercely engaged in hand-to-hand combat with bayonets. The artillery fire forced the Americans to disengage and allowed Cornwallis to reorganize and renew his attack, which drove Greene's men from the field of battle.

Q. According to historical tradition, a single American at Guilford Courthouse killed eleven British with his five-foot sword. Who was this man?

A. Peter Francisco killed the British with a sword that Washington had ordered made for him. Francisco was 6 foot, 8 inches tall and weighed 260 pounds. He was believed to have been the strongest man in both the American and British armies. He was found lying among the dead on the battlefield, but recovered to fight again. In another fight in Virginia, he was surrounded by nine of Tarleton's dragoons and fought his way clear after killing two of them.

Q. Did Cornwallis fight Greene again after Guilford Courthouse?

A. No. As a consequence of his severe losses in the battle, Cornwallis retreated to Wilmington, North Carolina. He then left North Carolina for Virginia, thereby abandoning the Carolinas for the duration of the war.

Q. What future president of the United States was captured in a fight at Waxhaws in April?

A. Andrew Jackson. He also received wounds when a British officer with a sword struck Jackson on his arm and head after Jackson refused an order to clean the officer's boots. Jackson hated England for the remainder of his life.

Andrew Jackson
(1767–1845)
President of the United
States, 1829–1837

Q. What idea of Hezekiah Maham enabled Henry Lee and Francis Marion to force the surrender of the 120-man garrison of Fort Watson on April 23?

A. It was Colonel Maham's idea to build a tower out of log cribs, with a platform on top to allow riflemen to shoot down into the fort. This type of tower was later used with similar success in several other instances, including the siege at Augusta, Georgia.

Q. After the American defeat at Hobkirk's Hill on April 25 in South Carolina, which American general wrote, "We fight, get beat, rise, fight again"?

A. General Nathanael Greene wrote these words to the French envoy, the Chevalier de la Luzerne.

Q. Name the British commander Greene fought against at Hobkirk's Hill.

A. Lord Francis Rawdon commanded 900 British and Loyalist troops against Greene's 1,300 troops and 250 militia; Rawdon obtained only a limited victory by exploiting the First Maryland Regiment's mistaken withdrawal during the battle. Afterwards, due to his losses and tenuous supply lines, Rawdon abandoned Camden.

Q. In less than a month after the defeat at Hobkirk's Hill, Greene's army captured Forts Watson, Motte, Granby, and Orangeburg, and with them 800 men. What weapon did Francis Marion and Henry Lee use to induce Fort Motte to surrender?

A. They shot flaming arrows to start the fort on fire.

Q. What was "Ninety-Six"?

A. A British fort located in the interior of South Carolina. Tory lieutenant colonel John Cruger commanded the 550-man garrison and successfully withstood a siege by Nathanael Greene from May 22 until June 20. When Lord Rawdon drew near with 2,000 troops to relieve the garrison, Greene's army withdrew from the fort. The British destroyed the fort and then retreated to the South Carolina coast.

Q. In early June, on orders from Cornwallis, Tarleton descended on Charlottesville, where the Virginia legislature was meeting. He managed to capture several legislators. Unluckily for him, what more important prize eluded him?

A. Virginia governor Thomas Jefferson escaped on horseback only minutes before Tarleton's men arrived at his Monticello estate.

Q. How did Jack Jouett earn the title of Virginia's Paul Revere?

A. Jouett noticed Tarleton on his way to Charlottesville. He rode hard to warn Jefferson of Tarleton's approach.

Q. In what battle did a retreating Cornwallis turn around and set a trap for Lafayette's pursuing army?

A. At Green Spring Farm by the James River in Virginia. Cornwallis nearly bagged a substantial portion of Lafayette's army. A bayonet charge, ordered by Anthony Wayne, delayed the British advance long enough to prevent pursuit as darkness approached.

Q. What apparent victory turned into defeat when the Americans stopped and plundered the British rum supply in an overrun camp? A fortified house held by the British also stymied the Americans.

A. At the September battle of Eutaw Springs, the Americans first drove the British out of their own camp. The British recovered, counterattacked, and eventually turned the tables on the Americans.

Q. Who commanded the British army of 1,200 men at Eutaw Springs, South Carolina?

A. Lieutenant Colonel Alexander Stewart commanded in the well-contested battle. His army suffered the loss of 693 men, the highest rate of loss by any regular British army during the war. As with other costly victories, the British afterwards retreated from the battlefield to a base along the coast, in this instance Charleston.

Q. What important American cavalry leader was captured at Eutaw Springs?

A. Colonel William Washington was captured after the enemy bayoneted him.

Q. Where did the French and Americans finally trap Cornwallis's army?

A. With 16,000 men, the allies trapped Cornwallis and his army of 8,000 men at Yorktown, Virginia. Clinton had ordered Cornwallis to send him reinforcements, so Cornwallis had withdrawn to Yorktown, surmising that he did not have enough strength to hold the entire peninsula. He chose Yorktown and fortified his position so he could protect the British fleet when they came to the harbor there.

Q. On his way to Yorktown from New York, Washington stopped at his home at Mount Vernon from September 9 to 12. How many years had passed since he had last been home?

A. Washington had not been home for over six years, since he left for Philadelphia on May 4, 1775.

Q. Name the commander of the 6,000-man allied French army that assisted Washington in cornering Cornwallis's army at Yorktown.

A. Comte de Rochambeau, whose army had been sitting at Newport, Rhode Island, since July 1780. He agreed to march south with Washington's army to trap Cornwallis. Actually, Rochambeau had urged Washington on several occasions to move his army to the Chesapeake. In addition, Rochambeau had also urged de Grasse to bring his fleet there. Washington had been determined to capture New York, but the British defenses were very strong. Once he learned that de Grasse had arrived at the Chesapeake, he made the decision to march. The combined allied army of 4,000 to 5,000 French and 2,000 Continentals marched 500 miles, averaging 15 miles a day.

Q. What French naval victory sealed off Cornwallis's army from any further supplies or reinforcements?

A. In the battle of Virginia Capes, French admiral de Grasse's more powerful fleet defeated an English fleet under Admiral Graves. Graves then withdrew and sailed back to New York. The victory was made possible because de Grasse had disobeyed orders by retaining his entire fleet instead of sending half of it home.

Q. For weeks Lafayette's surrounding army mustered fewer men than Cornwallis's. Cornwallis uncharacteristically did not respond aggressively to the situation. Finally, Tarleton convinced him to make a night attack on the Americans at Williamsburg. The British could still break out of their position before Washington arrived with the rest of the army. What dissuaded Cornwallis from making the attack?

A. Cornwallis received two dispatches from Clinton. The first assured him that reinforcements were being sent. The second informed him that 4,000 troops had already embarked. Soon after Cornwallis's decision to stay, Washington arrived with the rest of the army and Cornwallis's fate was sealed.

Q. Cornwallis hastened his own doom by abandoning his outer works without a fight; thus, he saved the allies time and lives. The allies started one parallel of siege lines and then a second. What strong points had to be captured before the second parallel could be completed?

A. Taking Redoubts 9 and 10 would ensure the surrender of the British army.

Q. Washington first softened up both redoubts with artillery barrages. He then issued orders for two 400-man columns, one French and one American, to storm the redoubts in a night attack. Who led the American attack on Redoubt 9?

A. Colonel Alexander Hamilton overwhelmed the redoubt, held by 70 men, with a bayonet charge in which 9 were killed and 25 wounded. The French losses capturing Redoubt 10, manned by 120 men, were 15 killed and 77 wounded. The new line was only 250 yards from the British line.

Q. The oldest U.S. military decoration, and the first awarded without regard to rank, was given to Sergeant William Brown of the Fifth Connecticut for his part in the attack on Redoubt 9. What was this decoration?

A. George Washington authorized the awarding of the Purple Heart medal to Brown, who was wounded in the assault.

Q. After the capture of the redoubts, the British ventured out at night in a minor attack in which they attempted to spike allied artillery by breaking off bayonets in the touchholes. The guns were back in action after only six hours. The allied artillery began to demolish the British line. Soon Cornwallis attempted to escape. What prevented the British from escaping the siege?

A. In a desperate gamble, Cornwallis endeavored to send his army across the York River to Gloucester Point on the night of October 16–17. A violent storm arose and drove all the boats down the York River after about one thousand men had crossed to the other side. Unable to escape, too weak to break out, and unwilling to wait any longer for Clinton's rescue, Cornwallis accepted the inevitable. He sent out a man to accept surrender terms on

FACT

W hile at sea on October 24, Clinton first learned of Cornwallis's possible surrender on October 18 from three men who had escaped from Yorktown in a tiny schooner.

October 17, four years to the day after the British had surrendered at Saratoga.

Q. The British marched out to formally surrender on October 19. According to legend, what song did the British army band play?

A. They played "The World Turn'd Upside Down."

Q. Cornwallis ordered British general Charles O'Hara, who had also been at Saratoga, to surrender. In an endeavor to avoid the humiliation of surrendering to the Americans, O'Hara tried to surrender to Rochambeau, who then directed him to Washington. Who did Washington then direct O'Hara to surrender to?

A. General Benjamin Lincoln received the surrender as compensation for his humiliating surrender of Charleston to the British in 1780. Following the surrender, the Americans discovered that the British still had plenty of food and ammunition.

1782

Q. What was the fate of Cornwallis and most of the British officers after the surrender?

A. Most British officers were paroled. Cornwallis was exchanged for Henry Laurens in May 1782. Upon hearing of the surrender at Yorktown, Philadelphians had urged Congress to hang Cornwallis. In a close vote, a resolution for vengeance was defeated.

Q. Though the British will to continue the war was effectively sapped with the surrender at Yorktown, approximately how many troops did they still have in America at the time?

A. The British still maintained about thirty thousand men in all of the major American ports except Boston.

Q. Congress adopted a Great Seal of the United States in July 1782. The front of the seal showed an olive branch and an eagle with arrows and the motto *Annuit Coeptis*, meaning "He [God] favors our undertakings." The motto on the reverse side was *Novus Ordo Seclorum*. What did it mean?

A. The motto means "A new age now begins." The reverse also has a pyramid on it.

Q. On August 19, 1782, what battle was the Kentuckians' worst defeat of the war against the Native Americans?

A. At the battle of Blue Licks, 70 were killed and another 20 captured when 180 Kentuckians attacked a retreating war party, which had abandoned a siege of Bryan's Station, Kentucky. The Kentuckians attacked against the advice of Daniel Boone, who suspected a trap and wanted to wait for additional reinforcements. After he learned of the battle, General George Rogers Clark posted armed guards at Cumberland Gap and on the Wilderness Road to prevent anyone from fleeing Kentucky. He had done this in 1781 as well, to prevent flight and to force the raising of militia.

Q. Also in August, during an attack on Bryan's Station, Kentucky, an arrow landed in the cradle of what future vice president of the United States?

A. The arrow landed in the cradle of Richard Mentor Johnson, later acclaimed as a hero for supposedly killing Tecumseh in the War of 1812 and also elected vice president on the Martin Van Buren ticket in 1836.

Q. In what state did the war's last land engagement between regular British and American forces take place in which an American died in battle?

A. One American was killed in a minor fight on James Island in South Carolina in November 1782. The Americans were led by Colonel Tadeusz Kosciuszko. The war's last land engagement in North America is believed to have taken place at Fort Carlos III (Arkansas Post), Arkansas, April 17–24, 1783. There were no casualties in the siege, which ended when it was learned the peace treaty had been signed. South Carolina, Kentucky, and Ohio have also claimed to have had the war's last land engagement.

Q. Who was the last Continental army soldier killed in the war in the skirmish on James Island in November 1782?

A. The enemy shot and killed Captain William Wilmot, and wounded and captured two other men.

1783

Q. What was the subject of Washington's Newburgh Address of March 15, 1783?

A. Washington addressed his officers to prevent their rebelling against Congress. The officers wanted to settle their grievances about back pay (some were in arrears six years), food and clothing accounts, and provisions for their pension. They planned to march on Congress and get satisfaction by use of force if necessary. Washington exhorted the officers to retain their dignity and promised them his own support for their complaints. His words had little effect until he drew out a pair of glasses, which only his aides had seen him wear, and said, "You must permit me to put on my spectacles, for I have not only grown gray but almost blind in your service." At that moment, many broke down and began to weep. They reaffirmed their loyalty to Congress. Thus perhaps the most serious crisis of the war was averted. Afterwards Congress partially met the officers' demands.

Q. Did Washington ever seriously consider becoming a dictator?

A. In all likelihood Washington never even considered it privately, and definitely not publicly. Some soldiers saw Washington as their only hope for resolving their grievances with Congress and holding the country together. Many historians have opined that Washington's greatest contribution to the United States, overshadowing any of his military feats, was his refusal to assume a military-backed dictatorship. When Colonel Lewis Nicola asked Washington if becoming King George I of America would be a consideration for him, Washington retorted angrily that "no occurrence in the course of the war" had given him "more painful sensations." At the close of the war, a real king, King George III, asked American Benjamin West what he thought Washington would do now that the war was over. West told the king that Washington would resign and become a private citizen. "If he does that," George III responded, "he will be the greatest man in the world." Thus Washington demonstrated his greatness by his unwavering commitment to liberty.

Q. In what year did the Revolutionary War officially end?

A. The war officially ended on April 15, 1783, when Congress ratified the provisional treaty of peace. Irrespective of the French, the American peace commissioners Benjamin Franklin, John Adams, John Jay, and Henry Laurens signed a separate treaty with the British on November 30, 1782.

Q. Benjamin Franklin had lived in France since November 1776, when he arrived with Thomas Jefferson and Silas Deane to represent America. In what year did Franklin return to America?

A. Franklin was out of the country for ten years. In that time, he negotiated a treaty with allies, secured supplies, commissioned a number of ships for the navy, and raised loans. He did not return to Philadelphia until the fall of 1785. For almost thirty years, beginning in 1757, Franklin was absent from the country most of the time, yet always serving it. In addition to his time in France, from 1757 to 1762 and from 1764 to 1775 he was in London as an agent of the Pennsylvania Assembly. He also served as an agent for Georgia and Massachusetts. During the periods he was at home, he served as the first postmaster general in 1775–76, was a member of the second Continental Congress, and helped draft the

Declaration of Independence. After the war he remained active. In 1787 he became president of the Pennsylvania Society for Promoting the Abolition of Slavery and a Pennsylvania representative at the Constitutional Convention. Franklin died in 1790.

Q. What countries besides France fought against Britain during the war?

A. Spain, hoping to reconquer Gibraltar, declared war in 1779, followed by Holland, with the League of Armed Neutrality (Denmark, Sweden, Portugal, and Russia) in 1780. In 1779 France and Spain combined in a joint expedition to invade England. For the first time in ninety years, England lost control of the English Channel to an enemy. However, though the French and Spanish outnumbered the English, their fleets were poorly coordinated, and their invasion attempt was eventually thwarted by storms and a typhoid epidemic.

Q. According to the Treaty of Paris, signed on September 3, 1783, what were to be the future boundaries of the United States?

A. The boundaries were to be Canada to the north, Spanish Florida to the south, and the Mississippi River to the west. The United States would also maintain the right to fish off Newfoundland and Nova Scotia and have right of navigation on the Mississippi to the Caribbean Sea.

Q. What was the last American city to be evacuated by the British?

A. The last British garrison in America evacuated New York City in November 1783. The British had evacuated troops previously, from Savannah, Georgia, in the summer of 1782 and from Charleston, South Carolina, in December 1782.

Q. Approximately how many black people did the British take with them when they left America, 6,000, 13,000, or 19,000?

A. The British took about 19,000 black people with them, not all of their own free will, though many had served the British. The majority were taken to Jamaica and the other islands in the British West Indies.

Q. Is it true that perhaps as many as eighty to one hundred thousand Loyalists left America for Canada, Britain, and the West Indies during and after the war?

A. Yes. Eventually about four thousand of them later received compensation from the British government for their losses (3.3 million pounds of compensation was awarded).

Q. After the war ended, how did Congress reward the Native American allies?

A. Rather than reward the allied Native American tribes for their loyalty, Congress treated friend and foe alike, removing all Native Americans from their land and forced them to move west.

Q. Where did the last land battle of the war take place between the British and the French?

A. At Cuddalore, India, 11,000 men under British general James Stuart drove an approximately equal number of French, under Marquis de Bussy, into the town. However, before the battle could be decided, the opponents received word on June 28, 1783, that five months earlier both sides had agreed to end the war.

Miscellaneous

"First in War, First in Peace, and First in the hearts of his Countrymen."

Q. The Revolutionary War's bloodiest day, in terms of the number of casualties, occurred at what battle?

A. At Bunker Hill, where the British lost 1,054 men, with 226 killed. The Americans suffered 145 killed and 304 wounded.

Q. How did Joshua and John Mersereau help save Washington's army from General Howe's pursuit across the Delaware River in December 1776?

A. The Mersereaus observed local Tories sinking boats in the river to hide them. Howe could raise the boats later to ferry his men across the river to attack Washington's weakened army. The Mersereau brothers foiled the plan, however, by removing the boats from their hiding places so that Howe no longer had the means to transport his troops across the river.

Q. At what battle might history easily have been changed if British major Patrick Ferguson had taken advantage of the opportunity to shoot George Washington in the back?

A. Because it was against Ferguson's ethics to shoot a sitting bird, he didn't try to shoot Washington at the battle of Brandywine.

Q. What was the first American battlefield victory over an entire British army?

A. The battle of Saratoga.

Q. Although British general William Howe won many victories over the American army in New York and Pennsylvania, in which objective did he fail?

A. Howe failed to destroy Washington's army, allowing it to escape more than once and therefore permitting it to continue the war.

Q. In terms of number of men killed, what was the worst defeat for Americans during the war?

A. At Camden almost 900 men were killed and another 1,000 were wounded, missing, or captured.

Q. In what battle did more men die from the heat than from being shot?

A. Monmouth Courthouse. About 60 British of the 358 killed and wounded, and 37 Americans of the 356 killed, wounded, and missing, were reported to have died of sunstroke in the battle. Washington's white horse also died because of the heat.

Q. Despite losing four consecutive battles in 1781, General Nathanael Greene achieved his objective of regaining control of both Carolinas and Georgia for the colonies (excluding Charleston, South Carolina, and Savannah, Georgia). Name these four consecutive defeats.

A. Guilford Courthouse, Hobkirk's Hill, Ninety-Six, and Eutaw Springs.

Q. How many different commanders did Greene face in his four defeats?

A. Greene faced four different commanders: Lord Cornwallis, Lord Francis Rawdon, Lieutenant Colonel John Cruger, and Lieutenant Colonel Alexander Stewart.

Q. What was the last battle fought between the main American and British armies in the southern theater (south of Virginia)?

A. Eutaw Springs, fought on September 8, 1781.

Q. During the war, approximately how many men served in the state militias and with the Continental army?

a. 50,000

b. 100,000

c. 200,000

A. The answer is c. Though some historians have estimated that as few as 100,000 served.

Q. What was the peak strength of the Continental army during the war?

a. 10,000

b. 20,000

c. 50,000

A. The answer is b. The Continental army reached a peak strength of 20,000 men in 1776. If militia are included, the peak strength was 48,017 men, reached in October 1776.

Q. During the war, approximately what percent of the American army were militia?

a. Twenty percent.

b. Forty percent.

c. Sixty percent.

A. The answer is b.

Q. The largest army that Washington commanded during the war numbered, including militia, no more than 25,000 men. Where did he command this large army?

A. Washington commanded the army around New York City before Howe attacked him on Long Island.

Q. Did Americans pay for Native American scalps during the war?

A. Yes. In 1776 New Hampshire offered seventy pounds for the scalp of each hostile male Native American and thirty-seven pounds, ten shillings for the scalp of a woman or a child over twelve years old.

Q. What regiment has been considered the best in the Continental army during the war?

A. The First Maryland, which also contained some Delaware Continentals.

Q. What did the Continental army's fife and drum corps adopt as a rallying song?

A. "Yankee Doodle." A British army surgeon, Richard Schuckberg, originated the first version of the song in the French and Indian War.

Q. The first Continental Congress met from the spring of 1774 until October 26, 1774, in Philadelphia's Carpenter's Hall. Who was the first president of the Continental Congress?

A. Peyton Randolf of Virginia. The second Continental Congress met in the spring of 1775, and John Hancock of Massachusetts was elected president of the Congress on May 24, 1775.

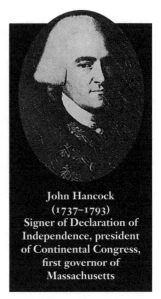

John Hancock
(1737–1793)
Signer of Declaration of Independence, president of Continental Congress, first governor of Massachusetts

Q. Did Congress adopt the Stars and Stripes as the flag of the United States during the war?

A. Yes, on June 14, 1777, Congress passed the Flag Resolution, which specified a flag with thirteen alternate red and white stripes and thirteen white stars in a blue field. The descendants of Betsy Ross claim that she made the first Stars and Stripes after George Washington showed her his striped flag and asked her if she could design one with white stars on a dark blue field instead of the British Union Jack. However, many historians do not believe Ross made the first Stars and Stripes, with its thirteen five-pointed stars in a circle on a blue field and its seven red and six white stripes.

Q. What color did Congress first adopt for the official uniforms in the Continental army?

A. In 1775 Congress adopted brown. In 1779 blue was adopted as the basic color of army clothing. France shipped over many blue coats, but not until the Yorktown campaign did a substantial body of the ragtag Continental army appear together in decent uniforms.

Q. In what year did the federal government begin to stamp "United States" on all arms, tools, and accoutrements that it owned?

A. In 1777. Items from the war owned by the federal government and in existence today are inscribed "US," "U States," or "United States."

Q. Did Congress vote a medal for anyone besides George Washington during the war?

A. Yes. Besides Washington for his 1776 capture of Boston, Congress voted medals for seven others: Horatio Gates for Burgoyne's capture; Anthony Wayne, John Stewart, and Teisedre de Fleury for Stony Point; Henry Lee for Paulus Hook; and Daniel Morgan and John Howard for Cowpens.

Q. In what year did the Continental currency collapse?

A. In 1781. By November 1777, Congress had authorized the issue of $241,552,280. Congress could not tax and could not back the money. By January 1778 the value of Continental currency was down 75 percent, and it kept going down. By mid-1781 only hard money was used in the market and the phrase "not worth a Continental" entered the language.

Q. What was the highest rank attained by a clergyman on either side during the war?

A. Virginia clergyman Peter Muhlenberg was brevetted to major general on September 30, 1783. He had started as a militia colonel in 1775 and fought throughout the entire war.

Q. Did women fight in the Continental army?

A. Not officially; however, one woman named Deborah Sampson disguised herself as a man. She went by the alias Robert Shurtleff and served from 1781 to 1783 in a Massachusetts regiment, without her sex being discovered. At least two women camp followers, Mary Corbin and Mary Hays, fought when their husbands fell in battle.

Q. Women camp followers (many were wives) performed many chores for the men in the army including the laundry, cooking, cleaning, and medical care. Women camp followers in both the American and British armies were also issued rations. What was the ratio of women camp followers to men in the American army?

A. The ratio was one woman camp follower for every fifteen men. In the British army the ratio was one to ten. Ironically, the romantic French did not have any women officially attached to their army in America.

Q. Did blacks fight in the Continental army?

A. Yes, black patriots usually fought as part of a white unit, although Rhode Island did have a small black regiment of 125 men, 30 of which were free slaves, officered by whites. Altogether, approximately 9,000 blacks fought for the patriot cause, most serving in the infantry. Black enlistment in the war became widespread after 1777.

Q. Many slaves gained their freedom by serving in the army. Some served as substitutes for others who had been drafted. Which two states never did allow slave enlistments into the army?

FACT

At first Washington did not want black men to serve in the Continental army. Washington feared that their enlistment would dissuade Southerners from serving. In fact, in September 1775, Congressman Edward Rutledge of South Carolina tried to have Congress discharge all blacks from the Continental army. However, when Washington's army began to melt away at the end of 1775, Washington wrote in favor of black enlistment and asked Congress to clarify official policy. Congress voted to permit the reenlistment of any black soldier who had already served. Eventually, the Continental army became the most integrated army until Vietnam.

> # F A C T
>
> **B**etween 1775 and 1800 the number of free blacks in the colonies increased from 14,000 to 100,000.

A. Georgia and South Carolina. Maryland was the only southern state that officially allowed slave enlistments.

Q. What was the first state to actually abolish slavery?
A. On March 7, 1780, Pennsylvania was the first state to abolish slavery. The act only applied to the children of slaves reaching their twenty-eighth birthday.

Q. Were Dick, Ned, and Peter Freedom related to each other?
A. No. They and Jefferey, Sharp, and Cuff Liberty, amongst others, were all blacks serving in a Connecticut regiment who took the names "Liberty" and "Freedom" for their last names.

Q. What slave, along with his family, did the state of South Carolina free as a reward for the service he performed relaying valuable information on enemy movement?
A. Antigua.

Q. During the war, who was the senior officer in the Marine Corps?
A. Samuel Nicholas, a Philadelphia tavern owner, was the senior officer. He led 268 marines in occupying the town and two forts in an attack on Nassau in the Bahamas in 1776.

Q. What state supplied the most signers of the Declaration of Independence?
A. Pennsylvania supplied the most signers with nine. Rhode Island had the fewest signers with only two. The most common profession for the signers was lawyer. Twenty-one of the fifty-six signers were lawyers. Among the rest were nine jurists, three office holders, nine planters or farmers, nine merchants, three millers, one carpenter, and one surveyor.

Q. George Washington was accused of being partial to the men of what state?

A. Virginia. Washington was a Virginian.

Q. Where did Lafayette exercise independent command in 1781?

A. Lafayette achieved independent command in 1781 in Virginia so that he could confront Cornwallis's army.

Q. Henri Gustave Rosenthal was his nation's only representative as an officer in the Continental army. What was his nationality?

A. Rosenthal was a Russian baron, born in modern Latvia, who had fled to America. He joined the army as Lieutenant Rose and served until 1783. He returned to Russia in 1784.

Q. Of the fourteen original generals that Congress had appointed in June 1775, how many were still in the Continental army at the war's end in 1783?

A. Three. George Washington, Nathanael Greene, and Horatio Gates.

Q. Name three ex-British officers who became generals in the Continental army?

A. Horatio Gates, Charles Lee, and Richard Montgomery.

Q. Name the eight Europeans who came to America to fight for the colonists and whom Congress commissioned as brigadier and major generals.

A. Thomas Conway, Philippe de Coudray (who died before serving), Louis Duportail, Johann Kalb, Tadeusz Kosciuszko (who was not commissioned until 1783), Marquis de Lafayette, Casimir Pulaski, and Friedrich von Steuben.

Q. How many major generals were there in the American army during the war?
a. Seven
b. Thirteen
c. Twenty-nine

A. The answer is c.

Q. How many generals were killed on the American side during the war?

A. Twelve. In proportion to the number of enlisted men, more generals were killed in the Revolutionary War than any other American war.

Q. In prisoner exchanges, how many privates were traded for a brigadier general?

a. 50
b. 100
c. 200

A. The answer is c.

Q. Was David Bushnell ever successful in destroying any British ships with his mines and torpedoes during the war?

A. Yes. In 1777 in the Hudson River, he attempted to use a line to draw a torpedo against the side of a ship. The crew of a schooner discovered it and hauled it aboard, where it exploded, killing three men and demolishing the vessel.

Q. What state paid more of the war expenses than any other state?

A. Massachusetts paid about as much of the war expenses as Pennsylvania, New York, Virginia, and Maryland combined, though its population was only 13 percent of America's total. Massachusetts also contributed the greatest number of troops to the Continental army, about 68,000.

Q. What state contributed the fewest troops during the war, including militia?

A. Delaware contributed only 3,386 troops, including militia. Its only regiment was organized in January 1776, under Colonel John Haslet. The troops were known as the Blue Hen's chickens after a company had charged into battle shouting, "We're sons of the Blue Hen, and we're game to the end!" The name "Blue Hen's chickens" originated from two gamecocks the men had brought with them when they marched to Philadelphia to join the Continental forces under General John Cadwalader. The cocks had been hatched from the eggs of a steel-blue hen and were never beaten in numerous cockfights.

Q. One of the largest Continental army brigades was known as the "Line of Ireland." Over half of the men and officers in this brigade were Irish. What state fielded this brigade?

A. Pennsylvania. Many Irish served in the army. Joseph Galloway of Pennsylvania stated that half of Washington's army was Irish, and he wasn't far from the truth.

Q. What state furnished the most troops in proportion to its population?

A. Delaware.

Q. In what state were the most engagements fought?

A. The most engagements were fought in New Jersey (238). New York was second with 228.

Q. Name the only colony of the original thirteen that the British never invaded during the war.

A. New Hampshire.

Q. Name the only colony of the original thirteen in which only two Americans died in battle during the entire war.

A. Maryland. One American each died in two different minor land engagements fought there in 1776.

Q. There were only three present-day states east of the Mississippi River in which no Americans died fighting the enemy during the course of the war. Name two of them.

A. Wisconsin, Michigan, and New Hampshire were the only states in which no Americans died in battle.

Q. Over half of all Americans killed in battle died in just three states. In which state did the most Americans die in battle against the enemy?
a. New York
b. Pennsylvania
c. South Carolina

A. The answer is c. In South Carolina 1,309 Americans died in battle, followed by New York with 1,136, and Pennsylvania with 1,028.

Q. What colony had the fewest Tories?

A. Connecticut.

Q. Is it true that Native Americans or Native Americans with British or Loyalist troops killed over 1,000 Americans during the war?

A. Yes. Native Americans by themselves or with British or Loyalist troops accounted for 1,029 known American military dead, one-sixth of the total.

Q. How many Americans were killed in naval battles involving the Continental or state navies?

    a. 432

    b. 832

    c. 1,232

A. The answer is a.

Q. Did more Americans die in battle or in prison?

A. Prison. By one estimate as many as eleven thousand men may have died in British prisons in New York City alone.

Q. Is it true that known battle deaths for the Continental army were more than 10,000 during the war?

A. No, the Continental army suffered anywhere from 4,435 to 8,000 battle deaths. Another 10,000 died in camp from wounds and disease, and 8,500 died in prison. The total number of known war-related deaths among the American armed forces was approximately 25,314, as compiled by historian Howard Peckham. Of course, statistics vary widely among historians. For example, while one historian asserts that ten times as many soldiers died of disease as in battle, another states that about the same number died of disease as in battle. Doctor James Thacher of the Continental army estimated that total deaths may have been equal to 70,000.

Q. Service-related deaths accounted for approximately what percentage of those who served?

    a. 2 percent

b. 12.5 percent

c. 20 percent

A. The answer is b. These are deaths from battle, from disease, or in prison.

Q. Did a greater percentage of men die in the Continental army and militias during the Revolutionary War than in the Union army in the Civil War?

A. No. Thirteen percent of the Union troops died, the greatest percent of all U.S. wars. As a percentage of population, the Civil War is also America's costliest war, with a 1.6 percent death rate. The Revolutionary War is second with 0.9 percent of the population dying in the war. In World War II, 0.28 percent of the population died.

Q. In what year were the most land engagements fought in North America during the war?

A. In 1777 the antagonists fought 265 land engagements. The second greatest number of land engagements was in 1776 (252). In total 1,331 military engagements were fought on land in North America. Naval engagements involving the Continental or state navies numbered 215.

Q. Name the five battles in the Revolutionary War in which the Americans suffered casualties of over one thousand men, including killed, wounded, missing, or captured.

A. Long Island, Fort Washington, Brandywine, Germantown, and Charleston. Many of the casualties were men captured. Americans lost the greatest number of actual killed and wounded in battle at Brandywine. The costliest single battle of the war for the British, in terms of killed and wounded, was Bunker Hill where they lost over one thousand men. In total casualties, Saratoga and Yorktown were the costliest battles for the British.

Q. Why may Revolutionary War veteran Daniel Frederick Bakeman be termed a survivor?

A. According to the records in the U.S. adjutant general's office, Bakeman died in Freedom, New York, on April 5, 1869, at the age of 109 years, 5 months, and 26 days.

Q. Of the known American military dead from the Revolutionary War, more men died with the last name of _____ than any other last name?

A. Ninety-nine men with the last name of Smith died in military service during the war. The next five most common last names of men who died were as follows: Brown (68), Jones (57), Williams (55), and White (46). Perhaps the unluckiest name of the war was John Brown. More men (18) with that name died than with any other name.

Q. What was the only state in which a legislative body convened to enforce royal authority after the Declaration of Independence?

A. Georgia, which became one of the Loyalist possessions.

Q. Who established the first permanent settlement in what became Kentucky?

A. James Harrod beat Daniel Boone by a few months when he established Harrodsburg near the Kentucky River in March 1775.

Q. Who was known as "Light Horse Harry"?

A. Lieutenant Colonel Henry Lee, as commander of Lee's legion, fought in almost every major engagement of the southern campaign. He was the father of Robert E. Lee and is also remembered for his famous toast to Washington, "First in War, First in Peace and First in the hearts of his Countrymen," which he gave at Congress after Washington's death in 1799.

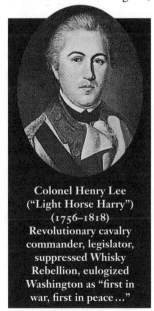

Colonel Henry Lee
("Light Horse Harry")
(1756–1818)
Revolutionary cavalry
commander, legislator,
suppressed Whisky
Rebellion, eulogized
Washington as "first in
war, first in peace..."

Q. Name the Royal governor who actually led the revolutionary movement in his own state.

A. Jonathan Trumbull of Connecticut.

Q. Did Americans manufacture their own cannons during the war?

A. Yes. Cannons were manufactured in Connecticut, Massachusetts, Pennsylvania, and Rhode Island. As many as three thousand cannons were cast at the Hope works in Rhode Island.

Q. Who became Washington's chief of intelligence?
A. Benjamin Tallmadge managed Washington's spies during the period from 1778 to 1783.

FACT

Especially valuable among Washington's New York spies were "the Culpers," Samuel Woodhull (Culper Sr.), Robert Townsend (Culper Jr.), and James Rivington, publisher of the *New York Gazette*, a pro-Tory newspaper. The Culpers' most important accomplishment was the discovery of a British plan to attack the vulnerable French army when it landed at Newport, Rhode Island. Washington frightened General Clinton into cancelling British troop movement toward Rhode Island by allowing the British to "accidentally" capture Washington's secret plans for an attack on New York City. The Culpers' secret identities were not discovered for 150 years, and no one proved that Rivington was really an American secret agent until 1959. Rivington's greatest intelligence coup was his theft of the British navy's signal book. Washington forwarded it to French admiral de Grasse. Washington also used double agents, of which only three are known for certain. They were Captains Elijah Hunter, David Gray, and Caleb Bruen. Washington usually handled all spy reports himself, yet was also kept in the dark as to his spies' real identities. Of all his staff officers, Alexander Hamilton is the only one known to have touched any of these reports.

Q. What American invented invisible ink?

A. James Jay, a doctor and the brother of John Jay, invented an ink that remained unseen until a chemical was rubbed over it. The British also had two secret inks, one revealed by acid and the other through heat.

Q. Name the Spanish governor of Louisiana who helped in assisting George Rogers Clark's campaign in the Northwest Territory by sending supplies. This governor also took British forts at Baton Rouge and Mobile in 1779, and captured Mobile in 1780 and Pensacola in 1781.

A. Bernardo de Galvez. His army of about two thousand Americans, French Creoles, free blacks, Native Americans, and Spanish regulars tied up thousands of British troops who otherwise may have tipped the scales for the British in their southern campaigns. Bernardo's success in conquering west Florida enabled Spain to obtain all of Florida and control the Mississippi River's mouth in the peace treaty of 1783.

Q. What was a spontoon?

A. A short stabbing spear carried by American officers as a defense against the bayonet. It was also used to signal troop movements.

Q. What was a timber fitted with iron spikes called?

A. Chevaux-de-frise.

Q. Of all the countries that fought against England during the war, which one's army had not virtually abandoned the pike as a weapon?

A. America's.

Q. Who were "Shirtmen"?

A. "Shirtmen" was the term the British applied to American riflemen; it originally applied to Virginia riflemen.

Q. What was a tricorn?

A. The tricorn was a triangular-shaped black-felt hat with a broad brim turned up on all three sides. Though usually considered the typical hat for a Revolutionary War soldier, it was mostly worn by the militia or minutemen.

Q. What term described a mounted infantryman?
A. A dragoon traveled on a horse and fought on foot. He was armed with a short musket or carbine, a sword, and pistols.

Q. The British used the term "Brother Jonathan" to designate whom?
A. Americans.

Q. Who suggested that the British army should be withdrawn from America and that the navy alone should be used to subjugate the colonies?
A. British secretary of war Viscount Barrington.

Q. After the fall of what fort did King George run into his wife's room, crying out that he had beaten all the Americans?
A. After Fort Ticonderoga fell to Burgoyne's army.

Q. In what year did the British change their base of operations from the northern to the southern colonies?
A. In 1778.

Q. When the British shifted the war south, from 1780 to 1782, how many South Carolina slaves joined the Royal Army?
   a. 5,000
   b. 10,000
   c. 20,000
A. The answer is c. An estimated 20,000 slaves joined the British army, hoping to gain their freedom.

Q. What were "kingbirds"?
A. British officers. Most British officers purchased their commissions and could not get the appointment without the king's personal approval.

Q. What was a jaeger?

A. Jaegers (literally huntsmen) were German light infantry troops (also called chausseurs) used for special missions, reconnaissance, or sniping. They wore green uniforms, carried rifles, and were expert marksmen.

Q. What were grenadiers?

A. Originally grenadiers were large and strong men selected to throw "hand bombs." Later, after they had ceased throwing grenades, they were formed into special companies of elite troops. Each regiment of the British army usually included a company of grenadiers.

Q. Did Butler's rangers fight for America or the British?

A. The British. In 1777 Governor Sir Guy Carleton authorized Tory colonel John Butler to raise eight companies. From their base at Fort Niagara, they partook in much of the frontier fighting in New York and Pennsylvania, including both the Wyoming Valley and Cherry Valley massacres.

Q. According to information from Lord North's return books, in what year did the British army have the most men in North America, including officers and men in regular, provincial, and German units?

A. The British army had 52,561 men in North America in 1778, more than in any other year. The highest total number of men the other years is as follows: 6,991 in 1775; 14,374 in 1776; 23,694 in 1777; 47,624 in 1779; 44,554 in 1780; 47,301 in 1781; and 47,223 in 1782.

Q. Approximately how many American Loyalists took up arms for the British during the war?

    a. 9,000

    b. 19,000

    c. 50,000

A. The answer is c. Of the 3 million Americans who lived during the war, about 500,000 were Loyalists. Of these, about 50,000 served the British, but only about 10,000 served in organized units.

Q. Not counting Hessians or Loyalists, what was the average number of British troops maintained in the colonies each year during the war?

A. From 1776 to the end of the war, Britain maintained an average of 12,000 British troops in America. Of the seventy infantry regiments existing in the British army at that time, fifty-two English, Irish, Scot, and Welsh regiments served in America.

Q. What British colony did 1,000 ex-slaves, who had joined the British during the war, help to establish?

A. Sierra Leone. Seven years after 3,000 of these former slaves had settled in Nova Scotia, the British transported 1,000 of them to Sierra Leone. They had requested to go back to Africa after experiencing segregation and difficulty in obtaining decent land.

Q. Is it true British general Cornwallis was only defeated once during the war?

A. Yes. Cornwallis's only defeat occurred at Yorktown. He is often considered the most competent of the British generals in the war. However, his surrender at Yorktown is historically considered the British army's greatest defeat until Dunkirk in World War II.

Q. What strategy did Generals Gage, Clinton, and later Benedict Arnold favor to win the war?

A. They favored what has been called "The Line of the Hudson" strategy. Proponents of this strategy argued that controlling the Hudson River would cut New England off from the rest of the colonies and win the war.

Q. Did Benedict Arnold die in Canada, England, or the West Indies?
A. Arnold died in London, England, in 1801, a poor man.

Q. How many troops did France send to the American mainland altogether?
a. 8,000
b. 16,000
c. 24,000

A. The answer is b. France sent troops in three different groups. D'Estaing brought 4,000 in 1770 for the siege and attack on Savannah; Rochambeau landed 5,000 at Newport, Rhode Island, in 1780; and 6,074 came from the West Indies with Comte Claud Henri Saint-Simon for the Yorktown campaign (joining the 5,000 of Rochambeau's troops).

Q. Louis XVI reigned in France during the American Revolutionary War. He agreed to support the colonists in the first three years of the war and was finally convinced by his foreign minister Charles Vergennes, to openly declare war on England after the surrender of Burgoyne's army at Saratoga. Siding with the Americans resulted in what personal tragedy for Louis ten years after the war ended?

A. Louis XVI lost his head. The expenditures of the war effort caused an economic crisis in France in the years following the war. The French started their own revolution in 1789. They abolished the monarchy in 1792, and in 1793 guillotined Louis XVI and his queen Marie Antoinette.

Naval Facts

"I have not yet begun to fight."

Q. Prior to the Revolutionary War, did American shipbuilders build warships?

A. Yes. At least four warships were built for the British beginning with the fourth-rate *Falkland* (54 gun) at Portsmouth, New Hampshire, in 1690 and *Bedford*, a galley, built a year later. The two latest warships were the 24-gun *Boston*, at Boston, and the 44-gun *America*, at Portsmouth, New Hampshire, both built between 1745 and 1749. All the American warships built for the British were considered inferior. By the outbreak of the Revolution, American shipbuilders were constructing about one hundred ships a year.

Q. How many guns did a first-rate ship of the line in the Royal Navy carry?

A. Ships of the eighteenth century were rated as follows.

	Guns	*Men*
First-Rate	100	850–950
Second-Rate	98 or 90	750
Third-Rate	80, 74, or 64	720, 640, 490
Fourth-Rate	50	350
Fifth-Rate	44, 40, 38, 36, or 32	320, 300, 250, 215
Sixth-Rate	28, 24, or 20	160–200

Ships under 60 guns were not usually considered acceptable for the line of battle. Frigates varied from 20 to 40 guns; the most common British frigate carried 32 guns, followed by 28, 44, and 36.

Q. Name two other types of warships.

A.
Sloops	three-masted, 8–20 guns
Brigs	two-masted, square-rigged
Brigantines	two-masted, square rig on foremast and fore-and-aft rig on mainmast
Schooners	fore-and-aft rigs on two masts
Bomb Ketches	masts in aft, designed to carry one or two heavy sea mortars

Q. In contrast to the largest battleship of World War II (Japan's *Yamamoto*, at 64,000 tons and 863 feet long), the largest ships of the line during the Revolution were about 2,700 tons, 226 feet long, and 50 feet wide. A ton was equal to the displacement of 35 cubic feet of seawater. Did it take more or less than one thousand trees to build the hull for a ship of the line?

A. It could take up to four thousand trees to build one ship of the line. Oak was the most desired wood.

Q. New England pines were especially prized for masts, but only one in ten thousand trees was suitable. A mainmast for the largest ships could be over three feet in diameter and more than one hundred feet in length. Once Britain's supply was cut off, where did the Royal Navy obtain timber?

A. For a hundred years prior to the Revolutionary War, Britain obtained timber from New England. When the supply from there was cut, the British obtained timber from New Brunswick and the Baltic. At the beginning of the war, England suffered from a shortage of masts. Sometimes the British built a mast from more than one tree by binding the trees together with iron hoops.

Q. How many gun decks did the largest ships have?

A. Ships with over eighty guns usually had three gun decks. Other ships of the line had two decks, and frigates on down had one deck.

Q. Not counting swivel guns, cannon sizes ranged from the small 3-pounder, weighing 700 pounds, to the huge 42-pounder, weighing 6,500 pounds. In between there were 4-pounders, 6-pounders,

9-pounders, 12-pounders, 18-pounders, 24-pounders, and 32-pounders. Most calibers came in two sizes, long and short. The long gun was the more accurate and could shoot farther. What was the largest naval gun mounted on American vessels during the war?

A. The largest gun on an American vessel was an 18-pounder. The largest naval gun in general use on a British ship was a 32-pounder, though some did carry a 42-pounder. The *Warren* was the only frigate in the Continental navy to carry 18-pounders. Before the Revolution, Americans had not manufactured cannons. The original intent was to cast all of them in Pennsylvania, but this proved impractical. Naval cannons were mostly cast iron, made at foundries in Connecticut, Rhode Island, Massachusetts, Pennsylvania, and Maryland.

Q. What does "pound" refer to when a cannon is called a "12-pounder"?

A. "Pound" refers to the weight of the cast-iron shot fired by the cannon.

Q. What was the maximum range for a 32-pounder?

A. The maximum range was about 2,900 yards. A 32-pound shot would hit water at about 350 yards if fired at no elevation, which was considered point-blank range.

Q. Though a shorter gun had less range, it could fire a heavier projectile, which caused much more damage. What new type of short naval gun did the British introduce in 1779?

A. The carronade was first cast at and named for the Carron Iron Works in Scotland. To illustrate the difference in size, a long (9.5 feet in length) 32-pounder weighed 5,500 pounds and used a powder charge of 14 pounds. A short (8 feet in length) 32-pounder weighed 4,900 pounds and used a powder charge of 11 pounds. In contrast, a 32-pound carronade was 4 feet in length, weighed 1,700 pounds, and only needed a charge of 2 pounds, 10 ounces. The lighter and more rapid-firing carronade required only half the crew of a regular gun, and a carronade could also throw a much heavier projectile. One nicknamed "the Smasher" could throw a 68-pound ball. By 1781 the British had installed carronades on 492 vessels. Americans did not manufacture carronades, but may have obtained some from captured vessels.

Q. Gunpowder consisted of three ingredients: 75 percent saltpeter (potassium nitrate), 10 percent sulphur, and 15 percent charcoal. Which ingredient did Americans have to import to manufacture their own gunpowder?

A. Sulphur.

Q. What did it mean to have the weather gauge when a ship fought a battle?

A. A ship had the weather gauge when it attacked from the windward side. By assuming the weather gauge, the attacker could keep the initiative, deciding what distance to maintain for battle and moving quickly to close quarters. Also, the smoke of battle clouded the enemy and hindered his ability to maneuver, signal, or to aim his guns. Prior to battle, the British habitually maneuvered to gain the weather gauge, while the French mostly sought the lee position. From the lee position, the French could severely damage the British as they approached and could flee if they desired. Generally, in a battle line, opposing columns of ships sailed in the same direction in order to keep firing at each other. If the ships sailed in opposite directions, they might have no more than two minutes to fire their broadsides.

Q. In the Revolutionary War, it was considered good shooting to get off how many broadsides in a six-minute period?

A. Three.

Q. At sea, at what distance, approximately, could a man in the masthead of a medium-sized vessel spot another like vessel?
a. Five miles
b. Ten miles
c. Twenty miles

A. The answer is c.

Naval Facts

Q. With full sails in an average wind, approximately how many knots per hour did a ship of the line travel?

A. The ship could travel about six knots in an hour. A knot, or nautical mile, measures 6,080 feet.

Q. A ship's bottom had to be kept clean. Organisms, algae, and especially barnacles attaching themselves to a hull could add several tons in weight, which could reduce speed and maneuverability by as much as 50 percent. A ship's bottom had to be scraped about every six months to keep it clean. This was a time-consuming process, made especially difficult for the Continental navy because it did not possess a single dry dock. A ship had to be stripped and turned from side to side to clean it. What was one method of greatly reducing the frequency of hull cleaning?

A. Many methods were attempted to solve this problem and to protect the wood from worms, including covering the hull with tar, chemical substances, lead plates, and even hides. The best method was to sheathe the hull with copper. In 1761 the British 32-gun frigate *Alarm* was the first ship sent to sea with copper plates covering its hull. Yet, by the beginning of the war, the British had only a few coppered vessels. The French realized the strategic value of the method and began sheathing their ships after entering the war. The British began to sheathe their vessels in earnest in 1778. By the war's end, they had coppered every ship ready for service.

Q. Did America sheathe the hulls of any of its warships with copper?

A. Yes. Due to lack of funds, however, only one ship, the frigate *Alliance*, was sheathed.

Q. With how many naval vessels did the British start the war?
   a. 90
   b. 270
   c. 460

A. The answer is b. Included in this total were 131 ships of the line.

Q. After hostilities erupted at Lexington and Concord, America captured its first British warship, early in May 1775, on the southside of Cape Cod. The incident began when Captain John Linzee, in the British 16-gun sloop *Falcon*, seized a small American vessel belonging to smugglers. Nearby citizens pursued in a few vessels and recaptured the prize. They also took the *Falcon* after a brief engagement. In a more renowned incident, accredited as the first patriot resistance, what British sloop was seized in early June at Machias, Maine?

A. Boston merchant Ichabod Jones arrived at Machias with the sloops *Unity* and *Polly* to obtain lumber for the British troops in Boston. Midshipman James Moore escorted him in the British schooner *Margaretta*. A majority of the citizens, who had recently learned of the outbreak of hostilities, voted to trade with Jones for provisions. The Sons of Liberty, led by Jeremiah O'Brien and Benjamin Foster, attempted unsuccessfully to apprehend Jones and some of the *Margaretta's* officers during a church service. Moore escaped to his ship. The patriots next boarded *Unity* and with another vessel pursued *Margaretta* out of the harbor where they boarded and captured her.

Q. Who was the first person of Continental authority to commission a ship for Continental service?

A. While in command of the siege of Boston, George Washington realized the necessity of striking at British supply vessels and realized the availably they presented for filling his own needs. At this time British vessels sailed into Boston both unarmed and unescorted. Having intelligence of British arrivals and departures increased Washington's opportunity. In the fall of 1775, he began commissioning vessels to raid British ships.

Q. Washington eventually commissioned eight small coastal vessels. Name the first vessel, which was commissioned on September 2, 1775.

A. Washington obtained the schooner *Hannah* from Colonel John Glover of the Marblehead regiment and appointed Nicholas Broughton to command the vessel, which first sailed on September 5, 1775.

Q. On January 1, 1776, who did Washington name as America's first flag officer?

A. Washington named John Manley commodore of his squadron in recognition of Manley's accomplishments. While commanding the schooner *Lee*, Manley made his most noteworthy capture, the brig *Nancy*, which contained badly needed military supplies including 2,500 muskets, 100,000 musket flints, 31 tons of musket shot, and 30,000 round shot. Washington had just written to Congress requesting musket flints when the capture was made.

Q. How many prizes did Washington's fleet capture before the Marine Committee disbanded it in early 1777?

   a. 55
   b. 75
   c. 100

A. The answer is a. Before it was disbanded, the fleet captured fifty-five prizes. After Washington left for New York with the main army, Artemus Ward assumed command of the fleet. During the fleet's career, it lost only two vessels to the enemy, the brigantine *Washington* in December 1775 and the schooner *Warren* in the summer of 1776. Washington began to fit out another fleet after he went to New York in April 1776; however, the British arrival in August put an end to its operation.

Q. Name the first colony to commission a navy.

A. Due to the annoyance the British frigate *Rose* caused in Narragansett Bay, Rhode Island commissioned two vessels on June 12, 1775. Under Abraham Whipple's command, they went to sea and destroyed a tender of the *Rose* on the same day.

Q. Name the only two of the thirteen states that failed to fit out and arm their own fleets.

A. Only New Jersey and Delaware failed to assemble their own fleets. Some states operated substantial fleets. For example, South Carolina had fifteen seagoing vessels, several of which were larger than any ships in the Continental navy.

Q. What colony's general assembly sent a resolution asking Congress to build or equip an American fleet?

A. Rhode Island. The resolution was passed on October 13, 1775. Congress authorized the outfitting of two ships. Then, on November 2, Congress authorized the outfitting of four ships.

Q. Congress made a first step toward forming a navy when it appointed on October 5 John Adams, John Langdon, and Silas Deane to a committee to plan the interception of some munition ships bound for Quebec. On October 13 Christopher Gadsen replaced Adams on the committee overseeing the outfitting of two ships to intercept the transports. Finally, on October 30, 1775, Congress appointed a seven-member Naval Committee to manage naval affairs. Name three of the seven members.

A. The members were John Langdon of New Hampshire, John Adams of Massachusetts, Stephen Hopkins of Rhode Island, Silas Deane of Connecticut, Richard Henry Lee of Virginia, Joseph Hewes of North Carolina, and Christopher Gadsen of South Carolina.

Q. Name the first ship of the Continental navy.

A. In November 1775 the Naval Committee purchased the *Black Prince*, a merchantman, and converted it to a 30-gun ship named the *Alfred* in honor of the founder of the British navy. Three other merchant vessels were purchased, the *Columbus*, *Cabot*, and *Andrew Doria*.

The *Alfred*

Q. Identify the commander of the Continental navy's first fleet, chosen by Congress in November 1775.

A. Congress chose Esek Hopkins, brother of Stephen Hopkins, the original Naval Committee's chairman. Esek was a merchant captain and had been a privateer in the French and Indian War.

Q. Is it true that according to the navy's rules and regulations a man could receive a maximum of twelve lashes with the cat-o'-nine-tails as punishment, unless he underwent a court-martial?

A. Yes. A court-martial could impose the death penalty for desertion, mutiny, or murder. The commander in chief of the fleet had to confirm the sentence before it could be enforced.

Q. Who drafted the rules and regulations for the navy, which were adopted by Congress with only minor changes on November 28, 1775?

A. John Adams. Among the rules and regulations was the stipulation that divine services be performed twice a day, with a sermon on Sunday. Also, vinegar was to be rationed out to prevent scurvy, and a half of a pint of rum was to be issued to each man per day. For drunkenness a seaman could be put in irons and an officer would lose two days' pay.

Q. Congress established the Marine Corps in November 1775 and authorized two battalions, which were never raised. Who was the first marine officer, commissioned at the rank of captain?

A. Samuel Nicholas. He later became a major, the highest marine rank authorized during the war. The marines wore green uniforms and were modeled after the British marines, who had first been organized in 1664. It is estimated that close to two thousand enlisted men served as marines in the Continental navy. The Marine Corps was then disbanded after the war ended.

Q. Were any of the Continental marines black?

A. Yes. At least three served in the Continental marines. Former slave John Martin became the first black killed at sea in 1777. The three men were the last black Americans to serve officially in the marines until World War II.

Q. In December 1775, Congress approved the construction of thirteen frigates to be built in seven different colonies. They were to be three different types, five 32 guns, five 28 guns, and three 24 guns. What colony built the most of the new frigates?

A. Pennsylvania built four, more than any other colony. All four, *Randolph* (32 gun), *Washington* (32), *Effingham* (28), and *Delaware* (24), were built in and around Philadelphia. The rest were built as follows: *Raleigh* (32), in Portsmouth, New Hampshire; *Hancock* (32) and *Boston* (24) in Newburyport, Massachusetts; *Warren* (32) and *Providence* (28) in Providence, Rhode Island; *Trumbull* (28) in Chatham, Connecticut; *Congress* (28) and *Montgomery* (24) in Poughkeepsie, New York; and *Virginia* (28) in Baltimore, Maryland. Congress named the ships after dead and living American patriots, the first president of the Continental Congress, two Englishmen, and for American geographical places.

Q. How many of these frigates made it to sea in 1776?
   a. none
   b. one
   c. four

A. The answer is a. The frigates were expected to be completed by March. However, there were delays in getting started, and once built, obtaining all the supplies needed to fit the ships out and to man them proved difficult. Rhode Islanders launched the first frigate, *Warren*, on May 15, 1776. The first frigates to get to sea were *Boston* under Hector McNeill and *Hancock* under Joseph Manly in February 1777. The *Hancock* had to return back to port soon afterwards when two rotten masts broke.

Q. Why did Congress choose to build frigates rather than ships of the line?

A. Congress planned the navy primarily for the purpose of commerce raiding. Single-decked frigates suited this purpose best since they were less costly than ships of the line (which had two or three decks and sixty-four or more guns), required a smaller crew, and were fast and efficient in single-ship engagements. These frigates were about 140 feet long, mounted twenty-four to fifty guns, and were manned by a crew of two to three hundred men.

Q. In early 1776 Congress dispatched orders to Esek Hopkins to sweep the Chesapeake and the coasts of the Carolinas and Virginia of enemy vessels, then to head for Rhode Island. Instead, Hopkins disobeyed orders. Where did Hopkins take his fleet of eight ships, 114 guns, 700 sailors, and over 200 marines for the first foreign amphibious landing by American forces?

A. In March 1776 Hopkins attacked Providence, now Nassau in the Bahamas, in the navy's only major planned operation during the war. It also proved to be the most successful American naval operation of the war, netting a considerable amount of badly needed military supplies. Hopkins captured over 100 cannons when the marines, in battle for the first time as an organized unit, under Captain Samuel Nicholas, took Forts Montagu and Nassau. However, Governor Montfort Browne managed to remove 150 casks of gunpowder to St. Augustine.

Q. What incident marred the return trip of Hopkins's fleet?

A. In a running battle with almost all of Hopkins's fleet, the 20-gun frigate *Glasgow* escaped with only one killed and three wounded, while inflicting casualties on four of the American vessels.

Q. The poor performance of the fleet against *Glasgow* resulted in much criticism. What Continental navy captain underwent the navy's first court-martial of the war in order to defend his conduct and to clear his name?

A. Abraham Whipple, commander of *Columbus*, was vindicated and continued in the service. Though Hopkins also was criticized for his actions, he was not suspended from command until March 1777, after all of the officers under his command signed a petition. He was formally dismissed on January 2, 1778. His failure to capture the grounded frigate *Diamond* in January 1777 began his downfall.

Q. Who was the first captain dismissed from service as a result of a court-martial that was also instigated because of his conduct against *Glasgow*?

A. Captain John Hazard, commanding the *Providence*, was found guilty of neglect of duty in his preparation for battle and for embezzling some of his ship's stores. At least nine captains underwent court-martials from the spring of 1776 through 1780; most of the trials were convened because of the loss of a ship. Three captains, Abraham Whipple, John Manley, and Hoystead Hacker, were acquitted.

Q. What was the first British warship captured by a Continental navy vessel?

A. The British schooner *Hawke* was captured in Narragansett Bay by part of Hopkins's returning squadron, as was the bomb brig *Bolton*. Both were taken with very little struggle.

Q. The flagship of Hopkins's fleet was the 24-gun *Alfred*. Lieutenant John Paul Jones hoisted its colors for the first time on a regular United States naval vessel. What was the motto written on the yellow flag?

A. There was "a lively representation of a rattlesnake" with the motto, "Don't tread on me." Upon obtaining command of the 18-gun *Ranger* on June 14, 1777, Jones may also have raised the new official U.S. flag, with thirteen alternating red and white stripes and thirteen stars in a blue field, for the first time on a U.S. warship; however, the flag may have had red, white, and blue stripes.

John Paul Jones
(1747–1792)
Naval officer in
Revolutionary War

Q. What Continental captain fought the first engagement of the Revolution in foreign waters?

A. Captain Lambert Wickes, in the 16-gun brig *Reprisal*, fought HMS *Shark* in July of 1776 near St. Pierre, Martinique, in an inconclusive engagement. Wickes was also the first Continental captain to cruise European waters. He carried Benjamin Franklin to France in November 1776. Afterwards Wickes took five prizes in the English Channel. In the summer of 1777, he led a squadron of the *Reprisal*, *Dolphin*, and *Lexington*, which captured between fourteen and twenty-five prizes in the Irish Sea. Wickes and his crew all perished without a trace on their voyage home in the fall of 1777.

Q. In November 1776 Congress voted to build three 74-gun ships of the line, five frigates, a brig, a packet boat, and soon afterwards, three sloops. How many of these frigates ever saw service in the Continental navy?

A. Only one frigate, the 36-gun *Alliance*, and two sloops, *General Gates* and *Saratoga*, saw Continental service.

Q. Almost all of the captains chosen to command the frigates resided in the area where the ships were built. They were chosen by patronage, favoritism, and to satisfy sectional feelings. Of the twenty-six senior officers Congress accepted on October 10, 1776, who was listed as the senior captain?

A. James Nicholson, captain of the *Virginia*, was listed as the senior captain. He had not even been commissioned in the Continental navy until June 1776. John Manley was second and Hector McNeill third on the list, while John Paul Jones was eighteenth.

Q. The lack of an existing navy meant no corps of naval officers to draw upon for service. Name the sole Continental naval officer who had previously served professionally as an officer aboard a British warship?

A. Nicholas Biddle, who had rubbed shoulders with Horatio Nelson, previously served as a midshipman in the Royal Navy. Three other officers had served in the Royal Navy: Hector McNeill, John Manley, and Samuel Tucker. George Washington had almost begun a stint at the age of four-

Nicholas Biddle
(1750–1844)
Naval officer

teen. Washington's brother Lawrence obtained a berth for him, but at the last moment, with his bags already packed, his pleading mother dissuaded him from joining.

Q. What was the first Continental frigate captured by the British?

A. The *Hancock*. Captained by John Manley, *Hancock* began its first cruise, in conjunction with the frigate *Boston*, captained by Hector

McNeill, and some privateers. The squadron captured a brig on May 29, 1777, and the British 28-gun frigate *Fox* in early June. When three British warships chased the American squadron, it split up. After being fired upon, Manley disgracefully surrendered the *Hancock* to the 44-gun frigate *Rainbow*, under Commodore George Collier, in July, after a chase of thirty-nine hours. Manley thought the 64-gun ship *Raisonable* was chasing him.

Q. Only four American frigates made it to sea in 1777: *Randolph*, *Boston*, *Hancock*, and *Raleigh*. How many Royal Navy warships did they capture or destroy?

A. They only captured one, the frigate *Fox*, which was almost immediately recaptured.

Q. What was the largest ship the British lost to the Americans during the war?

A. American artillery destroyed the 64-gun *Augusta* when it ran aground in the Delaware river during the attack on Forts Mifflin and Mercer in October 1777.

Q. In the greatest single disaster for the U.S. Navy up until 1941, what Continental frigate blew up in the midst of battle?

A. In a brief, hard-fought battle between Continental frigate *Randolph* and the British *Yarmouth* off the coast of Barbados, all but four of the 315-man crew, including Captain Nicholas Biddle, died when the *Randolph* blew up on March 17, 1778. Ironically, Biddle may have previously served aboard the *Yarmouth*.

Q. Name the first naval battle between the British and the French after France declared war in July 1778.

A. The battle of Ushant was fought to a draw on July 23 by French admiral d'Orvilliers, who had been ordered to cruise the English Channel, and British admiral Augustus Keppel. Both fleets of approximately thirty ships of the line inflicted a great deal of damage, though no ships were captured or sunk on either side. Keppel at least insured that there would be no French invasion of England in 1778. Unfortunately for England, third in command Admiral

Hugh Palliser accused Keppel of throwing away a victory. After a court-martial acquitted both of them, Keppel refused to serve in the navy any longer. Many of his fellow Whig party naval officers followed his example.

Q. In July 1779 the United States' largest amphibious operation, until Vera Cruz in the Mexican War, was sent out under the authority of the state of Massachusetts. The expedition lost all forty-two ships, over 500 lives, and cost $7 million dollars—in short it was a major colonial disaster. What had been the expedition's objective?

A. Penobscot Bay, Maine. Colonel Francis MacLean, with about 800 British troops, had occupied Penobscot Bay (then a part of Massachusetts), to secure timber for ship repair at the British naval base in Halifax. The people of Massachusetts feared renewed attacks by British vessels based there. Thus an expedition of twenty-two armed vessels and twenty transports—the entire Massachusetts state navy—privateers and a few Continental naval vessels, were organized to retake Fort St. George and destroy the British vessels there.

Q. Who commanded the doomed expedition to Penobscot Bay?

A. Unfortunately, the expedition was plagued by a divided command. Continental navy captain Dudley Saltonstall commanded the naval fleet while Brigadier General Solomon Lovell commanded over one thousand militia. An immediate, determined attack would probably have overwhelmed the British. However, Lovell and Saltonstall bickered over who should lead an assault first. Lovell wanted the British sloops in the Penobscot River destroyed before assaulting the fort, and Saltonstall insisted that the fort be captured before he attacked the British ships. Just when they had agreed on a joint attack, a British fleet of ten ships, which included a ship of the line and three frigates, arrived. After only brief resistance, the Americans scattered; twenty-eight ships were captured and fourteen destroyed. The British retained the post for the remainder of the war. Afterwards, Saltonstall was court-martialed and dismissed from the service.

Q. When asked to surrender in the midst of battle, what famous American sea captain replied, "I have not yet begun to fight"?

A. John Paul Jones. Originally from Scotland, John Paul assumed the name Jones when he arrived in America a few years before the Revolutionary War. He served in the Continental navy from the very beginning, earning a commission as a first lieutenant on the *Alfred*. In 1776 he was given command of the sloop *Providence*.

Q. What ship did Jones command in his fight with the *Serapis*, captained by Richard Pearson, in September 1779?

A. The *Bonhomme Richard*. In January 1779, the French presented a worn-out vessel, *Duc de Duras*, to John Paul Jones. Jones repaired and refitted the vessel and mounted it with forty-two guns. He then renamed it *Bonhomme Richard* (Franklin's French nickname) in honor of Benjamin Franklin. In perhaps the hardest fought battle of the war, half of Jones's crew of 300 was killed or wounded, and Jones had to abandon the *Bonhomme Richard*, which sank two days after the battle. The British lost 117 out of a crew of about equal size.

The capture of the Serapis *by the* Bonhomme Richard

Q. While Jones battled the *Serapis*, another ship in his squadron engaged a British ship. Name the American ship.

A. The *Pallas* fought and captured HMS *Countess of Scarborough*.

Q. Who captained the *Alliance*, which fired at the *Serapis* during the battle?

A. Captain Pierre Landais, the only French captain in Continental service, fired three broadsides into the *Serapis*, killing several men. Thought to be crazy, Landais later threatened Arthur Lee with a carving knife at a dinner on his return trip aboard the *Alliance* in 1780. Soon afterwards, Landais's officers and passengers forced him to abdicate his command. At a court-martial, he was dismissed from the service, the last Continental captain to suffer the ignominy.

Q. How many of the original thirteen frigates were still in the Continental navy by 1782?

A. None of the original thirteen remained by 1782.

Q. By the end of the war, 468 ships were serving in the Royal Navy. In contrast, how many were still serving in the Continental navy in 1782?

A. Only two ships were still in commission, the frigates *Alliance* and *Deane*. *Alliance* was the only frigate of the five additional frigates authorized by Congress in November 1776 to be completed before the war's end. *Deane* came to America from France in 1778.

Q. How many of the original thirteen frigates surrendered to the enemy?

A. Seven. The frigates *Congress*, *Montgomery*, and *Warren* were destroyed to avoid capture. The British burned the *Washington* and *Effingham*. And one frigate blew up in battle.

Q. The last of the original thirteen Continental frigates to be captured was the 30-gun *Trumbull*, under Captain James Nicholson. To what ship did Nicholson surrender to in August of 1781?

A. Ironically, he surrendered to the 32-gun frigate *Iris*, formerly the *Hancock*, the first Continental frigate to be captured. Nicholson gave up after fighting a mismatched battle.

Q. What captain fought the last battle in the war for the Continental navy?

A. John Barry, in the frigate *Alliance*, he demolished the British frigate *Sybil* in March 1783, more than a month after the official end of hostilities. Ironically he had been the first Continental captain to capture a Royal Navy vessel in a single-ship action. He had captured the 16-gun sloop *Edward* on April 7, 1776.

Q. On what frigate was a rattlesnake carved on the stern with the inscription "Don't tread on me"?

A. The *Hancock*, which one British officer described as "the finest and fastest frigate in the world."

Q. Congress approved the building of three ships of the line during the war. Though not stated by Congress, the ships were in fact too costly to build and required more men than America could supply. The ship of the line to be built in Philadelphia was never begun, and only a start was made on the vessel at Boston. Name the only ship of the line that was completed, at Portsmouth, New Hampshire.

A. *America* was begun in May of 1777, but due to lack of funds, was not completed until November 1782. In 1780 Congress had attempted to sell the half-completed ship to France, which declined. In 1781 Congress ordered Robert Morris to finish the ship, and they named John Paul Jones its commander. However, *America* never saw combat and was transferred to France as a gesture of good will. Most of the fittings used to finish *America* had come from the French ship of the line *Le Magnifique*, which had broken up in Boston Harbor after running aground. Congress had considered making John Paul Jones an admiral after his assignment to America; however, the senior captain of the navy, James Nicholson, lobbied against it.

Q. Did the British generally consider captured American ships well built?

A. Yes. Besides the *Hancock*, many were taken into service. The *Hancock* lasted in service until 1793, the last Continental vessel still afloat. Nevertheless, in the rush of war construction, many ships were built with green, unseasoned timber and did not last long. For example, the British did not take the captured frigate *Trumbull* into service. Also, the *America*, which was given to France in 1782, was found to be so rotten in 1786 that it was broken up.

Q. Were American ships painted?

A. Yes. The ships' sides were usually painted yellow with black mouldings or narrow stripes, or black with very narrow bands of red, white, and yellow.

Q. How many years on average did a ship in the Royal Navy last during the colonial period?
a. Ten years
b. Twenty years
c. Thirty years

A. The answer is a.

Q. What was a privateer?

A. A privateer was a privately owned vessel that the government commissioned to attack enemy merchantmen. Congress officially sanctioned the commissioning of privately armed vessels in March 1776. Congress did not directly issue commissions, but sent blank commissions to the states so they could take responsibility. The states also set up courts to regulate the distribution of the proceeds from prizes (that is, captured ships).

Q. From what state did Congress enlist the most privateers?

A. Massachusetts may have had as many as 626 privateers. After Massachusetts, Pennsylvania and Maryland commissioned the most privateers.

Q. In what year did Americans put to sea the greatest number of privateers?

A. In 1781 the Americans sent out 449 privateers carrying 6,735 guns. Also in 1781, the British suffered their heaviest ship losses of the war. Early in the war, privateers on average mounted ten guns and carried from thirty to sixty crewmen. Later, as a rule, they mounted twenty to twenty-six guns and carried 150 to 200 crewmen.

Q. During the war were more British warships taken by regular Continental navy vessels or by privateers and private enterprise?

A. Privateers and private enterprise accomplished the capture of sixteen warships while the Continental navy accounted for twelve.

Q. Which accounted for the loss of more enemy ships during the war, the Continental navy or privateers?

A. Though estimates vary, as many as two to three thousand privateers caused the loss of roughly six hundred British ships, while the Continental navy received credit for about two hundred.

Q. Approximately how many ships of all classes served in the Continental navy?

   a. 35
   b. 100
   c. 145

A. The answer is b, if all classes are counted, from lake galley to ship of the line.

FACT

At its peak the Continental navy never reached more than one-fourth the strength of the enemy navy in American waters.

Q. Is it true the practice of privateering provided a large trained pool of sailors to man the Continental navy?

A. No. The Continental navy had difficulty in obtaining crews because privateers paid almost double the salary the navy paid. Men could accumulate enough riches on one or two successful privateer voyages to retire for the rest of their lives. On the other hand, sixty privateers were commanded by men who later became captains in the Continental navy. About 55,000 men served on privateers throughout the war.

Q. Recruiting men to serve in the navy was a continual problem. What Continental navy captain suggested increasing enlistment by letting men sign on and leave when they wished, instead of signing on for a year, and giving the seamen all the proceeds from prizes?

A. John Paul Jones. Congress did increase the crew's share of prizes from one-half to all for warships and privateers, and from one-third to one-half for transports.

Q. What was the greatest number of seamen ever in Continental service at one time?
  a. 1,000
  b. 2,000
  c. 3,000

A. The answer is c. About 340 officers were commissioned.

Q. At what West Indian island did American merchantmen pick up most of the European goods needed for the American war effort?

A. St. Eustatius. The Dutch owned the island, which contained the busiest and richest port in the Americas. Admiral Lord Rodney finally attacked and closed the port in 1781.

Q. Each side impressed prisoners into service, sometimes with severe consequences. On what frigate did three-quarters of the crew (mostly impressed British seamen) refuse to fight in a battle, thus causing the loss of the ship?

A. The *Trumbull*, under Captain Samuel Nicholson, was forced to surrender to the British frigate *Iris*, formerly the American frigate

Hancock, and the *General Monck*, a former American privateer, after a brief battle. Three-fourths of Nicholson's crew were former British sailors. As prisoners, the sailors took the option of joining the Continental navy. During the battle, the British sailors refused to fight against their countrymen.

Q. What Continental navy captain captured the most British vessels?

A. Gustavus Conyngham in the *Revenge* was reputed to have captured sixty ships. He sent twenty-seven into port and sank or burned another thirty-three between July 1777 and the end of 1779.

Q. What American captain embarrassed the British by attacking the Scottish port of Whitehaven, spiking several guns and setting several vessels in the harbor on fire while he was there?

A. John Paul Jones. He also raided St. Mary's Isle, took Lord Selkirk's silver, and attacked and captured the 20-gun *Drake* at Carrickfergus, Scotland.

Q. Was it John Barry or John Paul Jones who coined the phrase "to go in harm's way"?

A. John Paul Jones.

Q. Identify the commander in chief of the British navy in America from 1776 to 1778 who was nicknamed "Black Dick."

A. British vice admiral Lord Richard Howe, brother of General William Howe.

Q. The first lord of the British admiralty during the war has been blamed for much of the British navy corruption at that time and for the decrepit condition of many of its ships at the beginning of the war. Who was he?

A. John Montagu Sandwich, Fourth Earl of Sandwich. Captain Cook named the Sandwich Islands, later renamed the Hawaiian Islands, after him.

Q. Who was the first commander in chief for the British on the American station?

A. Admiral Samuel Graves. He was hampered in early operations against the Americans because he had only twenty-nine ships to use to blockade the entire coast, when at least fifty ships were needed. Richard Howe replaced Graves in January 1776.

Q. Did Horatio Nelson ever fight against Americans during the war?

A. No. Nelson served under Sir Peter Parker in the West Indies. Nelson experienced his first action in the expedition to Nicaragua. His only other combat was against the French when his attempt to capture Turk's Island in the Bahamas was repulsed.

Q. During the war, the Royal Navy lost 203 ships from all causes. Were more lost to enemy action or to other causes?

A. The Royal Navy lost more ships to other causes. Only ninety were lost as a result of enemy action. Also, many more men were lost to disease and desertion rather than battle. Out of almost 176,000 men in the navy during the war, 42,000 deserted, 18,541 died of disease, and only 1,243 were killed in battle.

Q. What disease known as "the Scourge of the Sea and the Spoyle of Mariners" was caused by a vitamin C deficiency and has been estimated to have killed one million British seaman alone?

A. Scurvy. Fresh fruits and vegetables helped to prevent the disease, but could not be kept for long aboard a ship. In 1747 British surgeon James Lind proved that lemon juice was the best remedy; however, because of the expense, many captains ignored Lind's discovery until 1795 when the Royal Navy was ordered to serve each man one ounce of lemon juice per day. This virtually eliminated the disease. Other diseases also ravaged seamen and others, such as cholera, dysentery, typhus, smallpox, and yellow fever.

Q. Did the Royal Navy's average crew of seaman in wartime include more of men pressed into service against their will than volunteers?

A. The average crew contained 50 percent of pressed men, 23 percent volunteers, 15 percent from jails, and 12 percent foreigners. Due to poor pay and deplorable conditions, it was very difficult to keep men on a ship, so desertion was a huge problem any time a ship was in a port.

Q. Many American seamen were kept in British prison ships in New York Harbor during the war. Approximately how many died there?

A. Approximately eleven hundred American seaman died in British prison ships.

Q. What nation lost the most warships in the war?

A. The French lost sixty-five warships, while the Americans lost thirty-seven and the British twenty-three.

Q. What battle, fought on April 12, 1782, was the Royal Navy's greatest victory in the West Indies during the war?

A. In the Battle of the Saints, Admiral Sir George Rodney, with thirty-six ships of the line, inflicted severe damage on a French fleet of thirty-three ships of the line, under Comte de Grasse, capturing or destroying five ships (two more were captured later), killing or wounding 3,000 men, and capturing 7,980 while losing 261 killed and 837 wounded. Included in the captures was de Grasse in his flagship, the *Ville de Paris*, which, with 104 guns, was the largest and most powerful battleship in the world. The victory saved Jamaica, Britain's richest possession in the Caribbean, lifted morale, and had a decisive impact on peace negotiations.

Q. Name the French admiral who won the last naval battle of the war, on June 20, 1783, off of Cuddalore, India.

A. Admiral Saint-Tropez Suffren was the greatest and most successful French admiral of the war. He bested British Admiral Sir Edward Hughes in four of five naval battles in the waters near India in 1782 and 1783; they were Madras in February, Trincomalee in April and September of 1782, and Cuddalore in June 1783.

Between Wars: 1783-1811

"'Tis our true policy to steer clear of permanent alliances with any portion of the foreign world."

Q. George Washington was the first commander of the American army. Who succeeded him?

A. Major General Henry Knox succeeded Washington on December 23, 1783, when Washington resigned. Knox kept the command until June 20, 1784, when he resigned. Knox became the first secretary of war in 1785 (officially in September 1789 under the new constitution) and held the post until 1794.

Q. In a little over a year, in 1783 and 1784, the Continental Congress convened in five different cities in four states. Name three of the cities.

A. In order, they were Philadelphia, Pennsylvania; Princeton, New Jersey; Annapolis, Maryland; Trenton, New Jersey; and New York City, New York.

Q. In June of 1784 Congress reduced the army to only one company of eighty artillerymen. What duty did Congress assign them?

A. The eighty artillerymen were to guard the military stores at Fort Pitt and West Point. This original unit of artillerymen, known today as the First Battalion, Fifth Field Artillery, is the only United States military unit to have served continuously on active duty since the Revolutionary War.

Q. By 1783 there were already 25,000 people in the western lands. After the war, a flood of migrating settlers began to pour into the new lands. Congress had to decide how to divide and to govern the region. Who proposed that the West be divided into fourteen regions, giving them such names as Cherronesus, Pelisipia, Polypotamia, and Michigania?

A. Thomas Jefferson. Though Congress did not adopt Jefferson's recommendations, it did pass the Land Ordinance of 1785 and the Northwest Ordinance of 1787. The 1785 Ordinance regulated the sale, surveying, and governing of the western lands. It established six-mile-square townships of 36 sections of 640 acres each. Land could be sold only as a section for $640. The Northwest Ordinance specified the division and government of the land north of the Ohio and west to the Mississippi. The region was to be divided into at least three but no greater than five districts. As soon as a part of the territory had at least sixty thousand free inhabitants, it could become a state. Breaking the historical pattern of nations, these ordinances allowed for the expansion of the nation itself rather than colonization first.

Q. Which famous president's paternal grandfather was killed by Native Americans in Kentucky in 1784?

A. Abraham Lincoln's paternal grandfather, Abraham Lincoln.

Q. Name the independent nation that made up a portion of present-day Tennessee from 1785 to 1789.

A. Franklin. John Sevier was its governor, though other governments never recognized the nation.

Q. Beginning in 1786, who led a rebellion of farmers in Massachusetts over the issues of debts and taxes?

A. Daniel Shays, who had been a captain in the Revolutionary War, led the farmers, who called themselves Regulators, in an unsuccessful attack on the United States arsenal at Springfield, Massachusetts, in early 1787. Soon afterwards, General Benjamin Lincoln led 4,000 militia against them. He suprised them at camp in the early morning, captured 150 men, and scattered the rest. Afterwards the rebellion was broken, though in one pitched battle against militia, 100 men were killed or wounded. The rebellion provided impetus for the army's expansion and awareness of the weak federal government, so that the states convened a Constitutional Convention in Philadelphia in May of 1787.

Q. What was the name given to the first constitution, prepared by a committee headed by John Dickinson in 1776, then adopted by Congress in November of 1777, and finally ratified on March 1, 1781?

A. The Articles of Confederation enabled Congress to govern throughout the Revolution. A civil service had been established, a peace treaty with England concluded, and a method for settling western lands decided. However, the Articles proved inadequate for molding a nation because there was no federal executive or judiciary, and the federal government could not directly raise revenue. In addition, any amendment to the federal government's powers required the agreement of all thirteen states, which was extremely difficult to achieve. Under the Articles, Congress had attempted to furnish revenue by providing a 5 percent customs duty, but Rhode Island and then New York had defeated this. Instead, Congress estimated its own needs and made requisitions from the states, which levied their own taxes.

Q. What was the first state to ratify the new federal Constitution, adopted by Congress in 1787?

A. Delaware ratified the Constitution on December 12, 1787. With nine states needed for ratification, President of the Congress Cyrus Griffin did not announce the Constitution to be official until July 2, 1788. Rhode Island, the only state that did not send a delegation to the Constitutional Convention, became the last state to ratify the constitution in May 1790.

Q. The Connecticut Compromise, or Great Compromise, broke a deadlock on what issue at the Constitutional Convention?

A. The Great Compromise broke a deadlock on the issue of representation in Congress. The large states wanted representation based on population; the small states wanted equality. The terms of the compromise gave every state an equal vote in the Senate, but based representation in the House on the free population plus three-fifths of a state's slave population. At one point before the compromise, Benjamin Franklin had moved that the sessions be opened with prayer. The motion lost only because the Convention did not have the money to pay a chaplain.

Q. In what year did Washington become the first president under the new constitution?

A. Washington was inaugurated as the first president of the United States in New York on April 30, 1789. He would be the only person the electoral college would elect unanimously for president, not just once, but twice.

Q. While Washington waited to be inaugurated, Congress debated a proper title for him. Of the titles being debated, which one of the following did Washington prefer?
a. His Highness
b. President of the United States of America
c. Protector of the Rights of the United States of America
d. No title at all

A. The answer is d.

Q. Washington was the first among American presidents to have fought in battle. How many presidents have endured the risks of battle?
a. Five
b. Eleven
c. Sixteen

A. The answer is c. They were Washington, Monroe, Jackson, William Henry Harrison, Taylor, Pierce, Grant, Hayes, Garfield, Benjamin Harrison, McKinley, Theodore Roosevelt, Truman, Eisenhower, Kennedy, and Bush.

Q. The Continental Congress met for fifteen years, from the spring of 1774 until the spring of 1789. Of the 342 different members, only one delegate participated in every important session. Name him.

A. The secretary from Philadelphia, Charles Thomson, was present almost every day.

Q. In 1790 the capital was moved to Philadelphia. In June of the same year, a compromise was made to locate a permanent capital on the Potomac River. What were the terms of the compromise?
A. Southerners agreed to allow the federal government to assume state debts (which were mostly northern) left over from the Revolution in exchange for the location of the capital.

Q. What was the first state accepted into the Union after the original thirteen?
A. Vermont became the fourteenth state in March 1791.

Q. In 1787 Congress passed the Northwest Ordinance, opening up territory north of the Ohio River to settlement. The Native Americans resisted the intrusion of settlers onto their land. Who then led an expedition against the Native Americans in 1790?
A. General Josiah Harmer led almost 1,500 men, mostly militia, near what is now Fort Wayne, Indiana. They were defeated and lost 20 men.

Q. In 1791 another expedition was sent against the same Native Americans. Who led it?
A. General Arthur St. Clair, governor of the Northwest Territory, led a force of about fourteen hundred men, primarily militia, to the greatest defeat ever suffered by the white man against the Native American.

Q. Name the Miami chief who inflicted the defeats on both Harmar and St. Clair.
A. Little Turtle led Miamis, Shawnees, Potawatomis, Chippewas, and Wyandots to victory both times. Only 580 men of St. Clair's army made it back home after Little Turtle attacked.

Q. What territory's demand for statehood was refused by Congress for eight years before being accepted?

A. In 1792 Kentucky became the fifteenth state. It had been Virginia's Kentucky County before.

Q. On March 14, 1792, a reward of $500 and a gold medal was offered to whomever submitted the winning design for the President's House, to be erected on the site George Washington chose for the new capital. Three judges awarded James Hoban the reward over nine other entries, including one by Thomas Jefferson. Construction began on October 13 of the same year. Was the house completed in time for Washington to live in it?

A. No. John and Abigail Adams were the first to occupy the house. They moved into the house on November 1, 1800.

Q. By what act was the president authorized to raise six-month volunteer levies and appoint all the commissioned officers of the levies, in addition to calling out state militia?

A. The Militia Act of 1792 gave the president this authorization. In 1803 governors were given the power to appoint the commissioned officers of the levies. In addition, every able-bodied white male citizen was to enroll in the militia and furnish his own weapons and equipment within six months of enrollment. The Dick Act repealed the Militia Act during the Spanish American War.

Q. Name the minister of the French Republic whose actions in the United States in 1793 threatened to instigate a war against England?

A. While in the U.S., Edmond Charles Genet commissioned four privateering ships to raid against the British and armed another captured British ship, *Little Sarah*, in Philadelphia. Genet also sent funds to George Rogers Clark and commissioned him to lead an expedition against Spanish Louisiana. Washington asked the French government to recall Genet and prohibited sanctuary for privateers in American ports. Still, war with Britain loomed as the British began to seize American ships.

Q. In 1794 Little Turtle advised the Native Americans to seek peace when he saw the quality of the commander and army now invading their territory. The commander fortified his camp every night with trenches and breastworks. He also screened his movements with numerous Native Americans and white scouts. The Native Americans could not mount a surprise attack against him. Little Turtle said of him, "The Americans are now led by a chief who never sleeps." Who commanded this new army?

A. General "Mad Anthony" Wayne had taken the time to discipline and train his new army of 3,000 men. He surprised the Native Americans by moving toward their population center at Au Glaize.

Q. Name the battle where Wayne's army defeated the Native Americans, a battle in which the Native Americans had taken command away from Little Turtle and fought under Turkey Foot.

A. Wayne defeated them in the battle of Fallen Timbers with the loss of a little over one hundred killed and wounded. The battle raged in an area of fallen timbers felled by a tornado. After the Native Americans initially attacked and drove away the militia, Wayne's disciplined regulars advanced with fixed bayonets. The Native Americans fled to a British fort, but the British would not allow them to enter. By that action, British influence over the Native Americans was broken. The Native Americans had been led to believe the British would join them in war on the Americans.

Q. Because of their defeat in the battle of Fallen Timbers, British duplicity and Wayne's devastation of their villages afterwards, the Native Americans signed a treaty. Name the treaty.

A. The Treaty of Greenville, which twelve principal tribes signed on August 3, 1795. By ceding most of Ohio and much of Indiana, the tribes acknowledged the sovereignty of the United States. The treaty ended twenty years of almost continuous warfare on the frontier. Westerners also appreciated the role of the federal government in solving their Native American problem.

Q. What was the former name of the Wyandots?
A. They were called Hurons.

Q. Where was the first national armory established?

A. In 1794 an armory was established at Springfield, Massachusetts. Another one was established at Harpers Ferry, Virginia, later in the year.

Q. A federal tax on what product fomented a rebellion in western Pennsylvania?

A. Whiskey. Westerners feared the East was trying to dominate them. Whiskey was one of the few products Westerners could transport over the mountains for a profit. Gangs soon accosted federal officials who attempted to collect a tax, and marched on Pittsburgh. Washington sent Major General Henry Lee into the area with an army of 13,000 men. The rebellion collapsed after very little fighting largely because Wayne's victory at Fallen Timbers and the Treaty of Greenville assuaged western grievances. Two out of the 200 rebels arrested were convicted of treason but later were pardoned.

Q. By what treaty did the British finally agree to withdraw from the forts they occupied in the American Northwest Territory?

A. Jay's Treaty, signed in 1794 by American envoy John Jay and passed by Congress in 1795, helped avert a war between the United States and Britain. The British agreed to withdraw from the eight forts they occupied with about one thousand troops by June 1796. Captain Moses Porter finally occupied Detroit for the Americans on July 11, 1796, and Major Henry Burbeck occupied Fort Mackinac on October 2, 1796. American ships were also allowed to resume trade with Britain's Caribbean colonies, which had been prohibited since the Revolution.

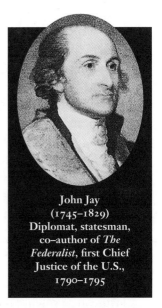

John Jay
(1745–1829)
Diplomat, statesman, co–author of *The Federalist*, first Chief Justice of the U.S., 1790–1795

Q. What coveted goal of Westerners was achieved in the 1795 Treaty of San Lorenzo, signed by Washington's emissary, Thomas Pinckney, with Spain?

A. Americans were granted freedom of navigation of the Mississippi and the right of deposit at New Orleans. They finally had a trade route to the sea. Also, Spain abandoned claim to all territory east of the Mississippi to a point south of Natchez.

Q. When the Revolutionary War ended so did the American navy. In what year—and why—did Congress authorize construction of ships for a permanent navy?

A. Congress passed a Naval Act in 1794 in response to Algerian depredations on American merchant shipping in the Mediterranean. The act designated that six ships be built in six different places: Boston, New York, Philadelphia, Baltimore, and Portsmouth, New Hampshire, and Portsmouth, Virginia. A peace treaty was signed with Algiers in March 1796. As a part of the treaty, a tribute in the form of four ships—a 32-gun frigate, a brig, and two schooners—was paid to Algiers.

Q. The Naval Act of 1794 mandated a halt to ship construction in the event of peace. Washington then persuaded Congress to continue ship construction, and a year later three frigates, *United States* (44-gun), *Constitution* (44), and *Constellation* (36), became the first war-ships of a permanent American navy. What was the first ship to be launched in the new navy?

A. The *United States* was the first, launched on May 10, 1797. Because of trouble with the French in 1798, Congress appropriated funds for the building and completion of three additional frigates, which had been authorized in 1794. *President* (44), *Congress* (36), and *Chesapeake* (36) were all launched by April 1800.

Q. Did Washington favor Britain or France in his foreign policy?

A. Washington favored neither one; instead he favored a policy of strict neutrality, warning against involvement in any European affairs. In his farewell address, he made the following statements: "Observe good faith and justice towards all nations"; "Even our commercial policy should hold an equal and impartial hand"; "Tis our true policy to steer clear of permanent alliances with any portion of the foreign world."

Q. The presidential election of 1796 was the first one in which opposing political parties supported candidates. In 1789 Washington had been chosen informally, without opposition and by a unanimous vote. Name the two political parties of 1796 from which the president and vice president were elected.

A. The Federalists supported John Adams, who garnered seventy-one electoral votes to win the presidency. The Democratic-Republicans fielded Thomas Jefferson, who obtained sixty-eight electoral votes to win the vice presidency. There were a total of thirteen candidates running including Thomas Pinckney, who received fifty-nine votes, and Aaron Burr, with thirty votes. Adams was the first president to occupy the presidential palace (known later as the White House) and the only one to have a son who also became president. John Quincy Adams won the election of 1824.

Q. In contrast to today's funding of ship construction, the Act of June 30, 1798, allowed the navy to accept ships built by public subscription, to be paid for in bonds carrying 6 percent interest. Also, cities were encouraged to build vessels and donate them to the navy as gifts. How many frigates were added to the navy in this manner?

A. Five new frigates were added, the *Philadelphia*, *Essex*, *New York*, *Boston*, and *John Adams*, along with several other smaller vessels.

Q. From 1794 until 1798, Henry Knox ran the navy. In April 1798, a new cabinet office was created. Who became the first secretary of the navy?

A. Benjamin Stoddert would run the navy until 1801. He inherited three frigates in 1798; when he left in 1801, there were fifty ships in the navy.

Q. In what year was the Marine Corps officially established?

A. The Marine Corps was officially established on July 11, 1798, with William Burrows in command. Continental marines had existed under Samuel Nicholas in the Revolutionary War, but they had been discontinued. The marines kept discipline aboard ships, led boarding parties, and manned coastal installations. No "Negroes, Mulattoes or Indians" could enlist.

Q. In 1797 President John Adams sent Charles Pinckney, John Marshall, and Elbridge Gerry to France to secure a treaty. In what was known as the XYZ affair, French Foreign Minister Charles Maurice de Talleyrand had three French agents request a bribe of $240,000 and asked for a $10 million loan before negotiations could begin. Is it true that the bribe was paid and that the loan was made?

A. No. When Congress learned the details, it began taking measures to prepare for a possible war, repealing the treaty of alliance made with France during the Revolutionary War. In the spring of 1798, Congress began to order ships out to sea to protect American commerce, and the undeclared naval war with France began.

Q. What was the name of the undeclared naval war the United States fought with France from May 1798 until February 1801?

A. The Quasi War. In 1794 John Jay signed a treaty settling differences with Britain. France, then at war with Britain, viewed this as a hostile action and began seizing American ships without compensation. An undeclared war was then fought until the Treaty of Mortefontaine was signed.

Q. How many warships did the United States Navy possess at the beginning of the Quasi War?
a. Five
b. Ten
c. Fifteen

A. The answer is c. The United States Navy possessed one 36-gun frigate, two 44-gun frigates, and twelve ships with 18 to 24 guns each. The first warship put to sea was the *Ganges*, with 24 nine-pound guns, under Captain Richard Dale, in late May.

Q. Name the first French ship captured by the United States during the Quasi War.

A. Stephen Decatur Sr. captured the first prize of the war, the 12-gun *La Croyable*, in late June 1798. While commanding the *Delaware*, a converted merchantman with 24 nine- and six-pounders, Decatur brought *La Croyable* to Philadelphia. The federal government bought it, added it to the navy, and renamed it *Retaliation*. Ironically, *Retaliation* became the first and only warship the United States lost to the French during the Quasi War. Lieutenant William Bainbridge was forced to surrender the ship to the French frigate *L'Insurgente* in November 1798.

Q. Who was the senior captain in the U.S. Navy during the Quasi War, considered by many to be the father of the U.S. Navy?

A. John Barry. On February 2, 1799, aboard the *United States* in the Caribbean, he took the first prize of the war, the 10-gun *Sans Pareil*.

Q. The Royal Navy also fought the French in the Caribbean during the Quasi War. Which navy captured more French privateers in the Caribbean, the U.S. or the British?

A. The U.S. Navy captured eighty-six French privateers with an average of sixteen ships operating in the Caribbean in two years of war. The Royal Navy averaged eighty ships but took only twenty-nine privateers during the same period. The U.S. Navy lost one ship, the 14-gun schooner *Retaliation* (formerly the French *La Croyable*). During the war, forty-two ships sailed in the U.S. Navy. The maximum operational strength of thirty-two ships was reached in June 1800. From 1799 to 1800 America lost 159 merchantmen to the French. However, they captured 86 French merchantmen and recaptured 100 merchantmen.

Q. What captain of the *Constellation* won two victories over French warships during the war?

A. Thomas Truxton, who was the only one of the first six captains in the navy who had not fought in the Revolutionary War. He captured the French frigate *L'Insurgente* in February 1799 and defeated the more heavily armed *La Vengeance* a year later. Just after the French captain surrendered, the *Constellation*'s mainmast collapsed and *La Vengeance* escaped. Truxton also wrote a book on signals in 1797 which the navy adopted.

Q. Because of the possiblity of war with France when nearly thirty thousand Frenchmen resided in the United States, in addition to other possible alien enemies, the Federalists in 1798 passed what act that empowered the president to deport any resident aliens?

A. Congress granted the president power to banish aliens in a series of acts known as the Alien and Sedition Acts, passed in the summer of 1798. The residency requirement to obtain full citizenship was raised from five to fourteen years. Also provisions were made for fining and imprisoning persons who interfered with federal officials performing their duties, opposed the enforcement of national laws, or published false, scandalous, or malicious writing attacking the government. Under these acts, ten of twenty-five editors and printers prosecuted, all Republicans, were convicted, fined, or imprisoned. These acts helped Thomas Jefferson and the Republican-Democrats defeat Adams.

Q. In 1801 who declared war on the United States?

A. Pasha Yusuf Karamanli, the Bashaw of Tripoli, declared war after the American envoy James Cathcart rejected the pasha's demand for a large tribute payment. The U.S. fought an undeclared war until 1805. The war ended when President Thomas Jefferson paid $60,000 to bribe Tripoli to refrain from attacking U.S. shipping and to ransom 300 prisoners.

Q. In what year was the U.S. military academy established at West Point, New York?

A. In March 1802 the academy began with seven officers and ten cadets. Colonel Jonathan Williams was the first superintendent. Colonel Joseph Gardner Swift and one other were the first graduates, commissioned as second lieutenants on October 12, 1802.

Q. Besides Tripoli, what were the other three Barbary states along the northern coast of Africa that preyed on United States shipping?

A. Morocco, Algiers, and Tunis also practiced piracy on United States shipping until President Thomas Jefferson sent naval squadrons to the Mediterranean to force all of the Barbary states to sign peace treaties with the United States. It took from 1801 to 1805 to establish peace with all four states.

Q. What ship did America lose to Tripoli in 1803 without firing a shot in defense?

A. Chasing a smaller vessel while on blockade duty on October 31, the 36-gun frigate *Philadelphia* ran aground outside the harbor at Tripoli. The captain was afraid that he would be bombarded from a distance and surrendered without firing a shot or sustaining a casualty. Just two days later a high tide refloated the ship. He and his crew of over 300 men were then held in captivity for one year and nine months.

The stranding and capture of the Philadelphia

Q. Name the captain of the *Philadelphia*, who had previously suffered the indignity of being the first commander to surrender a U.S. Navy ship during the Quasi War with France in 1798.

A. Captain William Bainbridge had surrendered the 14-gun schooner *Retaliation* to French frigates also without firing a shot when he mistook them for British ships. In addition, in 1800 he had been forced to lower the flag and raise the Algerian flag on the frigate *George Washington* while carrying tribute from Algiers to

Constantinople. He also brought the U.S. flag to the Black Sea for the first time.

Q. For what action was Stephen Decatur promoted to captain at the age of twenty-five, the youngest American yet to hold that rank?

A. On the night of February 16–17, 1804, Decatur and seventy-five men entered the harbor at Tripoli, using a Tripolitan ketch that Decatur had captured. The renamed ketch, *Intrepid*, was disguised as a Maltese vessel. Feigning damage from a storm as it approached the *Philadelphia*, the crew asked permission to pull alongside for the night. At the last moment the Tripolitans discovered the ruse. Nevertheless, within five minutes and without any guns, Decatur's party captured the ship, killed twenty men, and forced the rest overboard during the melee. Then they burned the ship and escaped without the loss of a man. Decatur, who had been the second man to board and the last to leave, was instantly a hero. He was soon promoted to the rank of post captain. Horatio Nelson praised his feat as "the most bold and daring act of the age."

Q. Where did an American flag first fly over an Old World fortress?

A. Derna. William Eaton, with seven United States Marines and 400 other men, captured the fortress in April 1805 after a march of 600 miles from Alexandria, Egypt.

Q. After discovering that Spain had dealt with France under Napoleon, exchanging Louisiana for a part of the Italian peninsula in the Treaty of San Ildefonso on October 1, 1803, who wrote, "The day that France takes possession of N. Orleans . . . from that moment we must marry ourselves to the British fleet and nation"?

A. Thomas Jefferson wrote it in a letter to Robert R. Livingston, the U.S. minister in France, with the intention that Livingston would relay it to the French government.

Q. In October 1802 the Louisiana intendent, Juan Morales, forbade Americans to deposit goods for trade in New Orleans. In December 1802, Napoleon had an army of 20,000 men ready to sail to New Orleans. What prevented the French fleet from sailing

FACT

In Egypt Eaton had enlisted Hamet (the brother of Yusuf the Bashaw of Tripoli) and his followers by promising him the United States's help in regaining his throne from his brother. In return Hamet promised to make perpetual peace with the United States, release the prisoners of the *Philadelphia*, and reimburse the United States for its expenses on his behalf. After Eaton's capture of Derna, Yusuf negotiated a peace treaty with the United States and released the *Philadelphia* 's captives for $160,000 instead of the originally demanded $200,000. He also retained his throne, while the U.S. Congress granted a pension of $2,400 a year to Hamet.

and what prevented the United States from marching on New Orleans?

A. Early ice held the French fleet at Dunkirk, and the U.S. Senate defeated the Ross Resolution by a vote of 15–11. The resolution would have authorized the president to call 50,000 militia from Georgia, South Carolina, Ohio, Kentucky, Tennessee, and the Mississippi Territory to assist the regular army in attempting to seize New Orleans.

Q. Why did Napoleon call off the expedition and decide to sell Louisiana, which included land all the way to the Pacific Ocean, north of Spanish territory, to the United States?

A. Napoleon's army had recently been decimated in Haiti while attempting to suppress a rebellion under Toussaint L'Ouverture. Also, he believed war with Britain was imminent and knew he would not be able to hold New Orleans because of the powerful British navy. Therefore, Napoleon sold the land for $15 million, and through the Louisiana Purchase in 1803, the United States doubled its territory.

Q. President Jefferson appointed his secretary, Captain Meriwether Lewis, who had lived in the President's House for the past two years, to lead an expedition to explore the new territory. Lewis was to seek an all-water route to the Pacific Ocean, make scientific observations of plants, animals, and resources, and make contact with Native Americans. Lewis chose William Clark (younger brother of George Rogers Clark) to be his co-captain (Lewis only received a lieutenant's commission) and to accompany him along with twenty-eight men. Did the Lewis and Clark expedition reach the Pacific Ocean?

A. Yes. The expedition left St. Louis in the spring of 1804, wintered with the Mandan tribe in present-day South Dakota, reached the Pacific Ocean at the mouth of the Columbia River in November 1805, and returned to St. Louis in September of 1806, after having traveled approximately eight thouand miles.

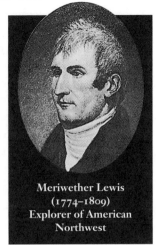

Meriwether Lewis
(1774–1809)
Explorer of American
Northwest

William Clark
(1770–1838)
Army officer, explorer of
American Northwest

Q. What was the official name of the Lewis and Clark expedition?
A. The Corps of Discovery.

Q. Lewis and Clark were very careful to cultivate peaceful relations with all the Native Americans they encountered and handed out many presents. In fact without the help of many different individual from various tribes, they never would have succeeded. Did they ever fight any Native Americans during their expedition?
A. Yes. Though Lewis threatened to kill Native Americans several times for thievery, they fought only once, when a party of Blackfoot tried to steal their horses and guns on the return trip.

> # FACT
>
> L ewis and Clark were not the first white men to reach the Pacific from the North American continent. Alexander Mackenzie of the North West Company and a party of six French Canadian voyagers and two Native Americans had reached the Pacific in July 1793.

One Blackfoot was killed and another shot in the stomach, with no loss to Lewis's men. They did have to be careful of the Sioux, who had stolen some meat and horses on one occasion and who threatened to kill them in any future meeting.

Q. Name the Shoshone (Snake) woman who served as an interpreter for much of the trip.

A. Sacagawea. She was the 15-year-old wife of French trapper Toussaint Charbonneau. She carried a young infant with her during the journey from the Mandan village and back.

Q. Was the Lewis and Clark expedition the first American-sponsored expedition sent out to find a route across the continent to the Pacific?

A. No. In 1793 the American Philosophical Society of Philadelphia had sponsored the French botanist Andre Michaux. Michaux, whom Jefferson had selected, was recalled when he reached Kentucky after Jefferson discovered he was a French secret agent. Eighteen-year-old Meriwether Lewis had applied to lead the expedition, but was passed over.

Q. Name the first U.S. Army fort established west of the Mississippi.

A. General James Wilkinson established Fort Bellefontaine in 1805. Wilkinson was also a spy for the Spanish and had informed Spain of the Lewis and Clark expedition. As a result, the governor of

New Mexico dispatched at least four parties from Sante Fe to attempt to capture Lewis.

Q. In leading an expedition of about eighty armed men down the Mississippi River in 1806, what former vice president and presidential candidate plotted to invade Mexico and to detach western territory from the United States?

A. Aaron Burr, who had run for president in 1796 and 1800. In 1800 he had tied Jefferson with seventy-three electoral votes on the first ballot. Jefferson was finally elected president on the thirty-sixth ballot, and Burr was elected vice president. About thirty miles above Natchez, Burr learned that General James Wilkinson had betrayed him and that Jefferson had declared any expedition against the Spanish illegal. Burr then fled, was apprehended, and went on trial for treason in Richmond, Virginia, where he was acquitted. He then escaped to Europe to avoid further trials, later returning to America in 1812.

Aaron Burr
(1756–1836)
Politician, U. S. Senator,
Vice President of U.S.,
1801–1805

Q. In 1807, just a year after the Lewis and Clark expediton returned to St. Louis, who led sixty men to the Yellowstone River to build a trading post and a fort and begin trapping fur in the mountains?

A. Manuel Lisa, a Spaniard living in St. Louis.

Q. Which side won the first engagement between Native Americans and the United States Army west of the Mississippi River?

A. Arikaras forced the Kimball-Pryor-Chouteau-Dorian expedition (fifty men) to retreat down the Missouri River after a sudden attack in which the Native Americans killed four and wounded nine. The expedition had been attempting to return the Mandan chief Shehaka (Big White) home. Shehaka had visited Washington at the invitation of Lewis.

Q. Impressment of seamen was a major irritant in relations between the United States and Britain and France. Which country impressed more sailors from the American merchant fleet in the years 1803–1812, Britain or France?

A. The British navy seized an estimated 6,000 sailors (James Monroe estimated 6,257) in their attempt to remedy a shortage of sailors caused by their war with Napoleon. Napoleon admitted to impressing at least 1,600 American sailors.

Q. Prior to and during the War of 1812, did the British consider anyone born in Britain but living in America a British citizen?

A. Yes.

Q. Name the 1807 "incident" that almost brought the United States and Britain to blows.

A. In the "*Chesapeake* incident" of June 22, the British frigate *Leopard* fired several broadsides on the U.S. frigate *Chesapeake* near Norfolk, Virginia, after Captain James Barron first refused permission to examine his crew. The broadsides killed three and wounded eighteen of the crew. Barron, who was totally unprepared to fight a battle, was forced to allow the British to board the *Chesapeake*. The Americans had managed to fire just one gun, and then only because Lieutenant William H. Allen had brought up a live coal to the deck. Four U.S. sailors—three of whom were unquestionably American—were taken from the vessel. Commodore Barron's punishment for neglect of duty was suspension from command for five years. The British eventually did make reparations to the families of those killed and wounded in the attack. They also returned two of the Americans taken from *Chesapeake* (one had died), but not until 1811.

Q. How did the U.S. respond to the *Chesapeake* incident?

A. President Jefferson influenced Congress to pass the Embargo Act in December 1807. The act forbade U.S. vessels to carry goods from any U.S. port to any foreign port. Rather than punishing Britain by decreasing British imports, the act hurt the American economy and was repealed on March 1, 1809.

Q. What were Britain's Orders in Council, which were one of the primary reasons for the American declaration of war?

A. In the 1807 Act, Britain declared that any trading ship on the ocean headed directly for any Napoleonic port would be seized unless it had first visited a British port, paid a fee, and obtained a certificate. The British enacted a series of Orders in Council in response to Napoleon's Berlin Decree of 1806, whereby Napoleon had proclaimed that any ship putting into a British port would not be received in a French controlled port. By 1812 the British captured almost four hundred American ships, some even within sight of the American coast, and cut America's trade to about three-fifths of its 1807 level. Britain announced suspension of the act on June 16, 1812, in an effort to avoid war. During the same period, France, Denmark, and Naples seized 434 vessels; others were seized by the Dutch and the Spanish. Britain returned about half of their seizures, while France only returned one-fourth of the seized ships to their owners.

Q. What was the Rule of 1756?

A. It was a British rule stating, "No neutral has a right to deliver a belligerent from the pressures of his enemies' hostilities by trading with his colonies in time of war in a manner not allowed in time of peace." British used it to partially justify the Orders in Council, since the United States had begun to carry produce from the French West Indies to France, a trade that France had monopolized in peacetime.

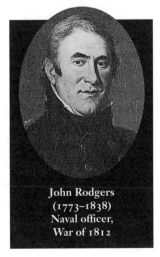

John Rodgers
(1773–1838)
Naval officer,
War of 1812

Q. In May of 1811, how did Captain John Rodgers, in the frigate *President*, revenge the *Chesapeake* incident?

A. Rodgers sighted a British sloop of war off of Cape Henry and gave chase. After sunset, he drew close to the other vessel and asked for identification. Instead, the vessel answered with cannon fire. The Americans replied likewise and demolished HMS *Little Belt*, killing thirteen and wounding nineteen, with only one slightly wounded on the American side.

Q. In the fall of 1811, Republicans in the legislature of Massachusetts created meandering state legislative districts to maintain their dominance. Gilbert Stuart, upon seeing a pencil cartoon in the office of the *Boston Centinel*, said one district looked like a salamander. The editor of the *Boston Centinel* called it a gerrymander. The term is still used today when legislative districts are redrawn. For whom was the term named?

A. Elbridge Gerry. During his career, Gerry had been part of the Continental Congress, had represented Massachusetts at the Constitutional Convention in 1787, was a Massachusetts congressman, served on the commission to negotiate with France in 1797, and was elected vice president in 1812. Today his name is mostly remembered by the term coined for the new legislative districts he signed into law as governor of Massachusetts in February 1812.

Q. Name the Shawnee chief who tried uniting all the Native American tribes east of the Mississippi to resist white advancement. Beginning in 1805, he asserted that no tribe had the right to sell land without the consent of all other tribes.

A. Tecumseh was born in 1768. He had extensive contact with white society in his youth and had learned the Bible and Shakespeare. Later, Tecumseh turned against whites and sought revenge for their treatment of Native Americans. He eventually traveled to

Tecumseh
(1768–1813)
Shawnee Indian chief

the Carolinas, Mississippi, Georgia, Alabama, Florida, and Arkansas, and attempted to unify the tribes to resist white expansion. He has been called "the greatest Indian who ever lived." William Henry Harrison said of him, "If it were not for the vicinity of the United States he would be the founder of an empire that would rival in glory Mexico or Peru."

Q. What great event occurred on December 16, 1811, which was predicted by Tecumseh as a sign for the tribes to join with him in war?

A. The New Madrid earthquake, which caused the Mississippi to flow backwards and change its course, was felt all the way to New England.

Q. In what 1811 battle, referred to as the first battle in the War of 1812, did then governor of Indiana Territory William Henry Harrison defeat an alliance of Shawnees, Delawares, Wyandots, Sauks, Ojibwas, Kickapoos, Potawatomis, and Ottawas under the command of Tecumseh's brother, the prophet Tenskwatawa?

A. Harrison defeated the Native Americans in the battle of Tippecanoe on November 7, 1811, near the present-day city of Lafayette, Indiana. The great Shawnee chief Tecumseh was away trying to recruit southern tribes to his alliance. Tecumseh had commanded Tenskwatawa to avoid a fight until he returned from his trip. However, when Harrison's army of 1,000 camped near Prophetstown, Tenskwatawa inspired between five and eight hundred warriors to attack by convincing them that bullets would not harm them. The men surrounded Harrison's camp in predawn darkness, but a sentry heard them before they could form for a surprise attack. After several hours of fighting, Harrison dispatched mounted men to encircle the tribes' flanks and break up their ranks. After the battle, Harrison burned the tribes' center of power at Prophetstown. He had lost one-fifth of his army in the battle, and fearful of further attack, he returned to Vincennes. The battle resulted in the weakening of Tecumseh's confederacy of tribes.

Q. Besides the taking of their land by whites, one issue that caused Native American hostility was the number of incidents in which whites who murdered Native Americans were never brought to justice. Was any white man ever convicted and hanged for killing a Native American in the United States prior to the War of 1812?

A. No. Not until 1824 was a white man ever punished with a death penalty for killing a Native American. A man named Hudson, one of a group of five men who murdered eight Senecas (two men, two women, and four children) in Madison County, Indiana, was hung for the crime.

Q. In March of 1812, General George Mathews of Georgia led a brief incursion into Florida hoping to inspire a rebellion against Spanish authority. Georgians believed the Spanish were inciting Native Americans to attack Americans and were also harboring runaway slaves. Mathews invaded in the belief that he would receive support from the Madison administration, as indicated in letters of instruction from Secretary of State James Monroe.

FACT

The result of the battle of Tippecanoe and the future of the United States may have been much different if not for a small act unrelated to any battle preparations by either side. Before retiring for the night, Harrison had hitched his gray mare to a near-by stake, for instant use if need be. His aide, Colonel Abraham Owen, secured his horse to the same stake. Troops moved Harrison's horse to make room for baggage. After the alarm sounded signaling the start of the battle, Harrison rushed out of his tent. He didn't see his own horse, so he jumped on Owen's horse. Owen ran out next, found his horse gone, and mounted Harrison's. Warriors in hiding instantly slew Owen with musket fire. Tenskawtawa had learned from a camp follower that the gray mare was Harrison's horse and had assigned several braves the task of killing Harrison as soon as he mounted. Instead, Harrison survived to rally his force, repel the attack, and be elected president of the United States in 1840, largely on the basis of fame won in this battle, which inspired his campaign slogan "Tippecanoe and Tyler too."

During this so-called Patriot's War, Mathews laid siege to the Castillo de San Marcos, the Spanish fortress in St. Augustine. Was he able to capture the fortress?

A. No. Though Mathews received aid from United States Navy captain Hugh Campbell and army colonel Thomas Adams Smith, he was forced to break off his siege after the United States Senate defeated a bill to annex Florida, thereby denying him any further governmental support.

1812

"The militia of Kentucky are alone competent to place Montreal and Upper Canada at your feet."

Q. Who were the War Hawks?

A. President Thomas Jefferson called Republican politicians who desired war with Britain War Hawks. War Hawks were primarily from southwestern interior and frontier states, including Kentucky, Tennessee, South Carolina, as well as areas of New York and New Hampshire. They blamed the British for supplying Native Americans with weapons, inciting them to war on the frontier, and depressing their economy through trade restrictions. They also coveted additional land, especially Canada.

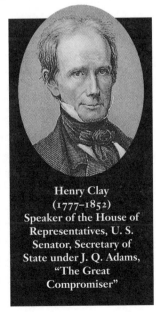

Henry Clay
(1777–1852)
Speaker of the House of Representatives, U. S. Senator, Secretary of State under J. Q. Adams, "The Great Compromiser"

Q. Who was the War Hawk leader and Speaker of the House who said when he addressed the United States Senate, "I verily believe that the militia of Kentucky are alone competent to place Montreal and upper Canada at your feet"?

A. Henry Clay was not alone in thinking that Americans could attain an easy victory. Thomas Jefferson claimed that the conquest of Canada would be "a mere matter of marching."

Q. Aside from their numeric inferiority to the United States, what was it about the Candian population that made Americans believe it would be so easy to conquer Canada?

A. They believed the Canadians would welcome the chance to throw off British rule and join the United States since two-thirds of the inhabitants of Lower Canada (Quebec) were of French descent and one-third of those in Upper Canada (Ontario) had emigrated from the United States.

Q. Did the French Canadians support the British or aid the Americans during the war?

A. The French majority feared Americanization (democracy and materialism). They demonstrated their support for the British government by joining the militia to defend against American invasions.

Q. Who was president of the United States in 1812?

A. James Madison, first elected in 1808 and reelected in 1812. He had defeated Federalist Charles Pinckney in 1808 by a margin of 122 to 47 in the electoral college. In the election of 1812, held after the war began, the vote was much closer, due to Madison's war policy. He defeated fellow Democratic-Republican De Witt Clinton by a vote of 128 to 89. Contemporaries sometimes referred to the war as "Mr. Madison's War."

Q. How many states were in the United States in 1812?

A. Louisiana was admitted as the eighteenth state in April of 1812.

Q. Name Madison's secretary of war in 1812.

A. He was William Eustis, who knew little about war. His only experience derived from serving as a military surgeon during the Revolution. He was replaced by John Armstrong in 1813.

Q. Who held two different cabinet posts during the war simultaneously?

A. Secretary of State James Monroe was also secretary of war, temporarily for a few months after Eustis resigned, and then permanently after the burning of Washington when he replaced Armstrong.

Q. Name the commander in chief of the American army at the start of the war.

A. Major General Henry Dearborn, a 61-year-old veteran of the Revolutionary War (he served as a major) was commander in chief. Dearborn weighed 250 pounds, and his soldiers called him "Granny." Since 1793, he had worked as a career politician. The only other major general in the army at the time was Thomas Pinckney. There were five brigadier generals of whom 55-year-old James Wilkinson was the senior. The other four brigadier generals were all about sixty. None had ever commanded a regiment in battle.

Q. Did New England initially favor war with Britain?

A. No. Though alleged impressment was a major reason for Madison's decision to declare war on Britain, the shipping center of New England did not consider it an overiding problem. The danger that a sailor, especially a bona fide American, would be impressed was actually remote. Shippers testifying to the Massachusetts legislature reported only thirty-five known cases of impressment among 68,700 seaman. The legislature also stated that the number of impressments had been diminishing.

Q. Is it true that New England states even refused to provide militia for federal service?

A. Yes. New England states opposed the war to the extent of refusing their militia for federal service unless their state was threatened with invasion. At one point, Connecticut governor John Cotton Smith refused to send troops out of the state, citing the Constitution, "Congress may provide for calling forth the militia to execute the laws of the Union, suppress insurrections, and repel invasions." As yet, there had been no invasions. Even before the war began, Governor Caleb Strong of Massachusetts refused Madison's request to use militia against Montreal. None of Massachusetts's men would officially participate in federal service throughout the entire war. Massachusetts's John Lowell actually proposed a secessionist plan that called for eliminating the West from the Union. The only states that gave full cooperation to the federal government during the war were New York, Kentucky, Tennessee, and Ohio.

Q. What state supplied most of the militiamen who fought in the West?

A. Kentucky not only supplied the most men but also shed the most blood. Though Kentucky supplied only 4.6 percent of the troops who fought in the war, 64 percent, or 1,200, of the 1,876 Americans killed in action were from Kentucky.

Q. What state supplied the most recruits for the regular army?

A. New York. Surprisingly, Massachusetts was second.

Q. Approximately how many men were in the regular U.S. Army at the start of the war?

A. There were approximately seven thousand men in the U.S. Army. At the time Britain had about forty-five hundred troops in all of Canada. The population of the United States was about eight million, compared to less than half a million in Canada.

Q. By 1812, how many cadets had graduated from the military academy at West Point?

a. 37
b. 71
c. 114

A. The answer is b. Of the 71 graduates, 23 had died or resigned, and 12 would die of wounds or disease during the war.

Q. Name three soldiers who fought in the war who were later elected president of the United States.

A. Andrew Jackson, 1829–1837; William Henry Harrison, 1841 (he died from pneumonia after serving only a month in office); and Zachary Taylor, 1849–1853 (elected because of his Mexican War victories).

Q. The federal arsenals at Springfield, Massachusetts, and Harpers Ferry, Virginia, were unable to provide what weapon for the army?

A. The federal arsenals could not produce artillery. However, private gun foundries manufactured sufficient quantities. The principal gun foundry for the army was at Georgetown. Naval guns came from the Dorsey works in Baltimore and the Foxall Foundry in Washington.

Q. King George III, who had reigned during the Revolutionary War, still occupied the throne in 1812; however, he was now insane. Because of the king's condition, who managed the war for England as secretary of state?

A. Henry Bathurst, who served under Prime Minister Robert Banks Jenkinson, Second Earl of Liverpool, who actually ran the government during the war. His administration was known as the Liverpool ministry.

Q. Initially, why couldn't Britain spare many soldiers to fight against the Americans?

A. They were occupied fighting against Napoleon's armies in Europe.

Q. The British had only four generals in Canada at the start of the war. Name two of them.

A. Isaac Brock, Roger Sheaffe, Sir George Prevost, and Baron Francis de Rottenburg.

Q. Who was in overall command for the British in Canada during the war?

A. Sir George Prevost, whose official title was captain general, governor in chief, vice admiral, lieutenant general, and commanding officer of His Majesty's forces in Upper Canada, Lower Canada, Nova Scotia, New Brunswick, Prince Edward Isle, Cape Breton, Newfoundland, and the Bermudas.

Q. Why did opposing armies generally try to form their battle lines about five hundred yards from each other?

A. This distance was roughly the effective range of artillery that fired solid shot. In addition to solid shot, cannon-fired canister shot up to 300 yards and grapeshot up to 200 yards.

Q. Describe canister and grapeshot.

A. A canister was a metallic cylinder filled with musket balls that scattered like a shotgun when fired. Grapeshot consisted of larger lead balls wrapped in cloth, which spread immediately after leaving the muzzle, hence its shorter range.

Q. What relatively new type of artillery ammunition, invented in 1784, also saw some use in the war?

A. In 1784 British officer lieutenant Henry Shrapnel invented a new type of shot, shrapnel, which was a hollow shell fitted with small metal balls and an explosive charge set off by a fuse. Shrapnel was a scattershot employed at close range.

Q. Until 1814, American infantry formations were placed in how many ranks to fight in battle?

A. They formed in three ranks until 1814. Thereafter, they fought in two ranks as the British did. Napoleon had adopted this formation in 1813.

Q. The United States Congress passed a bill declaring war on June 4, 1812, by a vote of 79–49. The Senate passed the House war bill on June 17 by a vote of 19–13, and President Madison signed it the next day. The war might have been avoided if the Senate had listened to Senator James A. Bayard of Delaware. Why?

A. Bayard asked that consideration of the war bill be postponed until October, as the people were not prepared for war. If the United States had waited to declare war, it would have learned that on June 16 Parliament had rescinded the Orders in Council, a primary cause of the war. Unfortunately, the slowness of communications prevented a reconciliation before it was too late. The war bill vote was notable for being the closest on a declaration of war in American history.

Q. Did the war prove to be very popular in America once it began?

A. No, only in the West and the South was the war popular. Congress voted to increase the army to 50,000 men, but only 5,000 volunteered in the first six months. In addition to New England's resistance to the war, antiwar riots occurred elsewhere.

Q. What famous Revolutionary War general was left for dead after a beating in a Baltimore riot?

A. Henry "Light Horse Harry" Lee. Lee had helped defend Federalist Alexander Hanson, editor of the *Federal Republican*, from a mob in which one rioter was killed. After Hanson and his defenders agreed to surrender and were locked up behind bars, a mob stormed the jail and attacked the Federalists. They beat them and left them for dead, killing Revolutionary War general James M. Lingan in the process. Lee never fully recovered from the wounds he sustained in the beating.

Q. To encourage enlistees to join the army, Congress gradually offered increasingly lucrative bonuses. How long did it take an unskilled laborer to earn the equivalent of the bonus amount?
   a. Six months
   b. One year
   c. Two years

A. The answer is c. Congress offered as much as $124 and 320 acres of land, worth approximately fifty cents an acre, as a bonus for enlistees signing for the war's duration.

Q. Who on the northwestern frontier learned about the declaration of war first, the British or the Americans?

A. The British, under Major General Sir Isaac Brock, commander of Upper Canada, learned of the declaration on June 26. The Americans, under Brigadier General William Hull, did not learn of the event until July 2. Early British strategy originated with Prevost and Brock in Canada. The British government in London did not learn of the declaration of war until July 29.

Q. What American fort fell to a hostile British force before the defenders even knew war was declared?

A. Fort Michilimackinac (Mackinac) surrendered without a fight to British captain Charles Roberts.

Q. Who was the American commander at Fort Mackinac?

A. Lieutenant Porter Hanks commanded about sxity men at the fort. After he estimated the enemy force to be about nine hundred men, including Native Americans, he surrendered on July 17. The fort's surrender swayed many Native Americans of the Northwest to the British side.

Q. Dearborn, Eustis, and Madison planned the American strategy for 1812. They planned to invade Canada in three places. Where did the American army invade first on July 12?
a. Lake Champlain to Montreal
b. Along the Niagara River
c. At the Detroit River
A. The answer is c.

Q. Who led the invasion across the Detroit River?
A. Fifty-eight-year-old general William Hull, the governor of Michigan Territory since 1805, accepted the assignment. He had earned a commission as a lieutenant colonel in the Revolutionary War and later organized territorial militia. Hull received intelligence that told him that less than 100 British regulars were at Detroit. He estimated that 20,000 British regulars were west of Montreal, but in fact there were only 2,257.

William Hull
(1753–1825)
Army officer, first
governor of
Michigan Territory

Q. What was significant about the British capture of the American schooner *Cuyahoga Packet* on the Detroit River in early July?
A. Because Americans on the frontier did not the war's beginning, the British caught the Americans by surprise, captured the schooner, and confiscated William Hull's personal papers on board. The papers contained all the details they could possibly desire to know concerning Hull's army, including troop numbers and Hull's war strategy.

Q. What British fort was Hull's objective after he crossed the Detroit River?

A. Hull sought to capture Fort Malden (Amherstburg); however, he hesitated to attack and lost his opportunity while he waited for additional men and supplies and worried about Native Americans cutting his supply line. Though he outnumbered the British 2,000 to 500, he recrossed the river on August 6, without mounting any serious attack, and holed up in Fort Detroit.

Q. On two occasions General Hull forwarded troops to meet his supply train while he threatened to attack Fort Malden. Both times combined British and Native American forces ambushed them. What Native American chief commanded the combined forces?

A. Hull's troops were ambushed by forces under the great Shawnee chief Tecumseh at the Battles of Brownstown and Maguaga. In both instances, the Americans outnumbered the combined British and Native American forces.

Q. Hull had relied on one tribe to help him, but this previously friendly tribe, not considered a part of Tecumseh's confederation, instead joined the British, thereby jeopardizing Hull's supply line. Name this tribe.

A. The Wyandots (formerly the Huron) were venerated by various other tribes in the Northwest Territory. When the Hurons committed themselves to the British, other tribes followed them into the British camp.

Q. By what name did frontiersmen call the Iroquois at this time?

A. Mingos.

Q. Which side was victorious in the battle for Fort Detroit?

A. The British were victors. Isaac Brock induced Hull to surrender the fort after a short bombardment and a trick. By dressing his entire militia as British regulars, Brock made Hull believe his army was much larger than it actually was. He also allowed a letter alluding to a force of 5,000 Native Americans on their way to joining him to fall into Hull's possession.

Q. Hull surrendered almost two thousand men on August 16. He broke down mentally prior to the surrender. Toward the end of the siege, he was seen stuffing chewing tobacco into his mouth until it began to run out of his mouth and onto his beard and vest. Hull's capitulation at Detroit remains the first and only time an American city has surrendered to a foreign foe. Was Hull later court-martialed for his surrender?

A. Yes. He was court-martialed two years later and sentenced to death. President Madison then granted him a reprieve due to his Revolutionary War services.

Q. Which side maintained naval superiority on the Great Lakes during the first year of the war?

A. Britain controlled the Great Lakes, thereby forcing the Americans to send all their supplies and men for the Western frontier via slower overland routes that were constantly threatened by Native Americans.

Q. Name the commander of the American naval forces on the Great Lakes in 1812.

A. Commodore Isaac Chauncey.

Q. What is the modern-day site of Fort Dearborn?

A. The city of Chicago is now located on the site of old Fort Dearborn.

Q. Did Captain Nathan Heald hold Fort Dearborn against Native American attack until the war ended?

A. No. General Hull ordered Heald to evacuate the fort. Though he had stocked six months' worth of supplies, he decided to vacate the fort against the advice of a friendly Potawatomi chief and his own officers' council. On August 15, after Heald's party of fifty-four soldiers, twelve civilian men, and several women and children had traveled only a few miles from the fort, escorted by Captain William Wells with thirty Miami scouts, they were attacked by about five hundred Potawatomis and massacred. About eighteen victims of the massacre survived until the war's end, some living with their captors. The Native Americans burnt Fort Dearborn, which was not rebuilt until 1816.

Q. What was the first victory for the United States in the war on the frontier?

A. The U.S. won its first frontier victory on Lake Erie across from Black Rock, New York. Under the leadership of Lieutenant Jesse Elliott of the U.S. Navy, a party of about one hundred men captured the British schooner *Caledonia*, burned the brig *Detroit*, and rescued about thirty men in the process.

Q. What future commander in chief of the American army, in his first action against the British, was a participant in Elliott's enterprise?

A. Winfield Scott volunteered to join Elliott and fired on the British with artillery.

Q. In 1812 much fighting against Native Americans took place in Illinois and Indiana Territories. Who commanded the frontier troops after William Hull surrendered at Detroit?

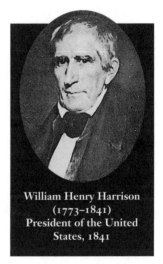

A. William Henry Harrison, then serving as governor of Indiana Territory, was commissioned a brigadier general in the U.S. Army and commanded all the troops in the West. He later resigned in 1814 after he was passed over for promotion and accused of profiting in his military district.

William Henry Harrison (1773–1841) President of the United States, 1841

Q. Where was the first victory on land for the Americans during the war?

A. At Fort Harrison, Captain Zachary Taylor with only 50 men, of which 38 were ill, withstood attacks from 600 Native Americans under Tecumseh during a thirteen-day siege, September 3–16, until a 1,200-man relief column led by Harrison himself arrived. Taylor was promoted to major for this action.

Q. After the botched invasion of Canada at Detroit, where did an American army next attack across the Canadian border?

A. The Americans next attacked Queenston, across the Niagara River from Lewiston, New York, in October.

Q. What event frustrated General Stephen Van Rensselaer in his first attempt to cross the Niagara River and attack Queenston?

A. A Lieutenant Sims proceeded ahead of the invaders in a boat loaded with the oars for the rest of the thirteen boats. He then disappeared and left the rest of the men waiting in the dark.

Q. Just as General James Wolfe had done at Quebec in the French and Indian War, a young 23-year-old army captain outflanked a British redan by climbing a supposedly impossible cliff, thus enabling the Americans to capture Queenston Heights. Name the officer.

A. John E. Wool, who was wounded in the battle, would finish the war as a lieutenant colonel.

Q. What British general was killed in the battle of Queenston Heights on October 13, 1812?

A. Isaac Brock. After Brock's death, General Roger Sheaffe led reinforcements, including Mohawk tribesmen into the battle. He then forced the surrender of the American troops on the Canadian side of the river. Approximately 900 Americans were taken prisoner and over 300 were killed or wounded, while the British lost 14 lives with 77 wounded and 28 missing. A commander of Brock's talent, however, was irreplaceable for the British army.

Q. If not for two Canadian officers' interference, what future general's career may have been ended by his Native American captors after he had gone forward to surrender his troops at the battle of Queenston Heights?

A. After Native Americans killed two couriers who tried to surrender, Lieutenant Colonel Winfield Scott attempted to surrender to prevent the Native Americans from butchering his routed troops. While he was struggling with two Native Americans, two Canadian officers rescued him. Scott had been sent over the river to command the troops with wounded officers after the Americans captured the Heights. Scott would later be exchanged and promoted to colonel in March 1813.

Q. Why did the British release one prisoner named Samuel Stubbs?
A. After seeing how old he was, Stubbs was in his sixties, a British officer told him to go home. Stubbs departed, but still stayed in the thick of the fighting all the way to New Orleans when he was sixty-six years old. He eliminated several British officers during his term of service.

Q. What reason did American general Stephen Van Rensselaer offer for the defeat at Queenston Heights?
A. He blamed the nearly one thousand militiamen who watched their fellow Americans battle the British on the other side of the Niagara River and refused to cross over to the Canadian side and fight. He also blamed Brigadier General Alexander Smyth for refusing to send reinforcements. Van Rensselaer resigned after the battle.

Q. Who replaced Van Rensselaer on the Niagara border after the battle of Queenston Heights?
A. General Alexander Smyth replaced Van Rensselaer. He made two aborted attempts to attack across the Niagara River in November. In disgust, his own soldiers then shot at him. He also escaped a duel unscathed. Afterwards, he left the army.

Q. In October, Illinois Territorial Governor Ninian Edwards marched with 360 men and destroyed the main town and one large village of what tribe located near the present-day towns of Bloomington and Peoria, Illinois?
A. The Kickapoos, who had been raiding and terrorizing frontier settlements all the way to the Ohio River.

Q. What American general made the last attempt to invade Canada and attack Montreal in mid-November?
A. Henry Dearborn led an army of over 6,000 men from Plattsburg to the border near Lake Champlain. After minor skirmishing

against a Canadian army of 1,900 men on the Lacolle River, he could not persuade two-thirds of his militiamen to cross the border. He retreated, then offered to relinquish his command, but was turned down.

Q. Did any Native Americans fight on the American side in 1812?

A. No. Though some favored the Americans, they did not help to fight against the British until 1813.

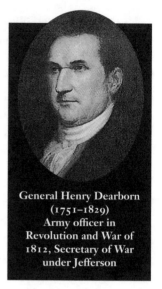

General Henry Dearborn (1751–1829) Army officer in Revolution and War of 1812, Secretary of War under Jefferson

1813

"We have met the enemy and they are ours."

Q. A few days after his soldiers captured Frenchtown, what American general was defeated and captured on January 22 in a surprise attack by 1,200 Native Americans, militia, and regulars commanded by British colonel Henry Proctor?

A. Brigadier General James Winchester was defeated in the battle of the River Raisin, or Frenchtown, in a predawn surprise attack. He shouldn't have even been there. Madison had instructed Harrison to advance only in the winter on ice, and Harrison had recommended Winchester abandon his march because he believed Tecumseh was in the vicinity. However, Winchester had responded to the residents of Frenchtown who had summoned him to defend them.

Q. Though he served in the Revolution and had earned a reputation as an "Indian fighter," what mistakes did Winchester make in securing his camp prior to the battle?

A. Though his encampment was only eighteen miles from British-held Fort Malden, Winchester did not build any fortifications or check on any pickets. Worse yet, he set up a camp that was divided by a river. Two-thirds of the men were with him on the north side and the remainder were on the south side. After surrendering, many men were massacred by Native Americans in the following days. In the battle, 200 Kentuckians were killed or wounded and over 700 made prisoners. The battle halted Harrison's advance on Detroit. "Remember the Raisin" became the rallying cry for the Kentuckians for the remainder of the war.

Q. The acting secretary of war, James Monroe, prodded Harrison to resume the offensive. What prevented Harrison, with his 4,000 men, from attacking Fort Malden in mid-February?

A. When he reached Lake Erie, he discovered he could not cross it because a two-week warm spell had caused the ice to break up.

Q. What British ally offered to mediate the differences between the United States and Britain?

A. Russia had offered to mediate between the British and Americans in the Revolutionary War, and it did so again in the War of 1812. This time, Czar Alexander I made the offer to John Q. Adams, the U.S. Minister at Petersburg, in September of 1812. President Madison learned of the offer on March 8, 1813. He quickly sent James Bayard and Albert Gallatin as peace commissioners to Russia, where they arrived in July. British foreign secretary Viscount Castlereagh, however, had already declined mediation, and the Czar, occupied with Napoleon, did not see the U.S. representatives. Finally, in November, Madison was informed that the British would meet with American negotiators.

Q. The only permanent land acquisition of the war, that of west Florida, resulted from the capture of Mobile from the Spanish. Who commanded the expedition that obtained Mobile's surrender in April?

A. General James Wilkinson. With a force that outnumbered the Spanish by five to one, he was able to induce the Spanish commander, Captain Con Cayetano, to surrender without a fight.

Q. What capital of Upper Canada did the U.S. seize in April?

A. Commodore Isaac Chauncey's fleet of fourteen vessels landed 1,600 men near York, Ontario (present-day Toronto). York, with its 625 inhabitants, was the capital of Upper Canada. The American fleet pounded the British artillery and Fort York. In face of a superior force, the 300 British regulars, 300 militia, and about 100 Native Americans retreated after a brief fight.

Q. Name the American brigadier general, already famous for his western exploration, who died at York when a British powder magazine blew up.

A. Brigadier General Zebulon Pike, who led the attack. The explosion killed 53 Americans and 40 Canadians and wounded 150 and 23, respectively.

**Zebulon Pike
(1779–1813)
Army officer, Western
explorer, discovered
Pikes Peak**

Q. American retaliation on York for the explosion would influence the outcome of what future battle in favor of the Americans?

A. The battle of Lake Erie. The Americans burned part of York and destroyed supplies including twenty cannons, which were meant to build up the British fleet on Lake Erie. They also burned a half-built 30-gun frigate. These actions would cost the British dearly in the battle for Lake Erie. Unfortunately Dearborn failed to leave an occupation force at York to hinder the flow of supplies to the British forces in the West.

Q. Who was appointed to command the Lake Erie fleet for the Americans in February?

A. Oliver Hazard Perry, who was only twenty-seven years old at the time. He had first joined the navy as a midshipman at the age of fourteen.

**Commodore
Oliver Hazard Perry
(1785–1819)
Naval officer,
War of 1812**

Q. Where did Perry build the American fleet on Erie? (In 1812 no American fleet existed on Lake Erie.)

A. The fleet of nine ships mounting fifty-four guns was built at Presque Isle and Black Rock. The Ontario fleet was built at Sackett's Harbor.

Q. What was the first British fort captured by the Americans during the war?

A. Fort George was captured on May 27 in an assault led by Winfield Scott; however, the British army escaped after Major Morgan Lewis ordered Scott to halt pursuit. The fall of Fort George, and British general John Vincent's subsequent withdrawal from Fort Erie, allowed the Americans to move the five vessels at Black Rock down the Niagara River to join the rest of the Lake Erie fleet at Presque Isle.

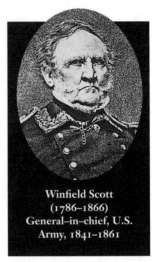

Winfield Scott
(1786–1866)
General–in–chief, U.S.
Army, 1841–1861

Q. After the Americans captured Fort George, they headed up the Niagara Peninsula. The British, under Lieutenant Colonel John Harvey, made a night attack against three times their number. The British captured Brigadier General John Chandler and his second in command, Brigadier General William Winder. The American army then retreated back to Fort George. What was the battle?

A. The battle of Stoney Creek, fought on June 5 and 6. Losses were about equal for both sides.

Q. Of what battle did Teyoninhokarawen (John Norton), the son of a Scottish woman and a Cherokee, who became a Mohawk chief say, "The Caughnawaga Indians fought the battle, the Mohawks got the plunder and Fitzgibbon got the credit"?

A. On June 24 in the battle of Beaver Dams, a party of Caughnawaga and British guerillas, outnumbered five to one by the Americans, managed to induce Lieutenant Colonel Charles Boerstler and 500 men to surrender after a brief fight. It was the last battle fought under Dearborn's overall command as he was removed after this battle.

Q. Name the general who replaced Dearborn as commander in chief. He had already resigned from the army twice, once for his involvement in the Conway cabal against George Washington and again after he had faced a court-martial for treason, misuse of public funds, and conspiracy.

A. Major General James Wilkinson, who had been the senior general in the army at the start of the war. He was known as "the general who never won a battle and never lost a court-martial."

Q. What was the first tribe to fight in a battle on the American side?
A. The Senecas aided in the defense of Black Rock in July, helping to drive off a British raiding party.

Q. The War of 1812 found the Six Nations (Iroquois) divided in allegiance. Some lived in New York and some lived in Canada, mostly in the Grand River settlements established by Joseph Brant west of Niagara. The Iroquois fought against each other on opposing sides, though the confederacy had attempted to prevent such an occurrence. After what battle did the Iroquois on both sides withdraw from the war?
A. The Iroquois suffered eighty killed, mostly fighting against each other, during the battle of Chippewa. This disaster induced the majority to lay down their weapons for the remainder of the war.

Q. During the spring and summer, Tecumseh prodded British general Proctor to invade Ohio. Name one of the two forts Proctor attacked.
A. He attacked Fort Meigs twice and Fort Stephenson, and was repulsed each time. In the second attack on Fort Meigs, after Proctor did nothing to protect American prisoners from being murdered by Native Americans, Tecumseh is reported to have said to him, "Begone, you are not fit to command, go and put on petticoats."

Q. At Fort Stephenson, who became a national hero when, with only one 6-pounder, his 160 men repulsed five times their number after General William Henry Harrison had ordered him to vacate the fort?
A. Twenty-one-year-old Major George Croghan defeated the last real British offensive on the northwest frontier. General Proctor ordered only one assault on the fort, which cost 150 casualties.

Q. In June which side gained control of Lake Champlain by capturing the sloops *Eagle* and *Growler*?

A. The British gained control by forcing the sloops to surrender in a battle fought near the island of Isle aux Noix in the Richelieu River, which runs north out of Lake Champlain. Governor Prevost then sent an expedition to Plattsburg, which burned the American military storehouses there. Prevost claimed that this diverted the American effort toward invading Canada and helped to save the Great Lakes for the British.

Q. Primarily what tribe fought against the Americans in the southeastern United States during the war?

A. The Creek, located mostly in Alabama. Those who fought against the United States were called "Red Sticks," the name given to the Creek war club. Red Sticks inspired by Tecumseh killed a few Americans in 1812. The Creek National Council, led by Tustennuggee Thlucco (Big Warrior), which favored accommodation with the Americans, ordered executions for those guilty of the murders. A Creek civil war then ensued between the two factions.

Q. Half-breeds played a prominent role in leading the Creeks to war. Name the half-breed chief who was attacked as he returned from a trip to Pensacola, Florida, where he had acquired ammunition.

A. Peter McQueen was attacked in the battle of Burnt Corn Creek in July 1813. This battle started the Creek War against the United States. Some Creeks had also fought previously against Americans with Tecumseh at Frenchtown. Another important half-breed chief was William Weatherford, or Red Eagle, who was the most important leader of the Red Sticks. During the war, though Weatherford was defeated at Econochaca, he repulsed Andrew Jackson's advance at Emuckfau, attacked Jackson at Enotachopco Creek, and sent General John Floyd packing at Calabee Creek.

Q. At what fort did Creeks massacre over five hundred whites, friendly Native Americans, and slaves?

A. Creeks massacred the inhabitants of Fort Mims, located about thirty-five miles north of Mobile, on August 30. About one hundred Creeks led by Weatherford entered through an open gate while the inhabitants were eating their midday meal. Weatherford attempted unsuccessfully to stop the killing once victory was assured.

Q. Name a famous frontiersman who while serving in General Andrew Jackson's army against the Creeks, was described as "the merriest of the merry, keeping the camp alive with his quaint conceits and marvelous narratives"?
A. Davy Crockett, then twenty-seven years old, spent most of his time guarding horses, scouting, and foraging for Jackson's army.

Q. What American commander wrote in a message to William Henry Harrison: "We have met the enemy and they are ours, two ships, two brigs, one schooner and one sloop"?
A. Oliver Perry wrote it after his victory over a British squadron commanded by Robert Barclay in the battle of Lake Erie fought on September 10.

Q. For the first time in history, Perry achieved a feat never accomplished before in battle against the British navy. What was this admirable feat?
A. Perry's victory was the first in history in which an entire British fleet was defeated and captured intact by an enemy.

Q. Before battle, why did Noah Brown, who had supervised the building of Perry's fleet, tell him that the ships were only good for one battle?
A. Because the ships were constructed of green timber.

Q. At Presque Isle, where Perry built most of his ships, the harbor was protected by a sandbar covered by between four to five feet of water. What device did Perry use to get his two largest ships (*Niagara* and *Lawrence*) over the sandbar?
A. Perry removed the guns and the rigging from the ships first, then he used "camels" to lift the ships over the sandbar. Camels were watertight boxes attached to the hull. They would be pumped with enough water to lower them. Then large timbers would be

placed underneath the hull of the vessel to raise it and rest it on top of the camels. Perry's men could then pump out the water, and the camels' buoyancy would lift the vessel. Perry went three sleepless nights during the operation. If the British had appeared, without doubt, they could have destroyed Perry's vulnerable ships.

Q. What was Perry's flagship in the battle of Lake Erie?

A. Perry's flagship was the 20-gun *Lawrence*. For the first two hours of the battle, *Lawrence* bore the brunt of the British cannonade until every officer but Perry had fallen. Out of a crew of 100, 21 were dead and 63 wounded. Perry abandoned the ship, rowed to the 20-gun *Niagara*, and took command from Jesse Elliott. Near the end of the extremely hard fighting, every British commander and second in command was a casualty, unable to remain on the deck of the ship.

Q. Which side could shoot a heavier broadside in the battle of Lake Erie, the Americans or the British?

A. The Americans manning nine ships had the advantage. They could shoot 896 pounds, while the British manning six ships could only shoot 459 pounds. The British cannons shot mostly at long range while the Americans possessed a majority of cannons that fired at short range. The Americans possessed an advantage in manpower, 530 compared to arounnd 450 for the British. Also, the Americans were better trained.

Q. Forty-seven of Perry's fifty-four gun crews were commanded by men from what state?

A. Rhode Island.

Q. What was the significance of Perry's victory on Lake Erie for the American army around Detroit?

A. In the short term, the American army under Harrison was able to take the offensive. The British were forced to abandon the Detroit area because they could no longer bring supplies in by water. In the long term, the victory prevented the British from dominating the Great Lakes, shortened the war, and preserved all of the

Northwest Territory for the United States. In appreciation of Perry's feat at Lake Erie, the Pennsylvania legislature voted a gold medal for Perry and a silver medal for every man in his fleet.

Q. Is it true that Perry was killed later in a duel with Jesse Elliott after quarreling over the credit for the victory on Lake Erie?

A. No. Though Elliott challenged Perry to a duel, Perry ignored the challenge and brought charges against him. Perry died in 1819, after contracting yellow fever on the Orinoco River in Venezuela.

Q. After the British abandoned Detroit following Perry's victory, Harrison's army pursued them. On October 5, in what battle did they halt to fight the pursuing Americans?

A. The British turned to fight the Americans in the battle of the Thames (or Moraviantown). Outnumbered by the Americans 3,500 to 1,300, the British and their Native American allies were quickly put to flight. British losses included eighteen killed and twenty-six wounded, with thirty-three Native Americans also dying on the battlefield. The American losses were slight.

Q. Name the British commander General Harrison defeated in the battle of the Thames.

A. General Henry Proctor, who fled as soon as the battle began. Tecumseh was also killed. Due to the British defeat and the death of their great leader Tecumseh, thirty-seven chiefs representing six tribes signed an armistice with Harrison. One future president, one vice president, three governors of Kentucky, three more lieutenant governors, four senators, a score elected to the House of Representatives, and even Oliver Perry participated in the battle. Proctor was found guilty of negligence and was suspended from rank and pay for six months.

Q. Whose reputation as the slayer of Tecumseh helped him win election as vice president?

A. Though it was never proven, Richard Johnson ostensibly shot Tecumseh with a pistol as Tecumseh rushed toward him with an upraised tomahawk in his hand. One refrain during the 1836 campaign in which Johnson was elected vice president and Martin Van Buren president was

Rumpsey, dumpsey
Colonel Johnson killed Tecumseh.

Johnson did not even gain a majority of electoral votes. Instead, for the first and only time in a presidential election, the Senate elected the vice president.

Q. What unorthodox tactic taken by a Kentucky militia regiment quickly routed the British in the battle of the Thames?

A. About one half of Colonel Richard M. Johnson's regiment of 1,000 men charged through the woods on horseback right through the thinly held British line, all the while holding onto their long rifles, a most unusual cavalry weapon. They dismounted and fired into the rear of the British line. The British quickly surrendered, after being fired upon from front and back. The other half of Johnson's regiment, under his brother, Colonel James Johnson, also dismounted and fought the Native Americans. Thus the battle was mostly fought and won by Johnson's mounted regiment. During the battle, the Americans recaptured a cannon that had been taken from Burgoyne at Saratoga in 1777 and lost by Hull at Detroit in 1812.

Q. In what battle (really a skirmish) did a force of about 400 mostly French Canadian militia repel an army of 4,000 Americans advancing on Montreal under Major General Wade Hampton?

A. In October the battle of Chateauguay was fought. The Canadians lost only five killed and sixteen wounded, and the Americans suffered about fifty casualties.

Q. The American army made one last attempt to capture Montreal in November. Was it successful?

A. No. At the battle of Crysler's Farm, fought on November 11, a British force of 700, under Lieutenant Colonel Joseph Morrison, defeated Wilkinson's army of 7,000 (only 2,000 participated in the battle), under Brigadier General John Boyd. This ignominious defeat was the last American threat on Montreal for the remainder of the war. After the battle, the army retreated to New York even though Montreal was defenseless.

Q. The term "blue-light Federalists" was applied to those Americans whose opposition to the war resulted in their actually aiding the British. How did the term originate?

A. Someone in New London, Connecticut, signaled the British to inform them that Stephen Decatur was planning to escape from the harbor with his ships, *United States*, *Hornet*, and the captured British *Macedonian*. Decatur had recently moved the ships from the safety of the Thames River to the harbor so that he could escape the British blockade on the night of December 12. Learning that the British had been alerted by someone flashing blue lights, Decatur canceled the attempt and remained bottled up for the rest of the war. The term "blue-light Federalists" arose from this event.

Q. Is it true that on December 13 an American army finally won a battle on the Niagara frontier by capturing Fort Erie, across the river from Black Rock, New York?

A. No. Instead it was the British who crossed the Niagara River and captured Fort Niagara. After learning the password from a captured sentry, 560 men entered the fort in the middle of the night. They attacked with bayonets, killed or wounded about 80, and captured about 350 Americans, losing only 6 men themselves. They held the fort for the remainder of the war. The British also routed American militia and burned five ships that were part of Perry's fleet. After the fighting, the commanding American militia general Amos Hall said, "Experience proves that with militia a retreat becomes a flight, and the battle once ended the army is dissipated".

Q. In addition, the British burned everything in an eighteen-mile stretch from Fort Niagara to Buffalo and Black Rock. What reason did the British have for burning this entire area?

A. The burning of the American settlements along the Niagara River was in retaliation for the burning of Newtown by Brigadier

General George McClure, who had left about four hundred Canadians, mostly women and children, without any shelter in early December.

Q. Name the westernmost fort surrendered to the British during the war?

A. Fort Astoria, at the site of present-day Astoria, Oregon, at the mouth of the Columbia River. The fort had been established in 1811 by John Jacob Astor's Pacific Fur Company. When news of the war reached the fort in January 1813, the Americans sold out to the British Northwest Company because they knew a British ship was on the way and would seize all the furs. When the British sloop of war *Raccoon* arrived in December 1813, a British flag was raised over the fort.

1814–1815

"Is the flag still there?"

Q. In 1812 the generals in the regular army had averaged about sixty years of age. By the summer of 1814, nine new major and brigadier generals were appointed. They averaged thirty-six years of age. Name three of them.

A. Jacob Brown, George Izard, and Andrew Jackson were appointed major generals. Daniel Bissell, Edmund P. Gaines, Alexander Macomb, Eleazar W. Ripley, and Thomas A. Smith were appointed brigadier generals.

Q. What general's 37-year career ended in failure when he and his army of 4,000 men did not capture a blockhouse defended by 180 British?

A. General James Wilkinson ordered his army to retreat from La Cole Mill without even storming the blockhouse. Unbeknown to him, he had already been cashiered from the army prior to the battle.

Q. What American general executed the first militiaman in service since the Revolution?

A. In February Andrew Jackson executed John Woods for refusing to obey orders.

Q. Major General Jacob Brown's army of just under four thousand men crossed into Canada and captured Fort Erie. They began moving north along the Niagara River and soon encountered the enemy. What was the first battle fought in America's last invasion of Canada?

A. At the July 5 battle of Chippewa, General Winfield Scott, under the command of General Jacob Brown, fought an equal British force under General Phineas Riall and routed them from the battlefield. The British suffered the worst of it with 148 killed and 221 wounded, while Scott lost 48 killed and 227 wounded.

Q. In the Battle of Chippewa, what did Scott's troops accomplish for the first time in the war?
A. It was the first battle in the war in which U.S. regulars beat British regulars.

Q. What influence did the battle of Chippewa have for the future cadets at the U.S. Army Military Academy at West Point?
A. In honor of Winfield Scott's First Brigade, which wore army uniforms of gray cloth, used by the militia because the supply of blue cloth was exhausted, the cadets at the Military Academy were ordered to wear gray uniforms for the first time in 1816.

Q. What major battle, fought on July 25, was proportionately the bloodiest of the war?
A. Lundy's Lane was the bloodiest battle of the war. Americans losses numbered 850 men killed, wounded, captured, or missing out of 2,100, while the British lost 875 men out of 3,000. Fought to a stalemate, the inferior (in numbers) American army retreated to Fort Erie.

Q. Who commanded the British at Lundy's Lane?
A. Lieutenant General Sir Gordon Drummond commanded the British. Winfield Scott, again under the command of Jacob Brown, led the American army.

Q. How many American generals were wounded at Lundy's Lane?
A. Three. Winfield Scott, Jacob Brown, and Peter Porter of the New York militia were all wounded. Scott would not fight again in the war.

Q. What present-day Canadian city occupies the battle site of Lundy's Lane?

A. Niagara Falls, Ontario. The battle of Lundy's Lane was also called the battle of Niagara Falls. In America, though, it was first known as the battle of Bridgewater.

Q. At the end of the war did the Americans retain Fort Erie in Canadian territory?

A. No. Drummond unsuccessfully attacked the Fort in August, suffering 900 casualties. Then a sortie from the fort in September so damaged the besieging British, inflicting another 500 casualties, so that they withdrew. The Americans later abandoned and blew up the fort in November.

Q. Did Americans recapture Fort Mackinac?

A. No. Colonel George Croghan's attack in late July was unsuccessful. He retreated after a brief battle on the island after the loss of 19 killed and 45 wounded. British lieutenant colonel Robert McDougall repelled 700 American invaders with about 200 militia and infantry and 350 Native Americans.

Q. Name the commander of the American forces around Washington, D.C. in the spring of 1814.

A. Brigadier General William H. Winder, who had been captured in 1813 at the battle of Stoney Creek. Madison appointed him commander of the Tenth Military District shortly after he returned in a prisoner of war exchange.

Q. Who commanded the British fleet that had been raiding in the Chesapeake Bay region for over a year?

A. Rear Admiral Sir George Cockburn, under the overall command of Admiral John Warren and then Admiral Sir Alexander Cochrane. It was Cockburn's idea that the British march on Washington. A formidable foe would have troubled them, since they did not have any cavalry for reconnaissance and had brought for artillery only two 3-pounders and two little howitzers with them.

Q. In addition, the British brought Congreve rockets with them on their expedition to Washington, D.C.. What were Congreve rockets?

A. The rockets were about forty inches long and used a 16-foot guide stick. They had a range of about 2,000 yards and were meant to fill the gap between a musket and a 12-pound field gun. Sir William Congreve invented them in 1805. He based them on the rockets that the Indian prince Hyder Ali used in battles against the British in 1792 and 1799. The British used Congreve rockets for the first time in battle in 1806 in an attack on Boulogne Harbor. In 1807 Congreve directed a rocket attack against Copenhagen. About 25,000 of them were launched and left much of the city burning.

Q. Did the British use Congreve rockets against Americans for the first time during the war on the Washington expedition?

A. No. The British employed the rockets for the first time against Americans in a naval attack on Lowes, Delaware, in April 1813. The British first fired the rockets in a land engagement at the battle of Lundy's Lane, where one wounded General Jacob Brown. The rockets were very inaccurate. In George Cockburn's raid at Havre de Grace, Maryland, in May 1813, the only American in the war to die from a rocket attack was killed.

Q. Did Americans also use rockets during the war?

A. Yes. At Havre de Grace, where rockets were used for the first time on the American continent, parts of a dud were picked up. The pieces were sent to Professor Thomas Cooper at Dickinson College in Carlisle, Pennsylvania. Cooper succeeded in making a rocket. A chemist named Beath continued Cooper's work and managed to throw a 6-pound rocket 2,000 yards. After that, the Americans made use of the rocket during the war. Most armies abandoned the rocket during the 1850s because of the superiority of artillery.

Q. Name the only battle fought in defense of Washington, D.C.

A. On August 24, in 98 degree heat, the battle of Bladensburg was fought to defend the city at a bridge across the Potomac. In about an hour, a British army of 4,000 of the Duke of Wellington's veterans (brought over after Napoleon's defeat) routed an army (mostly militia) of 6,000 Americans. Many of the militamen panicked when the British began firing their Congreve rockets, and fled after throwing down their weapons, though not one rocket had even struck the American lines. General Winder retreated through Washington D.C. and across the Potomac without even making a stand and lost most of his army in the process.

Q. Who was the commander of the only American force (500 sailors and marines) that made a real stand against the British in the battle of Bladensburg?

A. Commodore Joshua Barney's men caused the majority of the casualties inflicted on the British during the battle. Before the British outflanked Barney's position, his sailors first rammed back the enemy in a charge in which they yelled, "Board 'em! Board 'em!" Against Barney's loss of 26 killed and 51 wounded, the British suffered 250 casualties. Barney was wounded, captured, and immediately paroled.

Q. Many high officials were at the scene of the battle, including President Madison, Secretary of State James Monroe, and Secretary of War John Armstrong. Which one of them came close to being captured by the British?

A. Upon arriving before the battle, President Madison and a small party rode through the American lines toward a bridge. William Simmons, a scout, stopped them from crossing to the other side, where the British probably would have captured Madison.

Q. What British army general commanded the expedition to Washington, D.C.?

A. British major general Robert Ross commanded the expedition. Were it not for Admiral George Cockburn, who accompanied the expedition, the British probably never would have entered Washington. After receiving orders to return to the waiting ships before attacking Washington, Cockburn convinced Ross to continue.

Q. What significant event took place in the nation's capital on August 24 and 25?

A. The British burned Washington, D.C. including all the public buildings and a few private ones. A violent storm put out the fires in the afternoon on the twenty-fifth, and the British left that night. Though the British encountered almost no resistance in the city, they suffered casualties of between twelve and thirty killed and forty-four injured at Greenleaf's Point when 150 barrels of gunpowder, dumped down a well, exploded. The Americans burned two new ships, the sloop *Argus* and the frigate *Columbia*, and destroyed two old frigates the *New York* and *Boston*, to keep them out of British hands. Thus, as one historian has noted, the British captured the capital of a modern major power with the smallest army ever to accomplish the feat.

Q. The White House was also burnt. However, in those days it was not known as the White House. What was it called at that time?

A. The White House was called the President's House, the name preferred by George Washington. It was reconstructed by James Hoban from 1815 to 1817 and was painted in a gleaming white. By 1820 it had been nicknamed the White House. Finally in 1902, President Theodore Roosevelt officially named the President's House the White House.

Q. What did Dr. William Thornton save when he said to the British, "To burn what would be useful to all mankind would be as barbarous as to burn the Alexandria Library, for which the Turks have been condemned by all enlightened nations"?

A. Dr. Thornton, the superintendent of Patents, saved the Patent office, which occupied an empty hotel, by declaring that practically everything contained within was private property.

Q. The Library of Congress books were burnt during the British occupation in Washington. Who sold his personal library to the government to form the basis for a new collection?

A. Thomas Jefferson sold almost 6,500 books to begin the new Library of Congress.

Q. What major city did the British attempt to attack after Washington, D.C.?

A. Changing his plans to relocate to Rhode Island, Cochrane decided to attack Baltimore. Baltimore was the third largest city in the

United States and deserved retribution. Its privateers had sunk or captured 500 British vessels during the war. Additionally, Cochrane had just learned about American atrocities in Canada through a letter from Governor Prevost. This gave further justification for his plan to devastate the city and acquire wealth in plunder.

Q. Name the land battle fought in front of Baltimore by 3,200 militia under Brigadier General John Stricker, who was under the overall command of militia major general Samuel Smith.

A. At the battle of North Point, Stricker's militia fought about twenty minutes then fled from the approximately five thousand British regulars. At a loss of 163 killed and 50 wounded, they inflicted about 300 British casualties.

Q. The morning of the battle General Ross said, "I'll eat in Baltimore tonight or in hell." He was killed early in the battle, and Colonel Arthur Brooke assumed command. Why was Cockburn unable to persuade Brooke to attack the Americans the next day?

A. The British retreated after Brooke decided not to continue the fight when he learned that Cochrane could not stage a diversionary attack. He feared the fortified earthworks on Hampstead Hill, which he estimated were manned by about fifteen thousand men, (actually about thirteen thousand), could not be taken without help from the navy.

Q. While Ross attacked by land, Cochrane attacked by water. What fort guarding Baltimore did he bombard unsuccessfully, firing an estimated 1,500 rounds which killed four and wounded twenty-four?

A. Fort McHenry. Major General George Armistead commanded 1,000 men, who could not fire back at the British ships because they were out of range, two miles away. Armistead knew the fort's powder magazine was not bombproof and risked the whole fort blowing up. One bomb landed in the magazine but did not explode immediately. Fortunately, one brave man doused the fuse before it exploded.

Q. What prominent feature did Mary Pickersgill contribute to Fort McHenry?

A. She and her 13-year-old daughter made the 42 by 30 foot flag, for which she was been paid $405.90 in August 1813. The fifteen stars on the flag were each two feet from point to point, and the fifteen red and white stripes were each two feet wide. She also had made the 17 by 25 foot fort's storm flag for $168.54.

Q. Inspired by Dr. William Beanes, who kept asking: "Is the flag still there?," who wrote "The Star-Spangled Banner" while aboard an enemy vessel during the British bombardment of Fort McHenry?

Francis Scott Key
(1779–1843)
Lawyer, author of "The Star–Spangled Banner"

A. Francis Scott Key, a Georgetown lawyer, wrote the song during the bombardment. He was on a diplomatic mission to obtain the release of Dr. Beanes, whom the British had caught imprisoning their soldiers straggling out of Washington. It is not known for sure which flag was seen flying from the fort. The bombshells, fired from 10- and 13-inch mortars aboard five bomb ships, weighed over 200 pounds and had a fuse that was lit when the mortar was fired. They were very erratic in timing, so many did burst in the air before landing.

Q. Where was Francis Scott Key when he wrote "The Star-Spangled Banner"?

A. Prior to the battle, Key boarded the British ship *Minden* with the American prisoner of war exchange agent, John Shimmer. They visited the British to secure the release of Dr. Beanes, who had been held prisoner since the raid on Washington. Beanes was kept on the ship so he could not bring intelligence of British intentions in the ensuing campaign.

Q. What was the original title of "The Star-Spangled Banner"?

A. It was titled "Defence of Fort McHenry." Key first started writing it as a poem. His brother-in-law, Judge J. H. Nicholson, immediately determined that it could be sung to a popular drinking tune called "Anacreon in Heaven." He suggested publishing it, and it was published anonymously on September 20 in the *Baltimore Patriot*. Congress did not adopt the song as the American national anthem until March 3, 1931.

Q. In the autumn of 1814, after the British burned Washington, D.C., who recommended conscription in order to fight the British army?

A. Secretary of War James Monroe, who had replaced Armstrong after the burning of the city.

Q. Did the U.S. invade Spanish-held Florida during the war?

A. Yes. General Andrew Jackson, disobeying orders from James Monroe, invaded Florida with 4,000 men and captured Pensacola on November 6, with the loss of 7 killed and 11 wounded.

Q. Did the U.S. declare war against Spain in the War of 1812?

A. No.

Q. In late 1813 Generals Andrew Jackson and John Coffee defeated the Creeks at Talushatchee and Talladega, but had not broken their power. In what battle did Jackson's 2,000-man army, including 200 Cherokees and the yet-to-be-famous Sam Houston (severely wounded in the battle), crush the power of the Creeks, killing between 500 and 700 warriors at a cost of 200 casualties?

A. The Battle of Horseshoe Bend, fought on March 27 on the Tallapoosa River in Alabama. After an ineffective two-hour artillery bombardment, Jackson's army breached fortifications across a bend in the river, which the Creeks, under their leader Menewa, had built with the aid of white engineers from Pensacola. Jackson's men then slaughtered the Creeks, who could not escape and would not surrender. Afterwards, the half-breed Creek leader William Weatherford (Red Eagle), who had not been present at the battle, surrendered to Jackson. Another half-breed leader, Peter McQueen, led some of the Creeks to Spanish territory in Florida where they intermingled with the Seminoles.

In August 1814 the Creeks ceded 23 million acres of land to the United States at the Treaty of Fort Jackson, and never fought again as a nation.

Q. How were Jackson's Cherokee allies instrumental in helping Jackson to win a total victory at Horseshoe Bend?

A. During the artillery bombardment, the Cherokees shot fire arrows into the Creek village, to the rear of their fortified position. This distracted the defenders at the breastworks. Also, prior to the battle, Cherokees had slipped across the river and stolen the Creek canoes, thus denying the Creeks any means of escape.

Q. What American island signed a declaration with the British stating that they would stay neutral for the remainder of the war?

A. On August 23 the inhabitants of Nantucket Island agreed to become neutral so that they could import food. They also agreed to refrain from any warlike activities, to supply the British, and to pay no taxes to the U.S.

Q. In September George Prevost began an invasion of the United States with an army of over 10,000, mostly Wellington veterans. Prevost planned to move down Lake Champlain. Why did he decide to march his army down the New York side of the lake rather than the Vermont side?

A. Prevost chose to descend on the New York side to spare Vermont the ravages of war, since Vermont had demonstrated a reluctance to participate in the war and was supplying him with money and provisions. In fact, Prevost acknowledged that American contractors primarily from New York and Vermont supplied two-thirds of his army with beef.

Q. What naval battle fought on Lake Champlain (which is 136 miles long and from one-quarter to 13 miles wide) on September 11 saved New York from a 12,000-man British invasion force under George Prevost?

A. A British squadron was defeated in the battle of Plattsburg Bay. Without control of the Lake, Prevost decided to retreat because Americans swarming towards him would cut his line of supply.

Due to his decision, Prevost was recalled to England to face a court-martial. He died a week before the hearing.

Q. Who commanded the American flotilla, which included the frigate *Saratoga* (26 guns), the brig *Eagle* (20), the schooner *Ticonderoga* (17), the sloop *Preble* (7), and ten gunboats mounting 16 guns, in an unusual naval battle fought between two fleets while at anchor?

A. Lieutenant Thomas Macdonough defeated a squadron under Captain George Downie, which consisted of the frigate *Confiance* with 37 guns, the brig *Linnet* (16), the sloop *Chubb* (11), the sloop *Finch* (10), and twelve gunboats also mounting 16 guns. Downie's death in the opening shots of the battle hurt the British effort. The British were at a disadvantage in the battle because the two sides fought at close range and the Americans had a greater number of carronades (best at short range), which could throw a heavier weight of metal than the British guns. Macdonough's victory contributed greatly to the British decision to make peace. The British naval historian William Laird Clowes called Macdonough's victory, "a most notable feat, one which, on the whole surpassed that of any other captain of either navy in this war."

Q. While Downie engaged Macdonough, British general Frederick Robinson began to move almost 10,000 men against American general Alexander Macomb's 3,500 men defending a fortified position on the south side of the Saranac River. Before he could effectively engage all of his men, Robinson was recalled by Prevost, who thought the attack would be a waste of men since Downie's squadron was already defeated. Was Prevost's cancellation of the attack his most serious mistake of the campaign?

A. No. Even if Prevost had defeated Macomb, he probably could not have held Plattsburg without controlling Lake Champlain. He made his biggest mistake in not marching his army down the east side of the lake. This would have forced Macomb and Macdonough to withdraw from Plattsburg.

Q. In October General George Izard dispatched General Daniel Bissell with his brigade of 900 men to destoy a mill, in an attempt to move the British under Lieutenant General Gordon Drummond from their position. Bissell's men defended themselves in an attack by 750 British and then counterattacked, driving the British away. What was significant about the battle fought at Cook's Mills on October 19?

A. It was the last battle of the war fought between regular forces in Canada. Also, it was an American victory over Wellington's veterans.

Q. In November 1814 the British cabinet offered the Duke of Wellington command of British forces in Canada. What was his answer?

A. Wellington accepted but told the cabinet that he would not leave Europe until the spring. He also told them that his presence would do little good without British naval control of the Great Lakes. He believed peace could be concluded if England dropped demands for any territorial concessions from America.

Q. What future president led 330 men up the Mississippi River in September and made the last American effort to control the area west of Lake Michigan during the war?

FACT

One of the most lopsided victories of the war occurred on September 12, when the British bombarded Fort Bowyer in an attempt to capture Mobile. Five ships mounting seventy-eight guns bombarded the fort, commanded by Major William Lawrence. In imitation of Captain James Lawrence of Chesapeake fame, Major Lawrence inspired his men with the cry, "Don't give up the fort." His 130 men with twenty cannons didn't. They beat off the British naval attack, sinking *Hermes* in the fight, and inflicting 232 casualties, while sustaining 4 killed and 4 wounded.

A. Major Zachary Taylor led an expedition in an attempt to recapture Fort Shelby at Prairie du Chien, Wisconsin. The expedition retreated after being turned back at the Rock Island Rapids by about 20 British and 1,200 Native Americans under the Sauk Chief Black Hawk.

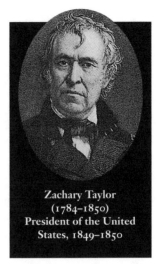

Zachary Taylor
(1784–1850)
President of the United States, 1849–1850

Q. What present-day U.S. state was essentially made a part of New Brunswick during a September invasion by Lieutenant General Sir John Sherbrooke and Major General Gerard Gosselin?

A. Sherbrooke's invasion of Maine, then a province of Massachusetts, brought the northern 100 miles of coastline under British control for eight months. Two-thirds of the population there took oaths of allegiance to the British crown. Massachusett's Governor Caleb Strong did not retaliate.

Q. Sherbrooke's expedition up the Penobscot River resulted in the loss of what American frigate?

A. Militia under Brigadier General John Blake destroyed the 28-gun frigate *John Adams* to prevent it from falling into British hands. The frigate had been at Hampden for hull repairs.

Q. Name the treaty which ended the War of 1812?

A. Signed on December 24, the Treaty of Ghent ended the war but did not address any of the issues that caused the war. Both sides agreed to stop fighting and restore the status quo. British influence and participation in the fur trade in the Upper Mississippi region in America was ended and the power of frontier Native American tribes was broken. Eventually boundaries with Canada were settled, the impressment issue faded away, and owners of slaves who had run away to the British were reimbursed. The last American prisoners held by the British were released in July 1815.

Q. Did the British navy ever impress American seaman after the War of 1812?

A. Yes. As late as 1847, during the War with Mexico, the British frigate *Columbia* created an international incident by impressing a seaman from the brig *Brookline*.

Q. Name three of the five United States peace commissioners.

A. John Quincy Adams, James A. Bayard, and Albert Gallatin were the original three commissioners sent to Russia in 1813. After Britain rejected Russian mediation and agreed to negotiate directly with the United States in January 1814, Jonathan Russell and Henry Clay were also appointed commissioners. Negotiations finally began in Ghent, Belgium, on August 8, 1814.

Q. Is it true that in 1814 the average age of the top nine U.S. generals was less than forty years old?

A. Yes. The average age was actually thirty-six. This compared with an average age of sixty years old for the top eight United States generals at the beginning of the war.

Q. In December it appeared that the federal government was no longer capable of carrying on the war or of at least defending New England. The General Court of Massachusetts called for a meeting of New England states to amend the Constitution. What was the name given to this convention, which was also rumored to be considering secession?

A. The Hartford Convention's delegates, from Massachusetts, Connecticut, and Rhode Island, along with two unofficial observers from New Hampshire and one from Vermont, met in a secret session from December 15 to January 5, 1815. Though the issue of secession was quickly ruled out, a series of resolutions was passed. The convention recommended seven Constitutional amendments; a two-thirds vote in Congress to declare war, admit new states to the union, or interdict trade with a foreign country; a limit of one term for a president; a sixty-day limit on government enforced embargoes; a repeal of the three-fifths rule for apportioning taxes and congressional representation; a rule disallowing a naturalized citizen from holding any office in the federal government; and a prohibition against electing a president twice in succession from the same state. Emissaries were sent to Washington to negotiate their demands with Madison. However, the capital was now favoring Madison as news of the American victory at New Orleans had recently arrived, setting off a wave of celebration. Therefore, Madison could safely ignore any federalist opposition.

Q. The city newspaper from what state made the following statement criticizing the Hartford Convention: "No man, no association of men, no state or set of states has a right to withdraw from this Union, of its own accord"?

A. Interesting in terms of future history, the statement appeared in the *Richmond Enquirer* of Virginia.

Q. Name the famous battle fought after the peace treaty had been signed.

A. The battle of New Orleans was fought on January 8. In the main assault on U.S. fortifications behind the Rodriguez Canal, the British army of 8,000 men lost about 2,000 killed or wounded in about one half hour. The American army of 5,700 lost 8 killed and 13 wounded.

Q. Name the commander of the American forces gathered in New Orleans to fight the invading British army.

A. Andrew Jackson was the commander. Though he was sick most of the time, his immense energy inspired the defense of the city.

Q. Jackson thought that the British would approach New Orleans by coming up the Mississippi or through Lake Pontchartrain. Did the British take one of the approaches Jackson expected of them?

A. No. The British came through Lake Borgne in the channels of Bayou Bienvenue. Jackson learned of the British approach from Major Gabriel Villere, who sighted the British, jumped out of a window in his own house to escape, and ran to notify Jackson. Jackson swiftly moved with 2,100 men to attack about 1,600 British at Villere's plantation on the night of December 23. He was repulsed. British General John Keane was reinforced the next

day and probably could have immediately fought his way into
New Orleans.

Q. Who commanded the five Jefferson gunboats that resisted a
British attack of forty-five rowboats and 1,200 men, commanded
by Admiral Cochrane, on Lake Borgne?

A. Lieutenant Thomas Ap Catesby Jones and his 180 men fought
valiantly. In the end he was wounded and lost all of his boats, yet
he had delayed the British, thereby giving Jackson additional time
to prepare his defenses.

Q. Name the fort that blocked the Mississippi River route to New
Orleans.

A. Fort St. Philip. Cochrane had ordered six vessels to attack on this
route.

Q. Identify the famous pirate who helped Andrew Jackson defend
New Orleans.

A. Jean Laffite rejected British navy captain Nicholas Lockyear's
overtures for an alliance. Instead Laffite informed Governor
William Claiborne and placed his 800 Baratarian pirates on the
side of the Americans. Though at first Jackson refused Laffite's
help, he relented upon Laffite's personal request and upon learning of how much artillery and artillery ammunition the pirates
possessed.

Q. Prior to the British attack on New Orleans, why had Jean Laffite
been held in prison by the Americans?

A. During the war, United States forces had fought against the
Baratarian Pirates under Pierre and Jean Laffite. From their base
in Barataria, located west of the mouth of the Mississippi River
and south of New Orleans, the pirates had been seizing United
States vessesls and those of other nations since 1805. Captain
Andrew Hunter Holmes captured the Laffite brothers in 1812,
and they had been imprisoned and then released on bond. Laffite
did not fight at the battle on January 8, 1815.

Q. On January 4, a brigade of approximately 2,300 Kentuckians arrived under the command of General John Thomas. Why couldn't Jackson put these men to good use?

A. Only about 700 of the Kentuckians came armed with weapons. A furious Jackson utilized only about 250 of them in the battle for New Orleans. Jackson condemned the Kentuckians, stating that they were, "The worst provided body of men perhaps, that ever went 1,500 miles from home to help a sister state."

Q. Who was the British commander in the attack on New Orleans?

A. Major General Sir Edward Pakenham. He was related to the Duke of Wellington and had served in the Peninsular campaign. Pakenham, along with two of the other three major generals, was killed in the battle. Wellington had once reproved Pakenham, who was hit about 300 yards from the American works, for exposing himself to the enemy needlessly.

Q. Behind what natural barrier did Jackson position his men?

A. The Rodriguez Canal. The British assault failed there. However, British Lieutenant Colonel William Thornton and about 450 men succeeded in pushing back 250 Louisiana militia and Kentuckians on the west bank of the Mississippi River, and in addition disabled thirteen guns and captured three bronze pieces. If British general John Lambert, who had replaced Pakenham, had sent more men across the river, the British army may very well have won the battle.

Q. What was the ratio of British to American casualties for the whole New Orleans campaign?
   a. Three to one
   b. Seven to one
   c. Ten to one

A. The answer is b. The British suffered 2,444 casualties against 336 for the Americans, a ratio of seven to one.

Q. What American fort surrendered to the British on February 11 after the war was officially over?

A. Fort Bowyer, thirty miles southeast of Mobile, Alabama. Lieutenant Colonel William Lawrence surrendered after the British, under Major General John Lambert, positioned their artillery. Two days later, news of the Treaty of Ghent arrived, thus sparing Mobile from a British attack.

Q. Is it true that the War of 1812 produced more regular U.S. Army generals who later became president than any other war?

A. Yes. Both Andrew Jackson and William Henry Harrison became presidents. Zachary Taylor, who only attained the rank of major during the war, was promoted to breveted general in the Mexican War and later became president. Among Civil War generals, two were voted into the presidency: Ulysses S. Grant and Rutherford Hayes. However, Hayes was only a militia general. Only five regular generals who have served in the regular U.S. Army have ever been elected president: George Washington, Andrew Jackson, William Henry Harrison, Ulysses S. Grant, and Dwight Eisenhower.

Q. Who was the only regular U.S. Army general in the war who also served as a general in the Mexican War and the Civil War?

A. Winfield Scott. He was the greatest military man of his era with a remarkable career that touched every major military event of his era.

Q. What officer serving in the War of 1812 would eventually set a record of forty-two years as quartermaster general, the longest tenure for any U.S. military staff officer?

A. Thomas Sidney Jesup. He was captured in Hull's surrender, exchanged, and later fought at Chippewa and Lundy's Lane, where he was severely wounded. Jesup became quartermaster general under Secretary of War John C. Calhoun in 1818 and held his post until 1860, when he died.

Q. Who were the only American brigadier generals who had also fought in the Revolutionary War?

A. Benjamin Howard and Thomas Paker, who were made generals in February 1813 by Secretary of War Armstrong.

FACT

Scott began the War of 1812 as a lieutenant colonel and retired from the army in 1861 at the rank of brevet lieutenant general. Besides participating and leading in many of the major battles on the Northwest Frontier during the War of 1812, he took part in the Black Hawk War in 1832 and the Seminole War in 1836. He virtually won the Mexican War, 1846–1848, when he conquered Mexico City in 1847, then served as a military governor. He formulated the Anaconda Plan, which was eventually adopted and helped the North win the Civil War. In addition, he led many diplomatic missions and ran as the Whig party candidate for president in 1852, losing to Franklin Pierce. He was called "old Fuss and Feathers" because of his penchant for formality and strict military decorum.

Q. Who was the highest ranking British officer captured by the Americans during the war?

A. Major General Phineas Riall was captured at Lundy's Lane after he was seriously wounded. Riall had been responsible for burning Buffalo and Black Rock, New York, in December 1813. He was exchanged in December 1814.

Q. Is it true that none of the fortifications that engineer graduates of West Point constructed were ever captured by the enemy during the war?

A. Yes. Major William McRee constructed the fortifications at Fort Erie, Captain Eleazer Wood constructed Fort Meigs, and Captain Joseph Gilbert Totten directed the fortifications at Plattsburg. The engineer graduates of West Point were the primary stars of the army during the war. The Duke of Wellington had noted that the absence of a professional officer at times was the greatest deficiency of U.S. forces during the war.

Q. What American city, assailed three separate times during the war, only once conducted a successful defense?

A. Mobile, Alabama. It surrendered to Wilkinson in April 1813, and Fort Bowyer (its only real defense) surrendered in February 1815 to the British. Major William Lawrence, with 160 men, conducted the only successful defense of the city when they defeated a force of over 800 British under Captain Sir William Percy of the Royal Navy and Colonel Edward Nicholls of the Royal Marines in September 1814. A cannon shot from Fort Bowyer cut the bow spring cable of HMS *Hermes*, Percy's flagship, and the fort's gunners were able to pound the ship, forcing Percy to destroy it and abandon his assault.

Q. During the war, the increasingly effective British naval blockade greatly restricted imports into the United States. Nitrate (saltpeter), a necessary ingredient in manufacturing gunpowder, became in short supply. Where did the United States finally obtain nitrate?

A. Mammoth Cave, Kentucky. The nitrate was developed from bat droppings.

Q. What was used to treat malaria during the war?

A. Peruvian bark, which is now known to contain quinine, the modern treatment for the disease.

Q. Many American slaves found their way to the British lines in the Revolutionary War. Did the British also employ black Americans in the War of 1812?

A. Yes. About 200 black soldiers fought at Bladensburg as a corps of colonial marines formed by Alexander Cochrane in May 1814. Between 3,000 and 5,000 former slaves went with the British when they departed from Chesapeake Bay. Repeating their actions after the Revolutionary War, the British brought many of them to Nova Scotia (2,000), and some were sold back into slavery.

FACT

F ew blacks served in the American armies during the war; however, Congress did authorize the enlistment of free blacks into the United States Navy in March 1813. The naval crews on the Upper Great Lakes eventually consisted of 10 to 20 percent blacks. Some blacks helped Perry win his decisive victory on Lake Erie.

Q. Which war cost more per capita to finance, the Revolutionary War or the War of 1812?

A. The War of 1812 cost only $15 per capita, about one-fifth the cost of the Revolutionary War.

Q. What major naval battle took place on Lake Ontario during the war?

A. None. Except for minor skirmishes, no naval battles took place on Lake Ontario.

Q. Name the commanders of the U.S. and British navies who conducted a shipbuilding race throughout the entire war on Lake Ontario.

A. Isaac Chauncey of the U.S. Navy and Commodore James Yeo of the British navy avoided battle. Each continually tried to gain naval superiority over the other.

Q. On Lake Ontario, Yeo constructed the largest ship in the world at that time, *St. Lawrence*, a three decker. How many guns did it mount?

A. One hundred and twenty guns. The Americans would have completed two ships of the line and a frigate on Lake Ontario if the war had continued. The ship of the line *New Orleans* was to have 130 guns.

Naval Action on the High Seas

"Don't give up the ship."

Q. Did the American navy of 1812 consist primarily of volunteers or conscripts?

A. Volunteers. In 1812 there were 4,010 enlisted sailors and 234 officers in the American navy.

Q. Approximately how many vessels did the U.S. Navy have at the start of the war?
a. Seven
b. Nineteen
c. Thirty-one

A. The answer is b. Only fourteen of the nineteen vessels were fit for service. Two or three of them were only useless hulks. There were no ships of the line. However, the seven frigates, of which the largest three, the *United States*, *President*, and *Constitution*, all rated forty-four guns, were the finest frigates afloat. Eight of the fit vessels were sloops or brigs and rated less than twenty guns. In comparison, the British navy had 116 frigates, 124 ships of the line, and various other warships totaling about 640.

The Constitution

Q. Is it true that Congress did not vote to increase the number of ships in the navy before it adjourned on July 6, 1812?

A. Yes.

Q. What frigate was called "Old Ironsides"?

A. *Constitution*, because the installation of her live-oak planks had been accomplished without undergoing the steaming process that was thought to weaken wood.

Q. Name the designer of the United States's frigates.

A. Joshua Humphreys designed the frigates to be able to fight any ship under sixty-four guns. Humphreys had previously designed frigates in the Revolutionary War. He was assisted by Josiah Fox, who was trained in England, and William Doughty. He was also inspired by the French, who had earlier cut down several of their seventy-fours to make large frigates. Humphreys recommended arming large frigates with 24-pounders instead of 18-pounders, as the British did. He also built frigates of live oak, which increased durability and strength. An American 44-gun frigate officially carried 400 men. The frigates usually carried about ten more guns than what their rating listed. For example, the 32-gun frigate *Essex* carried 46 guns.

Q. Just as the secretary of war knew relatively little about the art of war the secretary of the navy was ignorant of naval affairs. Name him.

A. Paul Hamilton. He had been a governor of South Carolina and a rice planter. Hamilton requested ten frigates and twelve 74-gun ships, but Congress voted against it in March 1812. Hamilton was succeeded by William Jones in December 1812. Jones proved very capable in the position.

Q. Three-fourths of the 89 officers on the U.S. Navy roster of January 1, 1813, including eleven of sixteen captains, served under this prewar navy captain. Name him.

A. Captain Edward Preble. Writer Fletcher Pratt called the navy's principle commanding officers of the war "Preble's Boys," noting that with the exception of Perry's victory on Lake Erie, Preble's subordinates, while he commanded the U.S. Mediterranean squadron from 1803 to 1804, later won all the naval victories of the war. Direct evidence proving Preble's sway over the future conduct of men who served under him is lacking. Few men knew him well, and other contemporary commanders also provided excellent models. However, Preble's training and his personal example undoubtedly exerted a powerful influence over the generation of officers who commanded during the war.

Q. Name the three different types of guns aboard U.S. Navy vessels during the war.

A. Long guns, carronades, and columbiads. U.S. guns were more likely to burst than those of the British, and the shot weighed about 7 percent less than equivalently rated British shot. Columbiads were short and large and made from rebored cannon. They were mostly 18-pounders and fired "bombshells," hollow shot. Long guns were eight to ten feet in length, weighed up to four tons, and were serviced by a crew of fourteen men in the U.S. Navy (nine in the British). A carronade was less than four feet long, weighed under two tons, and was serviced by nine men in the U.S. Navy (six in the British). Columbiads were the first U.S. shell guns, usually an 18-pounder, and were not utilized in large numbers.

Q. What was the largest gun used at sea during the war?

A. The British used a 68-pound carronade on some ships of the line, while the largest U.S. gun was a 42-pound carronade.

Q. Between 1803 and 1808, President Thomas Jefferson had pushed for the building of 278 gunboats to be used for defense. These craft were from 47 to 80 feet long, mounted one or two guns and were manned by twenty-five to thirty men. The gunboats were cheaper to build than larger vessels, which Jefferson feared might invite a British preemptive strike. The British had previously attacked a Dutch fleet at anchor in Copenhagen and seized eighteen ships of the line, eight frigates, and eighteen smaller vessels. Did the performance of the gunboats in the war prove the wisdom of Jefferson's decision?

A. No. Out of the 174 gunboats actually built in the decade before the war, only 62 were left in service in 1812. They proved to be practically worthless. In one instance, fifteen of them assaulted a becalmed British frigate for about a half an hour and scored a hit only once or twice. The gunboats all fled from the frigate when a breeze started. After the war, most of the gunboats were sold. Only one remained in service by 1822.

Q. What was the highest official rank in the navy?
A. Captain. Though the commander of a squadron was given the honorary rank of commodore.

Q. Was the average age of the captains who commanded frigates in the war greater or less than forty?
A. In contrast to the U.S. Army generals who averaged sixty years of age at the beginning of the war, the frigate captains were all in their thirties. Their ages at the start of the war, and the frigates which they commanded at sea, were as follows: Isaac Hull (39), *Constitution*; John Rodgers (39), *President*; William Bainbridge (38), *Constitution*; Charles Stewart (34), *Constitution*; Stephen Decatur (33), *Congress* and *United States*; David Porter (32), *Essex*; and James Lawrence (31), *Chesapeake*. In addition, all had served in the navy during the Tripolitan war.

Q. What did Portsmouth, New Hampshire; Charleston, Massachusetts; New York, New York; Philadelphia, Pennsylvania; Washington, D.C.; and Gosport, Virginia, have in common?
a. A naval yard was located in each city.
b. They were the six foremost cities for commissioning privateers.
c. The British attacked each one of them.
A. The answer is a. All the naval yards, except Gosport, were established in 1801. Only the Washington navy yard was manned when the war began.

Q. What happened to the approximately twenty-five hundred Americans who were in the British navy when the U.S. declared war?

A. They were regulated to British prisons because they refused to fight against the United States.

Q. Were many Royal Navy deserters serving on American ships?

A. Yes. One British source estimated as many as forty thousand British seaman had deserted and were serving on American ships. The deserters carried protection papers to prove their citizenship. Many paid to have someone vouch falsely as to their birthplace and residence, and thus carried fake papers.

Q. Like the Revolutionary War, the first squadron assembled during the war was the largest. Under Commodore John Rodgers, the frigates *President, United States, Congress*, along with the sloop *Hornet* and brig *Argus*, all departed from New York on June 21, 1812. Rodgers had sailed without waiting for orders within one hour of hearing war declared. He planned to intercept a British convoy homeward bound from Jamaica. Was the cruise a successful one?

A. Considering the number of ships, the cruise was not very successful. Rodgers battled the 32-gun *Belvidera* on June 23 but could not prevent its escape. Rodgers probably would have caught it were it not for a bursting gun that killed or wounded sixteen men and wounded him in the leg. The squadron chased the Jamaican convoy across the Atlantic and returned to Boston on August 31, 1812. The squadron captured only seven insignificant prizes, but its presence in English waters also kept single British ships from guarding American ports. Therefore, many American ships were able to make it home in the early days of the war. However, several historians have asserted that Rodgers and Decatur could have taken the squadron and swept a sixty-mile swath of ocean clean of British ships and probably have intercepted and captured the West Indies fleet.

Q. In October three separate squadrons were formed. Who were the commanders of these squadrons?

A. John Rogers, Stephen Decatur, and William Bainbridge. All three squadrons were under orders to sail to different areas of operations in the Atlantic Ocean. Nevertheless, most of the ships separated and some never joined their assigned squadrons. As Decatur originally advocated, most operated singly throughout the war.

Q. What was the first U.S. Navy ship captured by the British?

A. The *Nautilus* was captured on July 16 by a British squadron. Lieutenant Crane failed to escape even after throwing half of his guns overboard.

Q. Captain Isaac Hull in the *Constitution* performed perhaps the greatest sailing feat of the war between July 17 and 20 when he sailed into the midst of seven British ships and managed to escape without harm. He did this without throwing over his guns, an action sometimes resorted to in order to lighten the load and increase ship speed. Instead he used several inge-nious tactics including sending out his longboats to tow, draining off ten tons of his water supply to increase his speed by perhaps several hundred

Captain Isaac Hull
(1773–1843)
Naval officer, commanded
the *Constitution* in
War of 1812

yards a day, wetting his sails to catch the full impact of a breeze, and spreading or shortening sails at just the right moment. When the wind died and he found himself in shallow water (less than 150), he resorted to kedging. What was kedging?

A. A vessel kedged when its small boats carried a small anchor or anchors forward for a distance and lowered them. Then the ship was pulled forward by winching the anchor lines on a capstan. This method was especially effective in shallow water.

Q. What American navy captain had the honor of capturing the first British warship during the war?

A. Captain David Porter, in the 32-gun frigate *Essex*, obtained the surrender of the 20-gun sloop *Alert* after posing as a merchantman. When the *Alert* drew close he let loose one broadside and won the victory by wrecking the enemy vessel in only eight minutes.

Q. On August 19, 1812, the frigate *Guerriere* became the first British frigate since 1803 to haul down its flag in a single-ship action, and the first frigate ever to surrender to an American ship. Name the American ship.

A. The *Constitution* (44-guns), captained by Isaac Hull (nephew and adopted son of General William Hull), captured the British 38-gun frigate *Guerriere* after a half-hour battle. *Guerriere's* captain, James R. Dacres, had earlier issued a challenge to meet any American frigate of equal force off Sandy Hook. The *Guerriere* was so disabled that it was blown up afterwards.

Q. What was Hull's reward after he returned to Boston?

A. Because he had departed from Boston without authorization, he lost command of the *Constitution* and was appointed to supervise New York's harbor defense.

Q. Name Britain's only year-round North American naval base.

A. Halifax, Nova Scotia. The Americans never once mounted an attack on the base during the war.

Q. What was a letter of marque?

A. A letter of marque was a governmental commission authorizing private vessels to seize enemy vessels, their crews, and cargoes. It also bound the privateer to subject a captured vessel to the judgement of a prize court to obtain the captured property.

Q. For voyages to and from which port did British admiral Sir John Warren issue licenses to American merchant ships, granting them immunity from capture?

A. He granted licenses for voyages from Halifax and Bermuda to and from Lisbon, Portugal. Thus American shipping aided the British in supplying the Duke of Wellington's armies on the Iberian Peninsula, enabling him to continue the war against the French. Many unscrupulous British captains ignored the licenses and attacked American ships on their way home from Lisbon. Sometimes British captains would take the money earned by the Americans and then let the ship go. The trade to Portugal was illegal. Thus, even American cruisers and privateers seized a large number of the vessels engaged in the illegal trade. Yet, much silver and gold from the illicit trade was deposited in New England banks during the war, and this money helped to finance the development and expansion of American industry after the war.

Q. In the first year of the war, which navy dominated in engagements between the British and Americans?

A. The Americans dominated in the first year of the war defeating five British ships, the frigates *Guerriere*, *Macedonian*, *Java*, the *Frolic* (recaptured), and *Alert*. The British defeated three American vessels, in each instance with greatly superior force. The Americans lost only *Wasp*, 18 guns, to a 74-gun ship of the line after it had defeated the British sloop *Frolic*, 19 guns. *Nautilus* was captured by a squadron, and *Vixen*, 12 guns, by the 32-gun *Southampton*. In the previous twenty years of fighting against the French, Russians, Turks, Italians, Dutch, and others, the British had only lost 5 of 200 single-ship engagements in which forces were approximately equal. Thus the British suffered a substantial reversal of their previous success by losing the first five single-ship engagements of the war to the Americans.

Q. What invention allowed American naval gunners to fire their cannons three times as fast as their British counterparts?

A. Americans possessed a sheet lead cartridge, while the British had paper and flannel cartridges. The Americans also possessed a gun sight for their cannons, which the British did not have.

Q. What ship under Stephen Decatur achieved the honor of bringing into Newport the only British frigate ever brought into a U.S. port as a prize?

A. The frigate *United States*, 56 guns, defeated the frigate *Macedonian*, 49 guns, on October 25, 1812. The rapid-firing American crew outshot the British crew, commanded by Captain John S. Carden, by a margin of two to one. Not until World War II, when the U.S. Navy captured the German submarine *U-505*, would another enemy vessel be brought into a U.S. port.

Q. In the last naval battle of 1812, who captained the *Constitution*, 54 guns, in a victory over the British frigate *Java*, 49 guns?

A. In a two and a quarter hour battle that has been called the most fiercely contested of the war, William Bainbridge defeated the frigate *Java*, Captain Henry Lamber commanding, and destroyed her. Never again during the war did the U.S. Navy defeat a British frigate.

Q. How many British vessels were captured by American privateers in 1812?

    a. 54
    b. 108
    c. 219

A. The answer is c. In four months in 1812, approximately 600 American privateers captured 219 enemy vessels.

Q. To ensure success against American frigates, what orders did British frigate commanders receive?

A. They were ordered not to engage in any single-ship battles with American frigates. Instead they were to cruise in pairs or small squadrons when possible.

The United States *vs. the* Macedonian

Q. Who commanded the North American Station of the British fleet at the war's beginning?

A. Admiral Sir John Borlase Warren commanded the fleet until Admiral Alexander Cochrane took over in the spring of 1814.

Q. What American frigate was blockaded in the Chesapeake Bay for the entire war?

A. The *Constellation*, which was not ready to sail until early 1813. It did try to get to sea but found its way blocked by a British squadron. Captain George Stewart returned to Norfolk and anchored her. Twice British forces of up to two thousand men attempted to take *Constellation* by surprise, but were discovered and called off their attacks.

Q. In 1813 an American warship entered the Pacific Ocean for the first time and succeeded in devastating the British whaling fleet to the extent that the British whaling industry never recovered. Name this warship, which was also the only one to operate there during the war.

A. The *Essex*, a 32-gun frigate commanded by David Porter, captured twelve British whalers in a six-month period. Starting with one ship and 319 men, Porter captured fifteen prizes altogether. He kept himself supplied for all of 1813 with captured stock and placed crews on the best of the captured ships. At one point he commanded seven ships with eighty guns and 656 men.

Q. What was the first American frigate defeated by a British frigate during the war?

A. The 38-gun *Chesapeake* (in reality 50-guns) was captured on June 1, 1813, by the 52-gun *Shannon* under Sir Philip Broke. During the fighting American captain James Lawrence was mortally wounded. While dying, he uttered the now famous slogan, "Don't give up the ship. Fight her till she sinks." His men never did haul down the flag and only surrendered after all the American officers but one were wounded and a boarding party led by Captain Broke overpowered them. Out of the *Chesapeake*'s 349 men, 48 were killed and 98 wounded, and of 44 marines aboard, 32 were killed or wounded. The fight lasted only fifteen minutes.

Q. What U.S. Navy ship burned nineteen vessels in thirty-one days in the waters around England and Ireland in the summer of 1813?

A. The *Argus*, under the command of William Allen, caused British insurance rates to rise before it surrendered to the *Pelican*. At least one historian has judged the crew of the *Argus* to have fought the least credible single-ship action of the war on the American side. Capturing a prize with a cargo of wine proved be the *Argus*'s downfall.

Q. What particular area of the U.S. suffered from British amphibious operations beginning in 1813?

A. The Chesapeake Bay region. The British had gained supremacy in American waters and could attack as they pleased without much resistance. Under Admiral Cockburn, they ravaged the region. Though Cockburn burned homes and towns where residents resisted his men, he did offer payment for goods with bills on the British Treasury.

Q. In what year did the British blockade New England ports?

A. The British did not blockade New England ports until 1814, because New Englanders supplied them with necessary goods and Britain wanted to make use of their pro-British sympathy. With the war in Europe over, Britain changed their policy to keep Americans from trading and raising money to continue the war.

Q. While attempting to run out to sea from a neutral port in March 1814, Captain David Porter, in the *Essex*, was attacked by two British ships, *Phoebe* and *Cherub*. What port was he trying to vacate?

A. Porter was leaving the port of Valparaiso, Chile. He surrendered after a bloody battle in which more men died (58) than on any other American ship during the war. The *Essex*'s career had included the first U.S. Navy victory of the war over a British war-ship, the brig *Alert*, on August 13, 1812, and the seizure or destruction of forty enemy ships. British captain James Hilyer then paroled Porter and his crew and sent them back to the United States.

Q. What future first admiral in the Civil War served under Porter on the *Essex* as a midshipman at the age of thirteen?

A. David Farragut. He had been adopted by Porter at the age of ten when his mother died. Farragut actually commanded one of Porter's prizes, captured during the cruise, and served well during the fight against *Phoebe*. Incidentally, Porter's natural son, David Dixon Porter, became the second admiral in the U.S. Navy.

Admiral
David Glasgow Farragut
(1801–1870)
Union naval officer in
Civil War, hero of
battle of Mobile Bay

Q. Periodically British admirals declared the coast of the United States to be under blockade even when they did not have sufficient force to physically enforce a blockade. In response to their proclamations, what privateer captain declared a blockade of Great Britain?

A. During a cruise in the summer of 1814 in the English Channel, Captain Thomas Boyle of the *Chasseur* dispatched a handbill to Lloyd's of London stating: "I do therefore, by virtue of the power and authority in me vested (possessing sufficient force), declare all the ports, harbors, bays, creeks, river, inlets, outlets, islands, and seacoast of the United Kingdom of Great Britain and Ireland in a state of strict and rigorous blockade."

Q. In late September of 1814, anchored in the neutral port of Fayal in the Portuguese Azores, a single American vessel fought against more than a thousand men on three British ships— the 74-gun ship of the line *Plantagenet*, the 38-gun frigate *Rota*, and the 18-gun brig *Carnation*. Two Americans were killed and 7 wounded, against 63 killed and 110 wounded for the British, before the Americans abandoned their ship and scuttled it. Was the American ship a U.S. frigate, U.S. sloop, or a privateer schooner?

A. *General Armstrong* was a privateer schooner of nine guns and ninety men captained by Samuel C. Reid. While the privateer traded some shots against the *Carnation*, which could approach in the shallow water, the Americans fought mostly against attacking gunboats while at anchor. The British mounted one attack with twelve boats, each mounting one gun, and 400 men that was driven off. One English observer stated, "We may well say 'God deliver us from our enemies' if this is the way the Americans fight." Reid's men killed and wounded more British than did any U.S. frigate in a single encounter during the war. Finally, under fire from *Carnation*, Reid and his men abandoned ship and retreated to shore. Afterwards the British burned the ship. The British squadron was supposed to reinforce Edward Pakenham's invasion fleet headed for New Orleans. The delay caused by the *General Armstrong* gave Andrew Jackson a few more days to strengthen his defenses of that city.

Q. What kind of ship did Robert Fulton invent, launching it on October 31, 1814?

A. Robert Fulton built the world's first steam-propelled frigate, *Fulton the First* or *Demologus*. Constructed of sides five feet thick and mounting thirty 32-pounders, the frigate was designed for harbor defense. At 153 feet in length and with a beam of 56 feet, the *Fulton* was the world's largest steamer. The *Fulton* stayed in Long Island Sound and never saw action against an enemy vessel. It was finally launched after the war ended and Fulton had died. Fulton had also experimented with a submarine "turtle boat" during the war and attempted unsuccessfully to attach a torpedo (a floating mine at the time) to the British ship of the line *Ramillies* in New York Harbor. British captain Thomas Hardy discovered that the American attempt had failed only because the bolt used to attach a torpedo to the ship had broken. He then informed the Americans that he would keep prisoners of war on board all of his ships.

Robert Fulton
(1765–1815)
Engineer, inventor,
pioneer in steamboat
design, painter

Q. Is it true that the British blockade of American ports devastated American trade during the war?

A. Yes. The blockade was highly detrimental to American trade. In the year ending September 30, 1814, American exports fell to $7 million. They had been over $108 million in 1807. Imports fell from $138 million in 1807 to $13 million in 1814. The tonnage of American shipping engaged in foreign commerce dropped from over a million tons in 1807 to less than sixty thousand in 1814. The blockade also severely restricted coastal trade and the movement of goods within the United States. It was very expensive to move goods on the few woefully inadequate roads. One traveler reported it took thirty-eight hours to travel the fifty miles from Fredricksburg to Alexandria in 1813. Consequently, large price increases resulted.

FACT

The American merchant fleet reached its pre–World War II peak, in terms of tonnage per population, in 1810. That year has been noted as "the high water mark of the American merchant marine in foreign trade."

Q. Was the British public satisfied with the performance of their navy against the American navy?

A. No. The British public did not understand why the British navy couldn't prevent the Americans from harassing their trade to such a high degree, especially in the English Channel.

Q. During the war, the U.S. Navy had twenty-two fighting ships. How many British vessels did they capture during the war?
a. 45
b. 85
c. 165

A. The answer is c. By the war's end, the *Constitution* was the only original frigate that remained at sea.

Q. In eight single-ship encounters between American and British sloops of war, how many did the British win?
A. The British won only once when the *Pelican* defeated *Argus* in the summer of 1813.

Q. In twelve single-ship encounters of close to or approximately equal force, how many did the British win?
A. Only two. The *Pelican* defeated the *Argus*, and the *Shannon* defeated the *Chesapeake*.

Q. Did the U.S. Navy inflict more damage on the Royal Navy than did the French navy from 1812 to 1815?
A. Yes. In eight actions of approximately equal force between the French and British navies, the British won three victories and five contests were draws. Altogether, during this period, the British lost only three ships with 38 guns to the French. The French lost nineteen vessels with 830 guns to the British, including three ships of the line and eleven frigates. While the British defeated French ships at a six to one ratio, Americans defeated British ships at a four to three ratio. In total ship tonnage lost in battle on the ocean between ships mounting ten or more guns, the U.S. was the clear winner: Britain lost 8,451 tons and the U.S. lost 5,984 tons.

Q. Name the only U.S. Navy captain to sink two British warships during the war.
A. Captain Johnston Blakely, in the 22-gun sloop *Wasp* with a crew of mostly New Englanders, defeated and sunk the sloop *Reindeer* (18) under Captain William Manners on June 28, 1814, and the sloop *Avon* (18) under Captain James Arbuthnot on September 1, 1814.

Q. Is it true that during the course of the war American privateers captured over one thousand British vessels of all types?
A. Yes. Altogether, 517 commissioned privateers captured 1,345 British ships. They took 30,000 prisoners and inflicted a loss of over $45 million to British commerce.

Q. What state's privateers monopolized the name "Yankee," sending to sea the *Yankee*, *True Blooded Yankee*, *Yankee Lass*, *Yankee American*, and *Yankee Porter*?

A. Rhode Island. Captain Hailey in the *True Blooded Yankee* actually seized an island off the coast of Ireland and held it for six days.

Q. Which state commissioned the most privateers?

A. Massachusetts commissioned the most with 150 privateers. The next two most important states were Maryland with 112 and New York with 102. Maryland privateers captured one-third of the British ships taken during the war.

Q. Name the most successful U.S. privateer of the war.

A. The 14-gun *Yankee*, a brig from Bristol, Rhode Island, captured forty prizes in six cruises under several different captains. The ship seized an estimated $5 million worth of property and made owner James de Wolfe one of Rhode Island's wealthiest men.

Q. Is it true that both the United States and Britain agreed to ban privateering at the Treaty of Ghent?

A. No. Though most nations outlawed privateering by 1856, the United States did not renounce the practice until 1865, at the end of the Civil War.

Q. Name the only other U.S. frigate besides the *Chesapeake* and the *Essex* that was captured by the British during the war.

A. The *President*, under Commodore Stephen Decatur, attempted to slip past a British blockade of New York on January 14, 1815, after a storm had blown the squadron away. The next day Decatur found himself in the midst of the entire squadron. After defeating the frigate *Endymion*, he was forced to surrender to the remaining three ships of the squadron.

Q. A naval engagement fought on February 20, 1815, has been considered to be tactically the most professional of the war in which a United States naval ship was involved. Name the ship.

A. Captain Stewart won a victory for the U.S. with the *Constitution*, which fought against the small British frigate *Cyane* and a new sloop *Levant*. In an almost unheard of action, Captain Stewart raked both opponents while engaging them simultaneously. He avoided raking fire from either enemy ship. The opposing vessels had one more gun than the Constitution's fifty-two; however, they were mostly short-range carronades.

Q. What was the last American ship to fire its guns in the war?

A. The sloop *Peacock*, 18 guns. On June 30, it fired a broadside into a British vessel that refused to surrender, even though the British informed Captain Lewis Warrington that the war was over.

Q. What captured British frigate was repaired and commissioned in the U.S. Navy, where it remained in active service until 1871?

A. The *Macedonian*, which had been captured by the U.S. frigate *United States* in October 1812, was rebuilt by Joshua Humphreys in the early 1830s. Only a small part of the rotting original ship was actually incorporated into the new vessel.

Q. What was the bloodiest single-ship naval battle of the entire war between the U.S. and the Royal Navy in terms of the number of men killed and wounded?

A. In the battle between *Chesapeake* and *Shannon*, the Americans lost 148 and the British 83 killed and wounded. It was also the only single-ship battle where the victor was weaker in force than the opponent. The *Chesapeake*'s crew was inexperienced and suffered early in the battle from an explosion on the deck.

Q. What was the largest naval engagement of the war?

A. The largest and bloodiest engagement occurred on Lake Champlain at Plattsburg Bay. Sixteen British vessels with over 1,000 men and over 100 guns fought fourteen American vessels carrying 86 guns and 882 men. The British lost over 300 and the Americans about 200 killed and wounded.

Q. What was the only year in the war that the U.S. Navy lost more vessels on the oceans than the enemy?

A. The year 1813. It was also the year with the fewest naval engagements as most of the American warships were bottled up in ports.

The U.S. lost *Guerriere* to *Shannon*, *Essex* to *Phoebe*, and *Argus* to *Pelican*, winning only with *Enterprise*, which defeated *Boxer*.

Q. Approximately how many American ships other than U.S. naval vessels were lost during the war?
a. 300
b. 800
c. 1,400

A. The answer is c. Estimates for British vessels other than Royal Navy ships lost to the Americans range from 1,300 to 2,500.

Q. In January 1813, Congress authorized the building of four 74s and six additional frigates. Did any ships of the line fight in battle during the war?

A. No. None of the ships of the line were commissioned until after the war ended. They were *Franklin* at Philadelphia; *Washington* at Portsmouth, New Hampshire; *Independence* at Charleston, Massachusetts; and *Columbus* at the Washington Navy Yard. When the war ended, only *Philadelphia* was ready to sail. None of the authorized frigates saw action either. Yet, all of the six sloops authorized in March 1813 were launched within eleven months, and some were very successful. Four or five sloops could be built for the cost of one frigate.

Q. What same name was given to three different sloops of war, two of which were eighteen guns and one was five guns?

A. *Wasp.* The first (18) was built in 1806, captured in October 1812 by HMS *Poictiers* (74), and taken into the Royal Navy. The second (18) was built in 1813 and lost at sea in 1814. The third (5) was chartered on Lake Champlain in 1813 and returned to its owner in 1814.

Q. What U.S. frigate from the War of 1812 was burned and sunk in 1861 at Norfolk Navy Yard to prevent her capture by Confederates?

A. As the *United States* burned, flames spread from her rigging to nearby vessels, one of which was the steam frigate *Merrimack*. The Confederates raised and rebuilt the burned *Merrimack* and cov-

The Wasp *captures the* Frolic

ered it with iron sheets two inches thick, thus creating the first ironclad warship.

Q. How many U.S. Navy captains underwent a court-martial during the war?

A. None. This was in contrast to at least seven who underwent a court-martial during the Revolutionary War. Two captains died in battle, James Lawrence in the *Chesapeake* and William Henry Allen in the *Argus*.

Q. What American president, who had been assistant secretary of the navy, wrote a history entitled *The Naval War of 1812*?

A. Theodore Roosevelt, president from 1901 to 1909, wrote *The Naval War of 1812* at the age of twenty-three and published it in 1882. It is considered a classic and is still one of the best books on the U.S. Navy in the war. Roosevelt was an advocate of a big navy and believed twenty ships of the line would have prevented a successful British blockade and perhaps the war itself.

Q. What famous naval theorist, in his book *Sea Power in its Relation to the War of 1812*, also argued that the United States would have been better served by a navy more equal to that of the British?

A. Alfred Thayer Mahan. In contrast, Henry Adams in his work *The War of 1812* believed the United States should have concentrated on building sloops of war for commerce destruction. Though not as valuable, another prominent American, author James Fenimore Cooper also covered the war in his *Naval History of the United States.*

Q. In a toast, what veteran captain of the war uttered the famous words that virtually became a navy motto, "Our Country. In her intercourse with foreign nations, may she always be in the right, but our country, right or wrong"?

A. Stephen Decatur spoke the words at a banquet in April 1816. Decatur's already brilliant career ended prematurely when James Barron killed him in a duel on March 22, 1820. Decatur had been a member of the court-martial that suspended James Barron from the navy for five years because of his conduct in the *Chesapeake-Leopard* affair in 1807. Also, as a navy commissioner, Decatur opposed Barron's reinstatement into the navy.

Q. In what year did the United States Navy finally make dueling a violation of the law?

A. The U.S. Navy did not outlaw dueling until 1862, after many more unnecessary deaths.

Q. William Lowndes, a South Carolina congressman and a War Hawk, has been credited with establishing the principle that the generation which entered a war and created a war debt should be obligated to pay for it. Did the generation of the War of 1812 pay off the war debt they created?

A. Yes. The national debt created by the war was paid off in President Andrew Jackson's administration, twenty-three years later.

Appendix I

The following tables provide casualty numbers for selected Revolutionary War battles or engagements. No two historians seem to have the same figures when it comes to casualty figures from battles. The numbers here are not meant to be the final authoritative figures. There never will be any for the Revolutionary War as only incomplete and contradictory records are available. The statistics are just meant to illustrate the basic facts.

The battles are divided into two categories. The first tables illustrate sixteen major battles, defined as being those in which at least approximately four thousand men from both sides were engaged, with at least one hundred casualties sustained by either side and about four hundred total casualties for the battle. Casualties are divided into killed, wounded, missing, or captured and are broken down and tabulated as known. Of course this definition of a major battle is purely arbitrary.

The second set of tables contain twenty-five of the next largest battles, defined as battles in which the Americans suffered approximately one hundred casualties. Of course the list is not all inclusive. For example, Fort Mifflin is not included although about 250 Americans died there, primarily through a naval bombardment. Figures given for both the Americans and the British include anyone fighting on either side, whether they were French, Native American, militia, or regulars. Percents are rounded off to the nearest whole number.

Major Land Battles

	American	British	Victor
Lexington and Concord (April 19, 1775)			
Engaged	3,763	1,800	Americans
Killed	49	73	
Wounded	41	174	
Missing or Prisoner	5	26	
Total	95	273	
Percent lost	2	15	
Bunker Hill (June 17, 1775)			
Engaged	1,500	2,400	British
Killed	140	226	
Wounded	271	828	
Missing or Prisoner	30		
Total	441	1,054	
Percent lost	29	44	
Long Island (August 27, 1776)			
Engaged	5,000	15,000	British
Killed	200		
Wounded or captured	812		
Total	1,012	392	
Percent lost	20	3	
Fort Washington (November 16, 1776)			
Engaged	3,000	8,000	British
Killed	59	78	
Wounded	96	374	
Captured or Missing	2,837		
Total	2,992	452	
Percent lost	100	6	
White Plains (October 28, 1776)			
Engaged	1,600	4,000	British
Killed	25		
Wounded	125		
Total	150	231	
Percent lost	9	6	

Appendix I

	American	British	Victor
	Brandywine (September 11, 1777)		
Engaged	11,000	12,500	British
Killed	300	90	
Wounded	600	480	
Captured or Missing	400	6	
Total	1,300	576	
Percent loss	12	5	
	Bemis Heights (September 19, 1777)		
Engaged	5,000	2,100	Americans
Killed and Wounded	150		
Total	150	600	
Percent loss	29		
	Germantown (October 4, 1777)		
Engaged	11,000	9,000	British
Killed	152	70	
Wounded	521	450	
Missing or Captured	400		
Total	1,073	520	
Percent loss	10	6	
	Freeman's Farm (October 7, 1777)		
Engaged	3,000	4,400	Americans
Killed	65		
Wounded	218		
Missing	36		
Total	319	600	
Percent loss			
	Monmouth (June 28, 1778)		
Engaged	5,000	1,750	Draw
Killed	69	65 + 59 sunstroke	
Wounded	159	170	
Captured or Missing	130	64	
Total	358	358	
Percent loss	7	20	
	Savannah (October 9, 1779)		
Engaged	5,000	3,200	British
Killed	244	40	
Wounded	584	63	

	American	British	Victor
Savannah (October 9, 1779) continued			
Captured or Missing	52		
Total	828	155	
Percent loss	17	5	
Charleston (April 19 to May 12, 1780)			
Engaged	5,150	10,000	British
Killed	89	76	
Wounded	138	189	
Captured or Missing	3,371		
Total	3,598	265	
Percent loss	70	3	
Camden (August 16, 1780)			
Engaged	4,100	2,239	British
Killed	68		
Wounded	245		
Captured or Missing	11		
Total	750	324	
Percent loss	18	14	
Guilford Courthouse (March 15, 1781)			
Engaged	4,450	1,900	British
Killed	78	93	
Wounded	183	439	
Total	261	532	
Percent loss	6	28	
Eutaw Springs (September 8, 1781)			
Engaged	2,200	2,000	British
Killed	139	85	
Wounded	375	351	
Captured or Missing	8	430	
Total	522	866	
Percent loss	24	43	
Yorktown (September 28 to October 19, 1781)			
Engaged	20,000	9,750	Americans
Casualties	378	552	
Captured	8,000+		
Total	378	8,552	
Percent loss	2	100	

Appendix I

Smaller Battles

Battle	Year	Engaged	Casualties	% lost	Victor
Quebec	Jan. 1776	Am. 900	486	54	British
		Brt. 1,800	18	1	
Trois-Rivières	June 1776	Am. 2,000	400	20	British
		Brt. 6,000	17	0.3	
Harlem Heights	Sept. 1776	Am. 1,000+	130		British
		Brt. 5,000	168		
Danbury	Apr. 1777	Am. 600	95	16	British
		Brt. 2,000	171	8	
Hubbardton	July 1777	Am. 1,000	324	32	British
		Brt. 750	198	26	
Oriskany	Aug. 1777	Am. 700	200	29	British
		Brt. 450	100	22	
Bennington	Aug. 1777	Am. 2,000	80	4	Americans
		Brt. 1,462	895	61	
Paoli	Sept. 1777	Am. 1,500	370	25	British
		Brt. unknown	28		
Forts Clinton & Montgomery	Oct. 1777	Am. 600+	250	42	British
		Brt. 2,000	190	10	
Wyoming	July 1778	Am. 360	300		British
		Brt. 1,000?	11		
Newport, RI	Aug. 1778	Am. 1,500	211	14	Americans
		Brt. 5,000	260	5	
Savannah	Dec. 1778	Am. 850	547	64	British
		Brt. 3,500	13	0.4	
Briar Creek	Mar. 1779	Am. 1,500	370	25	British
		Brt. 900	16	2	

Battle	Year	Engaged	Casualties	% lost	Victor
Stono Ferry	June	Am. 1,200	301	25	British
	1779	Brt. 900	130	14	
Stony Point	July	Am. 1,200	100	8	Americans
	1779	Brt. 625	624	100	
Waxhaws	May	Am. 350	316	90	British
	1780	Brt. 270	17	6	
Ramsauer's Mill	June	Am. 400	150	38	Americans
	1780	Brt. 1,200	150	13	
King's Mountain	Oct.	Am. 900	88	10	Americans
	1780	Brt. 1,100	1,018	93	
Fishing Creek	Nov.	Am. 700	450	64	British
	1780	Brt. 160	16	1	
Cowpens	Jan.	Am. 1,040	72	7	Americans
	1781	Brt. 1,100	929	84	
Hobkirk's Hill	Apr.	Am. 1,551	263	17	British
	1781	Brt. 800	258	32	
Ninety-Six	May	Am. 1,000	147	15	British
	1781	Brt. 550	85	15	
Green Spring	July	Am. 900	145	16	British
	1781	Brt. 7,000	75	1	
New London	Sept.	Am. unknown	240		British
	1781	Brt. 1,700	193	11	
Blue Licks	Aug.	Am. 182	70–100	38	British
	1782	Brt. 240			

Out of the sixteen major engagements in the war, Americans clearly won only four, or 25 percent of them. Of the next twenty-five largest engagements, the Americans won six times, again approximately 25 percent of the total.

Appendix II

The American army has been greatly criticized for its often poor performance during the War of 1812, with its combination of untrained militia and inept generals. Nonetheless, it managed to win over 50 percent of the twenty engagements of the war.

War of 1812 Land Battles

Battle	Engaged	Casualties	% Lost	Victor
Detroit	Am. 2,200	2,200	100	British
Queenston Heights	Am. 1,150	1,100	96	British
October 13, 1812	Brt. 1,100	113	10	
River Raisin	Am. 975	975	100	British
January 22, 1813	Brt. 1,100	158*	14	
York	Am. 1,700	232	14	Americans
April 27, 1813	Brt. 800	146	2	
Fort Meigs	Am. 1,750	983	6	Americans
April 28 to May 9, 1813	Brt. 2,175	107	5	
Fort George	Am. 4,500	140	3	Americans
May 27, 1813	Brt. 1,100	350	32	
Sacket's Harbor	Am. 900	100	11	Americans
May 29, 1813	Brt. 750	260	35	
Stoney Creek	Am. 1,300	154	12	British
June 6, 1813	Brt. 700	214	31	
Thames (Moraviantown)	Am. 3,540	29	0.8	Americans
October 5, 1813	Brt. 1,330	632	unknown	
Crysler's Farm	Am. 2,000	440	22	British
November 11, 1813	Brt. 800	180	23	

Battle	Engaged	Casualties	% Lost	Victor
Horseshoe Bend	Am. 3,000	200	7	Americans
March 27, 1814	Crk. 1,000	800	80	
La Colle Mill	Am. 4,000	180	5	British
March 30,1814	Brt. 500	60	12	
Chippewa	Am. 1,500	325	22	Americans
July 5, 1814	Brt. 1,500	500	33	
Lundy's Lane	Am. 2,100	850	40	Draw
July 25, 1814	Brt. 3,000	875	29	
Bladensburg	Am. 6,000	70	1	British
August 24, 1814	Brt. 4,000	250	6	
Plattsburg	Am. 5,000*	100	2	Americans
September 11, 1814	Brt. 0,000*	350+	4	
Baltimore	Am. 3,200	215	7	Americans
September 12–13, 1814	Brt. 4,500	340	8	
Villere Plantation	Am. 1,800	215	12	Draw
December 23, 1814	Brt.1,600	275	17	
New Orleans	Am. 5,400	70	1	Americans
January, 8, 1815	Brt. 6,000	2,000	33	

Appendix III

With the demand for trade and supplies, the naval contests of the Revolutionary War were a vital component of the success of the military effort. Also, the coastal nature of the colonies made sea power essential, lest miles of border be left exposed. The number after each ship's name represents its number of guns.

Ships of the Continental Navy

Alfred, 24	Ship	Purchased, 1775	Captured by *Ariadne*, 20, *Ceres*, 16, 1778
Columbus, 20	Ship	Purchased, 1775	Driven ashore and burned, Point Judith, 1778.
Andrew Doria, 20	Brig	Purchased, 1775	Destroyed to prevent capture, Delaware River, 1777. Driven aground, captured. Taken in British service, 1777.
Cabot, 14	Brig	Purchased, 1775	Destroyed to prevent capture, Penobscot, 1779
Providence, 12	Sloop	Purchased, 1775	Destroyed to prevent capture, Delaware River, 1777.
Hornet, 10	Sloop	Purchased, 1775	Destroyed to prevent capture, Delaware River, 1777.
Wasp, 8	Schooner	Purchased, 1775	Destroyed to prevent capture, Delaware River, 1777.
Fly, 8	Schooner	Purchased, 1775	Destroyed to prevent capture, Delaware River, 1777.
Lexington, 16	Brig	Purchased, 1776	Captured by Alert, 10, 1777.
Reprisal, 16	Brig	Purchased, 1775-76	Lost at sea, 1777
Hampden, 14	Brig	Purchased, 1776	Sold, Providence, RI, 1777.
Independence, 10	Sloop	Purchased, 1775-76	Wrecked, Oracoke Inlet, NC, 1778.

Sachem, 10	Sloop	Purchased, 1775-76	Destroyed to prevent capture, Delaware River, 1777.
Mosquito, 4	Sloop	Purchased, 1775-76	Destroyed to prevent capture, Delaware River, 1777
Raleigh, 32	Frigate	Launched, 1776	Captured by *Experiment*, 50 Unicorn, 28, 1778.
Hancock, 32	Frigate	Launched, 1776	Captured by *Rainbow*, 44, 1777.
Warren, 32	Frigate	Launched, 1776	Destroyed to prevent capture, Penobscot, 1779.
Washington, 32	Frigate	Launched, 1776	Destroyed to prevent capture, Delaware River, 1777.
Randolph, 32	Frigate	Launched, 1776	Destroyed engaging *Yarmouth*, 64, 1778.
Providence, 28	Frigate	Launched, 1776	Captured at Charleston, SC, 1780.
Trumbull, 28	Frigate	Launched, 177?	Captured by *Iris* (ex-Hancock) and General Monk, 18, 1781.
Congress, 28	Frigate	Launched, 1776	Destroyed to prevent capture, Hudson River, 1777.
Virginia, 28	Frigate	Launched, 1776-77	Run aground, Chesapeake. Captured, 1778.
Effingham, 28	Frigate	Launched, 1776-77	Destroyed (unfinished), Delaware River, 1777.
Boston, 24	Frigate	Launched, 1776-77	Captured, Charleston, SC, 1780.
Montgomery, 24	Frigate	Launched, 1776-77	Destroyed to prevent capture, Hudson River, 1777.
Delaware, 24	Frigate	Launched, 1776	Captured, Delaware, 1777.
Ranger, 18	Ship	Launched, 1777	Captured, Charleston, SC, 1780.
Resistance, 10	Brigantine	Launched, 1777	Captured by Howe's fleet, 1778.
Surprise	Sloop	Purchased, 1777	Fate unknown.

Racehorse, 12	Schooner	Captured from British, 1776	Destroyed to prevent capture, Delaware River, 1777.
Repulse, 8	Xebec	Pa. State gunboat lent to Continental Navy	Destroyed to prevent capture, Delaware River, 1777.
Champion, 8	Xebec	Pa. State gunboat lent to Continental Navy	Destroyed to prevent capture, Delaware River, 1777.
Indien, 40	Ship	Built in Holland	Purchased by French. Acquired by S. Carolina. As South Carolina, captured in 1782.
Deane	Frigate	Built at Nantes, 1777	Renamed Hague, 1782. Decommissioned, 1783. (later Hague), 32
Queen of France, 28	Frigate	Purchased in France, 1777	Sunk as obstruction, Charleston, SC, 1780.
Dolphin, 10	Cutter	Purchased in Dover, 1777	Cruiser, packet, then receiving ship, 1777.
Surprise, 10	Lugger	Purchased in Dunkirk, 1777	Seized by French, 1777.
Revenge, 14	Cutter	Purchased at Dunkirk, 1777	Sold, Philadelphia, 1779. Captured as privateer, 1779.
Alliance, 32	Frigate	Launched, 1778	Sold out of service, 1785.
General Gates, 18.	Ship	Launched, 1777	Sold out of service, 1779
Retaliation	Brigantine	Purchased, 1778	Fate unknown.
Pigot, 8	Schooner	Captured from British, 1778	Fate unknown.
Confederacy, 32	Frigate	Launched, 1778	Sold out of service, 1779.
Argo, 12	Sloop	Purchased, 1779	Sold out of service, 1779.
Diligent, 12	Brig	Captured from British, 1779	Destroyed to prevent capture, Penobscot, 1779.
Bonhomme Richard, 42	Ship	Purchased in France, 1779	Sank after action with *Serapis*, 1779.
Pallas, 32	Frigate	Lent by France, 1779	French in Continental Service. Returned after war.
Cerf, 18	Cutter	Lent by France, 1779	French in Continental Service. Returned after war.

Vengeance, 12	Brig	Lent by France, 1779	French in Continental Service. Returned after war.
Serapis, 44	Ship	Captured by John Paul Jones	Sold, France, 1780.
Ariel, 20	Ship	Lent by France, 1779	French in Continental Service. Returned, 1781.
Saratoga, 18	Ship	Launched, 1780	Lost at sea, 1781.
America, 74	Ship of the line	Launched, 1782	Given to France. Broken up, 1786.
General Washington, 20 (ex-*General Monk*)	Ship	Captured, 1782	Sold 1784.
Duc de Lauzun, 20	Ship	Captured, 1782	Sold, France, 1783.
Bourbon, 36	Frigate	Launched, 1783	Sold, no service, 1783.

Naval Guns of the Revolutionary War

Class	Length (in feet)	Weight (in pounds)	Caliber (in inches)	Charge (in pounds)	Windage (in inches)
42-pounder	10	6,500	7.03	17	.35
32-pdr (long)	9.50	5,500	6.43	14	.33
32-pdr (short)	8	4,900	6.43	11	.33
24-pdr (long)	9.50	5,000	5.84	11	.30
24-pdr (short)	7.50	4,000	5.84	8.50	.30
18-pdr (long)	9	4,200	5.30	9	.27
18-pdr (short)	6	2,700	5.30	6.25	.27
12-pdr (long)	9	3,200	4.64	6	.24
12-pdr (short)	7.50	2,900	4.64	6	.24
9-pdr (long)	9	2,850	4.22	4.50	.22
9-pdr (short)	7.50	2,600	4.22	4	.22
6-pdr (long)	9	2,450	3.67	3	.19
6-pdr (short)	7	1,900	3.67	3	.19
4-pdr	6	1,200	3.22	2	.18
3-pdr	4.50	700	2.91	1.50	.14
1/2-pdr (swivel)	3.50	150	1.69	.25	–

Appendix III
Captains of the Continental Navy

(listed by seniority as established by Congress, October 10, 1776)

Captain	Command
James Nicholson	frigate *Virginia*
John Manley	frigate *Hancock*
Hector McNeill	frigate *Boston*
Dudley Saltonstall	frigate *Trumbull*
Nicholas Biddle	frigate *Randolph*
Thomas Thompson	frigate *Raleigh*
John Barry	frigate *Effingham*
Thomas Read	frigate *Washington*
Thomas Grinnell	frigate *Congress*
Charles Alexander	frigate *Delaware*
Lambert Wickes	sloop *Reprisal*
Abraham Whipple	frigate *Providence*
John B. Hopkins	frigate *Warren*
John Hodge	frigate *Montgomery*
William Hallock	brig *Lexington*
Hoysted Hacker	brig *Hampden*
Isiah Robinson	brig *Andrew Doria*
John Paul Jones	sloop *Providence*
James Josiah	no ship assigned
Elisha Hinman	ship *Alfred*
Joseph Olney	brig *Cabot*
James Robinson	sloop *Sachem*
John Young	sloop *Independence*
Elisha Warner	schooner *Fly*

Chronology

Pre-Revolution

1763   Treaty of Paris, ending French and Indian War, signed February 10
       King George signs Royal Proclamation of 1763, October 7

1764   Sugar Act enacted, April 5

1765   Stamp Act Congress convenes in New York, October 1–25

1767   Townshend Duties passed, June 29

1768   Two British regiments arrive in Boston, October 1

1770   Battle of Golden Hill, January 19
       Boston Massacre, March 5

1773   Boston Tea Party, December 16

1774   Lord Dunmore's War, June–October
       First Continental Congress meets, September 5 to October 26

1775   First permanent Kentucky settlement established at Harrodsburg, March

Revolutionary War

1775   The shots heard round the world at Lexington and Concord, April 19

Ethan Allen and Benedict Arnold captured Fort Ticonderoga, May 10

Crown Point was seized, May 12

Birth of U.S. Army, June 14

Washington commissioned commander in chief of the army by the Continental Congress, June 17

Battle of Bunker Hill, June 17

Washington assumed command of the army around Boston, July 3

Washington commissions *Hannah*, the first of eight vessels, September 2

Sir William Howe succeeded Gage as commander of the British in Boston, October 10

Congress authorizes beginning of a navy, October 13

Montgomery captured Montreal, November 13

Battle of Great Bridge, Virginia, December 9

Congress authorizes Continental navy with the building of 13 frigates, December 13

1776   American attack on Quebec under Montgomery and Arnold fails, January 1

Virginia's governor Dunmore bombards and sets fire to Norfolk, Virginia, January 1

Knox transports Fort Ticonderoga artillery 300 miles from Lake George to Cambridge, Massachusetts, January 7 to January 24 or 25

Patriots defeat Loyalists at Moores Creek Bridge, North Carolina, February 27

Esek Hopkins captures New Providence in the Bahamas, March 3–4

British evacuate Boston, March 17

Americans sent packing out of Canada at battle of Trois-Rivières, June 8

British repulsed at Charleston, June 28

Declaration of Independence adopted by Congress, July 4

British victory at battle of Long Island, August 27

Attack by David Bushnell's submarine the *Turtle* in New York Harbor, September 6

Part of New York City burned, September 21

Arnold's battle at Valcour Island in Lake Champlain, October 11

Battle of White Pains, New York, October 28

British captured Fort Washington, November 16

Americans abandon Fort Lee, November 20

British patrol captures General Charles Lee, December 13

Washington's victory at Trenton, December 26

1777   Battle of Princeton, January 3

New Hampshire grants independence to Vermont, January 16

Danbury, Connecticut, raided by British, April 26

Congress authorizes official United States flag, June 14

General St. Clair abandons Fort Ticonderoga, July 6

Battle of Hubbardton, Vermont, July 7

Howe leaves New York for Philadelphia, July 23

Militia under Herkimer are ambushed at Oriskany, New York, August 6

Stark destroys Hessians at Bennington, Vermont, August 16

Siege of Fort Stanwix, August 4–22

Battle of Cooch's Bridge, September 3

Washington defeated at Brandywine Creek, September 11

Engagement at White Horse Tavern, September 16

Battle of Freeman's Farm, September 19

Anthony Wayne's troops surprised at Paoli, September 20–21

Battle of Germantown, October 4

British capture of Forts Clinton and Montgomery on the Hudson, October 6

Burgoyne defeated at Bemis Heights, October 7

Burgoyne surrenders at Saratoga, October 17

Forts Mercer and Mifflin under siege by British, October 10 to November 21

The last significant engagement of the year at Whitemarsh, December 4

Washington's army go into winter quarters at Valley Forge, December 18

1778   Battle of the Kegs on the Delaware River, January 5

Alliance is signed between Americans and French, February 6

Randolph blew up, March 17

Carlisle Commission reaches Philadelphia, June 6

Clinton evacuates Philadelphia, June 18

Battle of Monmouth, June 28

Massacre of Wyoming Valley, Pennsylvania, July 4

George Rogers Clark captures Kaskaskia, July 4

Battle of Ushant, July 23

Battle of Rhode Island, August 29

Cherry Valley Massacre, November 11–12

British capture Savannah, December 29

1779   George Rogers Clark captures Vincennes, February 23

Spain enters the war against the British, May 8

Battle of Stono Ferry, June 20

Anthony Wayne captures Stony Point, July 15

American expedition up Penobscot River in Maine defeated, August 13

Henry Lee attacks the British at Paulus Hook, August 19

Sullivan wins victory against Iroquois at Newton, New York, August 29

John Paul Jones victorious over *Serapis*, September 23

Franco-American attack on Savannah fails, October 9

Clinton's expedition against Charleston leaves New York, December 26

1780   Tarleton victorious at Monck's Corner, April 14

Lincoln surrenders Charleston to British, May 12

City of St. Louis repels British-Native American attack, May 26

Battle of Waxhaws, May 29

Battle of Ramsauer's Mill, June 20

General Knyphausen raids into New Jersey June 7–23
Knyphausen defeated at Springfield, June 23
Rochambeau's French army arrives at Newport, July 11
Sumter victory at Williamson's plantation, July 12
Gates defeated at Camden, August 16
Battle of Kings' Mountain, October 7
Greene assumes command of Southern Department in Charlotte, North Carolina, December 3
William Washington obtains surrender of Rugeley's Mill, December 4

1781   The Pennsylvania line mutinies, January 1
Morgan annihilates Tarleton's force at Cowpens, January 17
Greene flees Cornwallis through North Carolina, February 1–14
Congress ratifies Articles of Confederation, March 1
Battle of Guilford Courthouse, March 15
Surrender of Fort Wanton to Lee and Marion, April 23
Greene loses to Rawdon at Hobkirk's Hill, April 25
Jefferson escapes capture by Tarleton at Charlottesville, June 4
Americans capture Augusta, Georgia, June 5
Greene unsuccessful in siege of Ninety-Six, May 22 to June 20
Lafayette defeated at Green Spring Farm, July 6
Trumbull, the last of the original thirteen frigates authorized by Congress, captured, August 8
Washington and Rochambeau begin march toward Yorktown from the Hudson River, August 25
De Grasse defeats Graves and Hood at Virginia Capes, September 5
New London, Connecticut, attacked by Arnold, September 6
Battle of Eutaw Springs, September 8
Siege at Yorktown begins, September 28
Redoubts 9 and 10 taken at Yorktown, October 14
Cornwallis surrenders at Yorktown, October 19

1782   Battle of the Saints, April 12
Capture of Pensacola by Spaniards, May 9
Battle of Blue Licks, Kentucky, August 19
First U.S. ship of the line, *America*, launched, November 5
Americans sign a separate treaty with British, November 30

1783   Washington's Newburgh Address, March 15
Congress ratifies provisional treaty of peace, April 15
Last fighting between French and British at Cuddalore, India, June 28

Treaty of Paris signed, September 3
Last British troops leave New York City, November 25
Washington retires from the army, December 23

Between the Wars

1784 Congress reduces army to eighty artillerymen, June 2
1787 Northwest Ordinance enacted, July 13
1788 New U.S. Constitution takes effect, July 2
1789 Washington inaugurated as first President of the United States,
      April 30
1790 Harmar expedition defeated by Ohio Native Americans, October 18
1791 St. Clair suffers worst defeat ever against Native Americans,
      November 4
1792 Militia Act of 1792, May 8
1794 Congress passes Naval Act authorizing establishment of United
      States Navy, March 27
      Whiskey Rebellion, July through November
      General Anthony Wayne defeats Ohio Native Americans at battle of
      Fallen Timbers, August 20
1795 Treaty of Greenville signed, August 3
      Washington signs Jay's Treaty, August 14
1798 U.S. Marine Corps officially established, July 11
      Quasi War with France, May 1798 to February 1801
1801 The Bashaw of Tripoli declares war on the United States, May 14
1802 Congress authorizes military academy at West Point, March 16
1803 Louisiana Purchase signed, May 2
      Philadelphia captured by Tripoli, October 31
1804 Lewis and Clark expedition departs from St. Louis, May 14
1805 William Eaton captures Derna, April 26–29
1806 Lewis and Clark return to St. Louis, September 23
1807 *Chesapeake* incident with *Leopard*, June 22
      Jefferson's Embargo Act enacted, December 22
1811 USS *President* v. HMS *Little Belt*, May 16
      Battle of Tippecanoe, November 11
      New Madrid earthquake, December 16

War of 1812

1812 Congress passes bill declaring war, June 4
      Senate passes House war bill, June 17
      Madison signs war bill, June 18
      Commodore John Rodgers departs from New York with a squadron,
      June 21
      Isaac Brock learns of declaration of war, June 26

Hull learns of declaration of war, July 2
Hull invades Canada, July 12
Hanks surrenders Fort Michilimackinac, July 17
Battle of Brownstown, August 5
Battle of Monguagon, August 9
USS *Essex* v. HMS *Alert*, August 12
Fort Dearborn Massacre, August 15
Hull surrenders Detroit, August 16
USS *Constitution* v. HMS *Guerriere*, August 19
Taylor defends Fort Harrison, September 3–16
Battle of Queenston, October 13
USS *Wasp* v. HMS *Frolic*, October 18
USS *United States* v. HMS *Macedonian*, October 25
USS *Constitution* v. HMS *Java*, December 29

1813 Winchester's troops capture Frenchtown, January 18
Battle of River Raisin (Frenchtown), January 22
USS *Hornet* v. HMS *Peacock*, February 24
Wilkinson captures Mobile, April 15
Battle of York, April 27
Siege of Fort Meigs, April 28 to May 9
Battle of Fort George, May 27
Battle of Sacket's Harbor, May 29
HMS *Shannon* v. USS *Chesapeake*, June 1
Battle of Stoney Creek, June 6
Battle of Craney Island, June 22
Boerstler surrenders at Beaver Dams (Beechwoods), June 24
Croghan successfully defends Fort Stephenson, August 2
Battle of Burnt Corn Creek, August 10
HMS *Pelican* v. USS *Argus*, August 14
Massacre at Fort Mims, August 30
USS *Enterprise* v. HMS *Boxer*, September 5
Battle of Lake Erie, September 10
Battle of the Thames, October 5
Battle of Châteauguay, October 26
Battle of French Creek, November 1
Battle of Tallushatchee, November 3
Battle of Talladega, November 9
Battle of Crysler's Farm, November 11
British capture Fort Niagara, December 19

Chronology

1814   Battle of Horseshoe Bend (Tohopeka), March 27
HMS *Phoebe* and *Cherub* v. USS *Essex*, March 28
Battle of La Colle Mill, March 30
Peacock v. *Epervier*, April 29
USS *Wasp* v. HMS *Reindeer*, June 28
Battle of Chippewa, July 5
Prarie du Chien surrendered to British, July 19
Battle of Lundy's Lane, July 25
Croghan repulsed at Mackinac, August 4
Treaty of Fort Jackson, August 9
British repulsed at Fort Erie, August 15
Nantucket Island becomes neutral, August 23
Battle of Bladensburg, August 24
British burn Washington, D.C., August 24–25
USS *Wasp* v. HMS *Avon*, September 7
Sherbrooke expedition up Penobscot River, September 1–18
Battle of Plattsburg Bay, September 11
Battle of Plattsburg, September 11
Battle of Baltimore, September 12–13
Fort McHenry bombarded, September 13
British fail to take Fort Bowyer, September 15
Battle of La Colle Mille, October 19
World's first steam-propelled frigate, *Fulton the First*, launched by
    Robert Fulton, October 31
Capture of Pensacola, November 7
Battle of Lake Borgne, December 15
Hartford Convention, December 15 to January 5
Battle at Villere Plantation, December 23
Treaty of Ghent, December 24, 1814

1815   Battle of New Orleans, January 8
HMS *Endymion*, *Tenados*, *Pomone* v. USS *President*, January 14
Fort Bowyer surrendered to the British, February 11
USS *Constitution* v. HMS *Cyane* and *Levant*, February 20
USS *Hornet* v. HMS *Penguin*, March 25
Massacre at Dartmoor Prison, April 15
USS *Peacock* v. HMS *Nautilus*, June 30

Bibliography

Abbot, Willis J. *Blue Jackets of 1812: A History of the Naval Battles of the Second War With Great Britain.* New York, 1887.

Adams, Henry. *The War of 1812.* Edited by H. A. DeWeerd. Harrisburg, Pennsylvania, 1944.

Alden, John R. *The American Revolution 1775–1783.* New York, 1954.

Allen, Gardner W. *Naval History of the American Revolution.* 2 vols. Boston, 1913.

Ambrose, Stephen E. *Undaunted Courage: Meriwether Lewis, Thomas Jefferson, and the Opening of the American West.* New York, 1996.

Bakeless, John and Katherine. *Spies of the Revolution.* New York, 1962.

Bass, Robert D. *Swamp Fox: The Life and Campaigns of General Francis Marion.* New York, 1959.

Berton, Pierre. *The Invasion of Canada 1812–1813.* Boston, 1980.

——. *Flames Across the Border 1813–1814.* Canada, 1988.

Boatner, Mark M. *Encyclopedia of the American Revolution.* New York, 1974.

Brookhiser, Richard. *Founding Father: Rediscovering George Washington.* New York, 1996.

Brown, Wallace. *The Good Americans: The Loyalists in the American Revolution.* New York, 1969.

Chapelle, Howard I. *The History of the American Sailing Navy: The Ships and Their Development.* New York, 1949.

——. *The History Of American Sailing Ships.* New York, 1935.

Clark, William B. *Ben Franklin's Privateers: A Naval Epic of the American Revolution.* Baton Rouge, LA, 1956.

Coggins, Jack. *Ships and Seamen of the American Revolution.* Harrisburg, 1969.

Coles, Harry L. *The War of 1812.* Chicago, 1965.

Commager, Henry S. and Richard B. Morris, eds. *The Spirit of Seventy-Six.* Indianapolis and New York, 1958.

Culver, Francis B. "Last Bloodshed of the Revolution." *Maryland Historical Magazine,* vol. 5, 1910: 329–37.

Davis, Burke. *The Campaign That Won America: The Story of Yorktown.* 1970.

Elliott, Charles Winslow. *Winfield Scott: The Soldier and the Man*. New York, 1937.

Fleming, Thomas. *Liberty! The American Revolution*. New York, 1997.

Flood, Charles B. *Rise, And Fight Again: Perilous Times Along the Road to Independence*. Binghamton, New York, 1976.

Forester, C. S. *The Age of Fighting Sail: The Story of the Naval War of 1812*. New York, 1956.

Fowler, William M., Jr. *Rebels Under Sail: The American Navy during the Revolution*. New York, 1976.

Freeman, Douglas Southall. *Washington: An Abridgement by Richard Harwell of the Seven-Volume George Washington*. New York, 1968.

Galloway, Colin G. *The American Revolution in Indian Country: Crises and Diversity in Native American Communities*. New York, 1995.

Hawke, David F. *Honorable Treason: The Declaration of Independence and the Men Who Signed It*. New York, 1976.

Hickey, Donald R. *The War Of 1812: A Forgotten Conflict*. Urbana and Chicago, 1989.

Higginbotham, Don. *Daniel Morgan, Revolutionary Rifleman*. Chapel Hill, North Carolina, 1961.

——. *The War of American Independence: Military Attitudes, Policies, and Practice, 1763–1789*. New York, 1971.

Hitsman, J. MacKay. *The Incredible War of 1812*. Toronto, 1965.

Ketchum, Richard M. *The Battle for Bunker Hill*. Garden City, New York, 1962.

Kipping, Ernst. *The Hessian View of America, 1776–1783*. Monmouth Beach, New Jersey, 1971.

Kyte, George W. "The British Invasion of South Carolina in 1780." *Historian*, vol. 14, spring 1952: 149–72.

Lancaster, Bruce. *From Lexington to Liberty*. Garden City, New York, 1955.

——. *The American Heritage History of the American Revolution*. Edited by Richard M. Ketchum. New York, 1971.

Lender, Mark Edward and James Kirby Martin. *A Respectable Army: The Military Origins of the Republic, 1763–1789*. Arlington Heights, Illinois, 1982.

Lippard, George. *Washington and the Generals of the American Revolution*. Philadelphia, 1856.

Lord, Walter. *The Dawn's Early Light*. New York, 1972.

Lossing, Benson J. *The Pictorial Field Book of the American Revolution*. 2 vols. New York, 1850–1852.

Mackesy, Piers. *The War for America, 1775–1783*. Lincoln and London, 1964.

Maclay, Edgar S. *A History of American Privateers*. New York, 1899.

Bibliography

Mahon, John K. *The War Of 1812*. Gainesville, Florida, 1972.

Messick, Hank. *King's Mountain: The Epic of the Blue Ridge "Mountain Men" in the American Revolution*. Boston and Toronto, 1976.

Middlekauff, Robert. *The Glorious Cause: The American Revolution, 1763–1789*. New York, 1982.

Miller, John C. *Origins of the American Revolution*. Stanford, California, 1957.

Miller, Nathan. *Sea of Glory: The Continental Navy Fights for Independence 1775–1783*. New York, 1973.

Mitchell, Joseph B. *Decisive Battles of the American Revolution*. New York, 1962.

———. *Military Leaders in the American Revolution*. McLean, Virginia, 1967.

Montross, Lynn. *The Reluctant Rebels: The Story of the Continental Congress*. New York, 1950.

Moore, Warren. *Weapons of the American Revolution*. New York, 1967.

Morgan, Ted. *Wilderness At Dawn: The Settling of the North American Continent*. New York, 1993.

Morison, Samuel Eliot. *John Paul Jones: A Sailor's Biography*. Boston and Toronto, 1959.

Nash, Howard P., Jr. *The Forgotten Wars: The U.S. Navy In The Quasi-War With France And The Barbary Wars, 1798–1805*. South Brunswick and New York, 1968.

Peckham, Howard H. *The War for Independence*. Chicago, 1958.

Peterson, Clarence Stuart. *Known Military Dead During the Revolutionary War, 1775–1783*. Baltimore, 1959.

Purcell, Edward L. and David F. Burg, eds. *The World Almanac of the American Revolution*. New York, 1992.

Quarles, Benjamin. *The Negro in the American Revolution*. Chapel Hill, North Carolina, 1961.

Rankin, Hugh F. *The American Revolution*. New York, 1964.

Roosevelt, Theodore. *The Naval War of 1812*. New York, 1927.

Scheer, George F. and Hugh F. Rankin. *Rebels and Redcoats*. Cleveland, 1957.

Seymour, William. *The Price of Folly: British Blunders in the War of American Independence*. London and Washington, 1995.

Smith, Page. *A New Age Now Begins: A People's History of the American Revolution*. Vol. 2. New York, 1976.

Sosin, Jack M. *The Revolutionary Frontier, 1763–1783*. New York, 1967.

Sprout, Harold and Margaret. *The Rise of American Naval Power 1776–1918*. Annapolis, Maryland, 1966.

Stagg, J. C. A. *Mr. Madison's War: Politics, Diplomacy, and Warfare in the Early American Republic, 1783–1830*. Princeton, 1963.

Thayer, Theodore G. *Nathanael Green: Strategist of the American Revolution*. New York, 1960.

Tourtellot, Arthur B. *William Diamond's Drum: The Beginnings of the War of the American Revolution.* New York, 1959.

Trevelyan, Sir George O. *The American Revolution.* New York and London, 1907–1908.

Tuchman, Barbara W. *The First Salute.* New York, 1988.

Tucker, Glenn. *Poltroons and Patriots: A Popular Account of the War of 1812.* Indianapolis and New York, 1954.

Van Doren, Carl. *Secret History of the American Revolution.* New York, 1941.

Van Every, Dale. *Forth to the Wilderness: The First American Frontier 1754–1774.* New York, 1961.

——. *A Company of Heroes: The American Frontier, 1775–1783.* New York, 1962.

——. *Ark of Empire: The American Frontier 1784–1803.* New York, 1963.

Wallace, Willard M. *Appeal to Arms.* New York, 1951.

Ward, Christopher. *The War of the Revolution.* New York, 1952.

Zobel, Hiller B. *The Boston Massacre.* New York, 1970.

Index

Index

Photo Credits:
All images not noted below courtesy of *The Dictionary of American Portraits*.

Chapter 1—pp. 4, 5: *Independence National Historical Park*; p. 7: *Colonial Williamsburg*; Chapter 2—p. 18: (Ward) *Independence National Historical Park*; Chapter 3—p. 34: *Bowdoin College Museum of Art*; p. 35: *Henry Francis Du Pont Winterthur Museum*; Chapter 4—p. 46: *Independence National Historical Park*; p. 54: *New-York Historical Society*; Chapter 5—p. 75: *Independence National Historical Park*; Chapter 6—p. 82: *Independence National Historical Park*; p. 90: *Metropolitan Museum of Art, Dick Fund*; Chapter 7—p. 113: *Independence National Historical Park*; Chapter 8—p. 128: *National Archives and Records Administration*; p. 132: *Independence National Historical Park*; p. 136: *National Archives and Records Administration*; Chapter 9—p. 158: *National Archives and Records Administration*; p. 165: *Independence National Historical Park*; p. 166: *Smithsonian Institution*; Chapter 10—p. 181: *Metropolitan Museum of Art, Stokes—Hawkes Collection*; p. 184: *Independence National Historical Park*; Chapter 11—p. 187: (Pike) *Independence National Historical Park*; Chapter 13—pp. 219, 227: *National Archives and Records Administration*; p. 231: *Independence National Historical Park*; p. 237: *National Archives and Records Administration*